Job Enrichment for Results:

Strategies for Successful Implementation

Roy W. Walters & Associates, Inc.

▲▼ Addison-Wesley Publishing Company
Reading, Massachusetts • Menlo Park, California
London • Amsterdam • Don Mills, Ontario • Sydney

ISBN 0-201-08492-9
BCDEFGHIJK-AL-798

Preface

Since World War II many books have been written on motivation theory. Prominent social science authors have been telling us what people are looking for in jobs and how to unlock their mainsprings of motivation. The theoreticians have given us nice neat frameworks for conceptualizing the problem.

However, little is available that can translate the theory and concepts into an actual program for implementation. Personnel people as a group have been roundly criticized because they have been unable to actually bring about solutions to the historical problems that exist.

Provoking change in organizations is slow, tedious, difficult work. This is so for one main reason: Organizations are made up of people and people resist change. Few managers or staff members are willing to go through the tortuous, agonizing efforts—to say nothing of the required follow-up—required to bring about changes in work processes, managerial styles, reward systems, and organizational relationships.

We really have no choice but to change unless we wish to pay the tremendous price for continued underutilization of our human resources. The waste of human effort is staggering.

Visits to hundreds of work locations in the last ten years have disclosed very sloppy work habits and lackadaisical attitudes. Workers think nothing about "calling in sick," being late for duty, permitting mistakes and errors to go by, taking excessive time for coffee breaks and lunch hours, and leaving work early.

Organizations are paying a very high price for all of this and most continue along their merry way, believing that this is a normal cost of doing business. Managers continue to damn the Personnel Department because "They hire us the wrong kinds of people." Or they criticize the youth because "They're not like we were when we were their age." Or

iii

they say "I can't understand employees' actions since we treat them so well."

A number of years ago, while still working for American Telephone and Telegraph Company, I began to suspect that the source of the trouble might be in the content of the work. Trials begun there have been continued at other locations and results have been truly amazing. We now know that most people are capable of doing far more than their current jobs either require or allow—and this means that vast quantities of resources are untapped.

Those who lead organizations, both profit and nonprofit enterprises, are not functioning solely to make people feel better about their daily activity, as admirable an objective as that might be. They are engaged in those enterprises to generate profits or give better service. They will be far more successful when they learn techniques for better utilization of their human resources. We do know that when this is done, the workers will feel better about their jobs and hence about the organization. What a gratifying by-product!

This book has been written out of the fruits of our labors. It is intended to bridge the gap between theory and practice. The line operating manager and the personnel manager who have to deliver operating results will find in these pages the key that can unlock their human resources. Those who wish to manage their way through this decade successfully will pay attention to the symptoms currently so visible. Failure to do so will place unnecessary strain on organizations, will make the job of managing far more difficult, and will surely depress profitability and quality of service.

Glen Rock, N.J.   R.W.W.
February 1975

Acknowledgments

This book represents the work of a great number of people. The philosophies, strategies, and procedures contained herein are ours, but they have evolved from the knowledge and information acquired from several learned professors, competent managers, pragmatic practitioners, and leaders of organizations to which we have been consultants.

I would like to thank our professional staff, who are true "action-agents" in performing the roles of catalysts for change. Robert Janson, W. Philip Kraft Jr., Kenneth Purdy, Frank Kaveney, Peter Landrigan and John Hickey worked and wrote prodigiously to place our experiences on paper.

Harold Dunkelman effectively handled much of the basic research and detailed the early chapters.

My long and pleasant association with Frederick Herzberg led to my commitment to work in this field. Francis Gramlich, at Dartmouth College at the time of his early death, helped me understand much about the human growth and development needs, a vital building stone for this work.

Robert Ford, retired from AT&T, bore a great load and contributed significantly to those original experiments while on my staff at AT&T.

Manuscript preparation was ably handled by Alma Nolan, Gwen Spencer, Jean Coleman, Lise Heptig and Evelyn Royce.

We consultants are deeply appreciative of the tolerance and support we have received from our wives who have learned to cope with husbands whose enriched jobs keep them away from their homes a great deal of the time.

R.W.W.

Contents

5 From Motivation Theory to Principles of Job Design

6 Preparing for Job Enrichment

7 The Education Phase

8 Organizing for Action

9 Problem-Solving and Installation of Motivational Job Changes

10 Halfway Home

11 Finishing the Pilot Project

12   Assuring a Successful Job Enrichment Project: A Checklist

13   Case Histories: Clerical

14   Case Histories: Manufacturing

15   A Pebble in the Pond: A Job Enrichment Model of Organizational Change and Development

16 Toward Enlightened Systems Design

chapter
ONE
The Motivation Problem

Historically, the citizens of the United States have experienced a steady
improvement in the standard of living. This is a tribute to their ability
to invent social organizations that satisfy human needs. But although
it is true that working conditions and real wages and benefits are better
than ever and that people are better educated and trained than they
have ever been, there is a growing gap between the way people perform
in organizations and the way they are expected to perform by their
employers. This difference between what people actually do and what
they are expected to (and could) do is a problem of human motivation.
Thus in recent years managers and administrators in government and
industry have been experiencing rapid changes in employee behavior
which not only reflect the growing tension of living within our modern
institutions, but also represent manifestations of the motivation gap.
This chapter explores in detail the dynamics at work in the labor force
as a whole and the underlying causes of personnel problems which are
related to employee motivation.

DYNAMICS IN THE LABOR FORCE

Organizations today are encountering growing monetary and human
costs that are associated with the disrupted production and diminished
quality that stem from heightened employee/management antagonism,
increased strike activity, and rising rates of turnover and absenteeism.
Each of these problems is considered in turn below.

Antagonism, Turmoil, and Strikes

Of 7,900 union members who were eligible to cast ballots in a recent
strike vote at a plant of one of the country's leading manufacturing

organizations, over 6,500 turned out and 97 percent of them voted in favor of the strike. This action formalized the antagonism that had been growing between plant management and the workers over many months. The initial turmoil was quite unexpected by management since the plant was modern and well-designed, containing what was considered to be the world's fastest assembly line, and the company paid good wages and had a competitive benefits program. Despite these factors of good design and working conditions, however, production results were running considerably below management's expectations. Therefore, in addition to reorganizing their operations, the management adopted a "get tough" attitude to obtain peak efficiency from the installation.

But both the union and management were surprised by the depth of resistance they encountered in the young people in the plant (whose average age was 24). Many young workers adopted the attitude that the tougher the company got, the more would they stiffen their resistance, even though jobs in the area are scarce and many of them were recently married and had young children. Unlike their parents or workers of an older generation, these young workers were not intimidated by threats of unemployment.

A particularly undesirable consequence of the struggle between management and the young workers had been a marked decrease in production quality to the extent that management believed itself to be the victim of industrial sabotage by its own work force. In addition to the direct costs associated with the production of defective goods, there was the cost of undermined public confidence in the organization's products. This can be particularly damaging when it comes, as it did in this case, during a time of rising consumer expectations and demands in the area of product quality and reliability.

The above is but one example of the growing number of authorized and unauthorized strikes and work stoppages that are leading to the loss of large amounts of work time in both the private and the public sectors of the economy.

Increased Turnover

A particularly costly problem for industry during extended periods of general economic prosperity with their concomitant labor shortages has been the high turnover of employees. The fact that jobs—especially in the clerical fields—are interchangeable among companies in many industries facilitates job switching during such periods. For example, figures from the United States Bureau of Labor Statistics indicate that "quit rates" in some industries jumped 80 percent from 1964 to 1973. Such high turnover of the labor force is costly not only in terms of the direct expenses involved in the continual hiring and training of new personnel, but also in terms of the hidden costs of diverted supervision, coaching and "break-in" time given by other employees, and in the low productivity during early on-the-job periods. Furthermore, once a high turnover situation develops in a company in a particular job category, it tends to create a climate that results in its self-perpetuation. This happens for several reasons. First, new employees (especially those with less than six months service) tend to have higher turnover rates than more experienced employees—so that the more people you lose, the faster you start to lose them as you hire replacements. Second, valued employees with longer service, who might otherwise stay with the company, are encouraged to take the plunge into the job market by the success experiences of their former co-workers in finding new employment. Finally, the loss of production and the diminished work quality levels that are attendant on our inexperienced work force cause the management to bear down more strictly in an effort to achieve satisfactory results (as in the plant strike described above), thus forcing out people who will not work under such stringent conditions.

In view of the likelihood of continued economic expansion and, over the long run, low national unemployment rates—especially in highly skilled occupations where turnover can be particularly costly—there would appear to be little hope for the natural diminution of this kind of turnover. Astute managers will, therefore, seek every means available to them to minimize the turnover of their force.

Absenteeism

If people are unwilling or unable to quit a job, one way they can show their displeasure with it is by staying away from it as often as they can. Thus absenteeism rates have been rising sharply over the past decade to the point where they have doubled in some companies. One of the country's largest manufacturing organizations has an average of five percent of its hourly workers absent without explanation every day, and on some days—particularly Mondays and Fridays—the rate can go as high as ten percent and more.

Closely related to absenteeism is the problem of tardiness. This too has been on the increase with the consequence that production lines have been prevented from starting up promptly when the shifts change in manufacturing plants and phones and desks go untended in offices. It is harder to leave a plant early than it is to come late, but if you have ever gambled with your life by standing in a plant parking lot at quitting time, you know just how anxious people are to be away from their workplace by the way in which they roar out of the lot.

For the company, the results of this increased absenteeism and tardiness are, of course, wasted manpower, lowered effectiveness, and increased costs.

Changing Composition of the Work Force

Problems such as strikes, turnover, and absenteeism were at one time primarily problems of the factory, and were commonly viewed as being peculiar to the blue-collar worker. But today these problems are as common to the office as they are to the shop floor. No employee group in the country is growing and changing as rapidly as the white-collar workers. One consequence of that growth has been the rapid erosion of the mutual loyalty that once bound white-collar workers and management together. Although white-collar workers once viewed themselves as being the elite of nonmanagement personnel, today's clerical worker—bookkeeper, secretary, or business machine operator—is more apt to consider himself or herself to be just another cog in the machine. In fact, as we move more and more toward a service economy, the keypunch operator, rather than the drill-press operator, seems more to typify the average American worker.

Evidence of the breakdown in the relationship between white-collar workers and management—and of the changes in the attitudes that white-collar employees have toward management and themselves—can be seen in the rapid growth of white-collar unionization: From 1958 to

1968 the number of white-collar union members increased by 46 percent. Currently there are over three million white-collar union members, or approximately 15 percent of the total white-collar force. There are several indications that this will become a growing trend. Since the white-collar work force shows rapid expansion over the long run, while the blue-collar force appears to be stagnating or even declining, union leaders are coming to recognize the white-collar force as being their likeliest area for growth in the future. In addition, a recent series of attitude surveys, taken across a broad cross-section of clerical employees in a variety of industries, has shown a marked and growing dissatisfaction among these workers toward the managers and companies for whom they work.

The attitudes of those white-collar employees who are engineers and other technical professionals might be expected to differ from the attitudes of other white-collar workers but such is not the case. In fact, over a period of time, the pattern of engineering dissatisfaction relative to other occupational groups appears to be independent of any particular set of economic conditions. Thus, the attitudes of engineers toward their companies, as surveyed in a variety of studies, are not unlike those of blue-collar workers or routine office employees; except that sometimes they are even less favorable than those groups.

In summary, it is a rare manager today who is not forced to cope with some, if not all, of the following personnel problems:

- High turnover or quit rates
- Absenteeism
- Tardiness
- Strikes, stoppages, and union grievances
- High training costs
- Low rates of productivity
- Generalized attitudes of employee dissatisfaction
- Industrial sabotage, both overt and covert.
- Alcoholism
- Drug addiction

UNDERLYING CAUSES OF EMPLOYEE BEHAVIOR

Only ten years ago a study made by the Survey Research Center of the University of Michigan[1] reported that the absence of a sense of personal fulfillment was not a major cause of dissatisfaction with their jobs for blue-collar workers. The researchers concluded that, whether blue-collar workers started out with minimal expectations of finding fulfillment in their jobs or became adjusted to the lack of it, they did not seem to be too frustrated about their situation. But today there are frequent signs of restlessness and discontent among workers, as has been described above, which have taken new forms in the labor movement. A new dimension has appeared in many of these incidents which suggests a pattern of causes which are not wholly economic and sometimes not economic at all. While slowdowns, protests, and walkouts are traditionally related to the usual issues of pay and benefits, they now increasingly reflect discontent among workers with the lives they lead within their organizations.

For example, at the heart of the young workers' strike described at the beginning of the previous section was the demand that they have a say in how their jobs were to be performed. They resented the constant, repetitive, unskilled nature of their work, and the recent efforts by management to increase efficiency resulted in making the jobs even simpler, removing the last traces of skill from the job's requirements.

It becomes clear that industry is going to have to do something to change the boring, repetitive nature of assembly line work if it would avoid the unrest that such work so often generates. Propagandizing is not the answer; all too often managements have tried to induce in employees a feeling that their jobs were important when, in fact, everyone knew that the jobs were routine and dull. All that does is add a credibility gap to the motivation gap.

To many managers it seems that the kinds of behavior we have been describing are simply a function of perversity on the part of employees. Perplexed by such behavior, managers characteristically respond to it with questions such as, "We treat them so well; why aren't they satisfied?" or, "Why won't they shoot for company goals?" Another question often voiced is, "Why can't they be like we were in the old days?" which is much like Henry Higgins' plaintive cry in George Bernard

Shaw's play *Pygmalion*: "Why can't she be like me?" (It is highly
doubtful that many managers would have the kind of success Henry
Higgins had were they to try to make over their employees into the
image of themselves.) The underlying assumption in all those questions,
of course, is that the fault inheres in the employee—and it is precisely
that assumption that we are challenging.

Robert N. Ford, formerly Personnel Director for Manpower Utilization of American Telephone and Telegraph, has commented on what he
calls "the obstinate employee" as follows:

> It appears to me that the employee as an audience—as someone with
> whom management is trying to communicate—is becoming more
> obstinate than ever. We have communicated like mad at him . . . but
> I'm afraid that he finished listening long before we stopped talking.[2]

Ford observed further that for 25 years or more we have made a
wide variety of attempts to make the employee feel better about his job
and company. Those efforts have resulted in: (1) higher wages, (2)
broader benefits, (3) better human relations, (4) varied employee activities, and (5) communication programs. These things have all been
very necessary and welcome additions to the work experience, but lasting motivation among workers is obviously still absent.

The Henry Higgins-type question raised by managers about the "obstinate" employee essentially asks, "What's the matter with him?" Management's traditional and authoritarian view of the employee permits the
assumption that there is something wrong with the employee whose goals
are different from those of the organization. Of course, few managers
would actually *say* that they believe most workers to have an inherent
dislike for work or responsibility and that the workers must be threatened with punishment in order to get them to produce—but many managers *act* as if they believed those things to be true. Unfortunately, such
a view fails to consider some facts about human behavior which recent
research has clarified.

Work is a natural expression of human existence, as natural as eat-
ing or sleeping, and most employees come to work in search of a good
job. The definition of "good job" may vary among individuals, but however it's defined, a good job is still the objective. The organization's purpose in hiring an employee, however, is to secure that person's contribu-

tion to its effort to provide a product or service to the satisfaction of its customers or recipients—and, in most cases, to do so at a profit. A newer view of this conflict of objectives is developing which acknowledges that employees may very well enter an organization with objectives different from those of the organization, or that they cannot simply be talked into adopting those objectives. Realizing this, managers must stop lamenting the fact that the objectives are different and accept a new managerial role for themselves: *The new function managers must undertake is to seek ways to create job experiences which will fulfill personal employee goals and, simultaneously, serve organization purposes.* It is simply too wide of the mark to say that there is something wrong with employees when their behavior does not seem to coincide with the organization's purpose. Instead of wishing that one's employees were more like oneself, or more like the employees of a bygone depression-wracked era, a manager might do better to assume that they *are* like him. Reflecting on what motivates and satisfies him, the manager might be able to determine those characteristics of his "real world" that are diminished or lacking entirely in the "real world" of his subordinates.

Who, then, is the obstinate employee? Well, the ferment and searching occurring in our society as a whole is most notable in the young, and the youthful segment of the labor force is expanding rapidly. (Of the total growth in United States population by 1980, two-thirds will be in the age group ranging from 20 to 34.) These young people are accustomed to a rising standard of living; they have had more and better education and training than any previous generation in our history. This combination of affluence and education has led young people to hold increasingly high expectations regarding what we might term the quality of their lives. Thus young persons are refusing to stay in organizations that do not give them work which will contribute to their leading a meaningful life. As we have seen, they refuse to work at jobs which (usually in the name of efficiency) have been stripped of interest for them and protest their situation by quitting in droves, or by frequently being absent, or by staying on but becoming more militant in their demands. With regard to absenteeism, for example, a recent study comparing several locations with varying absenteeism rates led to the conclusion that satisfactory attendance records were not so much a function of greater management emphasis on absence control as they were the consequence of the employees' greater interest in and involvement with the work itself.[3] The researchers concluded that management had too great a tendency to relate the frequency of absences to characteristics of the worker rather than to the characteristics of the work.

Dr. Frederick Herzberg, a behavioral scientist whose research lead him to formulate the Motivation-Hygiene Theory of work motivation to be described in Chapter Four, has provided some valuable insights into the underlying causes of current employee behavior.[4] He suggests that an existential view of life is on the rise in the United States as traditional religious and social systems recede or become transformed. Such an existential view makes it imperative for the individual to define for himself what constitutes a meaningful life. The definition of a meaningful life is conscious and sophisticated for some individuals. When meaning is absent from their experience, their response is immediate and articulate. For others, the need to find meaningful experience is less conscious and articulate. Should they fail to find it they are aware of their unhappiness and lack of fulfillment, but may not realize the reasons for those feelings. From the manager's point of view the cases are not much different, because the resultant behavior to be dealt with is much the same.

Many enlightened managers are already convinced that a central concern of any enterprise must be to provide work that not only meets economic needs but also satisfies and fulfills the people who spend so great a part of their lives in the organization. They realize that the failure to do so can only lead to frustration, bitterness, and even anger on the part of people who are required to perform narrow, constricting jobs—and that those feelings find expression in the catalog of personnel problems we described above.

Unions, too, have come in for their share of prodding in this new area of unmet worker needs. Paul Jacobs, a former union organizer and veteran observer and writer on unions has commented:

> (Unions) have to break with their pattern of not thinking about work, the nature of work, their relationship to work, and what they can do about work. What do we do about work now? Well, we say we're going to fix the wages, we're going to try to establish . . . minimal working conditions, we're going to slow down the line . . . But do we ever say: Hey, the whole concept of production of an automo-

bile on a line stinks; the whole thing is wrong; what we ought to be
doing is figuring out new ways of looking at the problem of work? [5]

Jacobs advocated that the United Auto Workers Research Department
stop spending its money researching wage problems and start spending
it on new ways of dealing with the problem of work at the workplace.
Walter Reuther, noting that young workers today are interested in a
sense of fulfillment as human beings, commented that:

> The young worker feels he's not master of his own destiny. He's
> going to run away from (work) every time he gets a chance. That
> is why there's an absentee problem ... The prospect of tightening up
> bolts every two minutes for eight hours for thirty years doesn't lift
> the human spirit. [6]

A fairly clear-cut pattern of understanding appears to be emerging,
then, from the seemingly aberrant changes in employee behavior that we
have been witnessing in recent years. Astute managers, behavioral scientists, business researchers, union officers, and workers themselves all
seem to be reaching the same conclusion: that the problem of motivation
lies in the nature of the work itself; that it is to the task and not to the
man or the environment that we must look if we want people to achieve
the performance of which we—and they—know they are capable. In addition to the understanding of the nature of the problem that many people have obtained through direct experience, there is a growing body of
theory and experimental evidence that documents the conclusion that the
nature of the task itself is at the heart of the motivation problem. Experience is beginning to accumulate on how to go about changing jobs
so that they will prove to be motivating for their incumbents. This process is known as "job enrichment."

SUMMARY

A large and growing proportion of the labor force consists of young
people who have been raised in an era of unparalleled economic prosperity. They do not share—certainly not to the same degree—their pred-
ecessors' concern with economic security; they are not easily intimidated
by threats of economic deprivation. In fact, they respond to such threats
with ever-increasing militancy. They are well educated and trained and

have come to expect that the work they do will not only put food into their mouths, but also put meaning into their lives. Thus, while in earlier eras *any* job was good enough for most workers, today's employees— white-collar as well as blue-collar—are telling us loudly and clearly that that is no longer the case. They are telling us not only with words, but with other forms of behavior that are proving increasingly costly—such as strikes, stoppages, turnover, absenteeism, reduced production rates, and diminished quality. It has become evident that the heart of the motivation problem is the nature of the work that people are required to do. Fortunately, knowledge has begun to accumulate that can assist managers in so changing their employees' jobs that the employees become motivated to perform at the highest levels of their ability.

REFERENCES

1. Robert A. Sutermeister, *People and Productivity* (New York, Mc-Graw-Hill, 1969), p. 21.

2. Robert N. Ford, "The Obstinate Employee," *Psychology Today* (November 1969).

3. Arthur N. Turner and Paul R. Lawrence, *Industrial Jobs and the Worker* (Boston, Harvard University Graduate School of Business Administration, 1965), p. 113.

4. Frederick Herzberg, B. Snyderman and H. Mausner, *Motivation to Work* (New York, John Wiley & Sons, 1959).

5. Quoted by Turner and Lawrence, *op. cit.*, p. 116.

6. Quoted by Judson Gooding, "Blue-Collar Blues on the Assembly Line," *Fortune* (July 1970), p. 112.

chapter
TWO
Historical Views of
Work Motivation
and Employee Behavior

INTRODUCTION

Imagine yourself in a factory at about the turn of the century. It is noisy, the light is dim, the work areas are crowded. The workers are poorly educated; many of them have not gone beyond grade school. Although there is in the country a general ethos—the Horatio Alger myth —that encourages the belief that a man can advance as far as his talents and ambition can carry him, these men have little faith in it. There is virtually no way for them to advance; this job—provided they don't get fired—is *it*.

The living conditions of these workers are not unlike their working conditions. The best they can hope for—the American dream—is that their children can live better lives than they—receive more education and get better jobs (the jobs unavailable to themselves). The vehicle for their dream fulfillment is money.

At the peak of the organizational pyramid are the men for whom the above-mentioned ethos has become a reality. They are the entrepreneurs, the men who are creating the industrial and societal revolution. Material success is the symbol of their entrepreneurial ability, the fruition of their ambition. These men commonly held a rather primitive view of work motivation. Were they to be asked what motivated them to success they would respond with the symbol rather than the reality: "Money," they would say, "of course."

It is no wonder that money was seen to be the controlling variable in worker motivation and industrial production. (In fact, that observation was somewhat in error, for the concept of motivation as such did not really exist at that time.) Money was seen to be directly related to productivity, either as a positive incentive in the form of reward, or as a negative incentive in the threat of unemployment. The worker was seen as another "black box" on which you manipulate certain levers to get certain responses. He or she was occasionally cantankerous, but essentially uncomplicated.

At the heart of this view of human nature—the concept of "economic man"—were two basic assumptions: the first, that the worker was a rational being who would always act in his or her own best interest; the second, that he or she worked primarily to satisfy economic needs: i.e., for food, shelter, clothing, and an occasional amenity. The conclusion drawn from these assumptions was that the formal reward/punishment structure of the firm was the sole determinant of a worker's behavior and that work effort could be controlled directly through the manipulation of that structure. The concepts and practice of "scientific management" were born out of this set of assumptions about the nature of man.

An alternative view of the worker—the concept of "social man"—arose out of research that was initially undertaken in the framework of the "scientific management" theory. While it could not be denied that people had to work to earn the money to satisfy their economic needs, this later view held that the worker was basically a social being and that economic rewards and punishments had to be understood in their social context. Productivity, for example, could be affected by a set of informal standards (informal in the sense that they were not sanctioned by management) developed and enforced by the work *group* as well as by the firm's formal reward structure. A key assumption of the "social man" viewpoint was that the worker was equipped with a wide range of emotional needs that would have to be accounted for in managerial planning and behavior.

What these two views had in common was the assumption that motivation was something that happened to a worker from "outside," and that variations in external factors would directly affect the effort of workers. Under the concept of "scientific management," financial incentives can be seen as a carrot-and-stick approach to motivation. For the human relations movement that grew out of the "social" man view, the connection is more complex and less explicit. The somewhat vague factor of "morale" was taken to be the key to employee motivation and was believed to be affected by various environmental factors such as the behavior of supervisors toward their subordinates.

Each of these views of man and the movements they gave birth to will be discussed in greater detail below. The chapter will conclude with a review of the work of Douglas McGregor, who provided a framework for the articulation of a philosophy about the nature of man at work.

SCIENTIFIC MANAGEMENT

The "scientific management" movement spearheaded by Frederick W. Taylor is generally conceded to be the most significant of early management theories. Taylor called his theory "scientific" because his aim was to replace rule-of-thumb operations with well-researched methods and a spirit of scientific inquiry. The name "scientific management" is generally found within quotation marks, however, because it was based on Taylor's assumptions rather than on a systematic method for developing and testing hypotheses about the nature of man and work. A key assumption in his theory is that worker behavior will conform to the "economic man" model previously described. One of the aims of the movement, in fact, was:

> to assure a happier home and social life to workers through removal, by increase of income, of many of the disagreeable and worrying factors in the total situation.[1]

As a young supervisor, trained in mechanical engineering, Taylor looked about the floor of the shop in which he worked and saw chaos. Workers operated their machines at different rates, used tools and methods of their own devising, and had no incentive to increase their production. In addition, he observed that workers were often placed in jobs for which they had insufficient aptitude and/or training, and that there was a continual struggle between supervisors and workers over what constituted "a fair day's output."

It was Taylor's belief that if management and labor cooperated in the application of "scientific methods" to their endeavors they would create the maximum possible good for themselves and for society.[2] He advocated the use of "scientific methods" for the placement and training of workers as well as for the setting of production standards and the establishment of work procedures. Furthermore, he argued that management relegated too many responsibilities to the workers that it should assume for itself. This included the planning, organizing, and controlling of production processes. Taylor believed that management's assumption of these responsibilities would increase production for two reasons: first, because workers would then have more time for productive effort; second, because management was better suited to make such decisions and would generate procedures which would improve productivity.

Taylor believed that performance standards should be set through timing of the various work stages with a stopwatch. A system of incentive payments would be geared to those standards, causing both productivity and the workers' income to be improved.

In addition to rationalizing the total job into its separate elemental components, Taylor also advocated the functionalization of supervision. Instead of establishing a single foreman over each group, Taylor argued that there should be a requisite number of supervisors, each an expert in a particular aspect of the production process. The worker would then consult with a given foreman depending on the nature of the particular problem he was having. There would be no need for a "whip man" type of supervisor, Taylor believed. Since each man's pay was to be tied to his output, he would therefore work as hard as he could because it was in his own best interest to do so.

At the time of its inception—as well as today—"scientific management" tended to be regarded as primarily a system for securing improved efficiency. But Taylor was most emphatic in his separation of the conceptual principles of "scientific management" from the techniques that derived from those principles. He truly believed that the *concept* of "scientific management" was nothing less than a "great mental revolution" in the basic attitudes of the worker and the manager about how work was to be accomplished. He felt that this transcended the use of stopwatches, the functionalization of foremanship, the establishment of incentives, and all the other manifestations of that "revolution."

It was this spirit of "scientific" inquiry that led to the pioneering efforts of Frank and Lillian Gilbreth in the area of work methods. Their primary concern was with the development of the most efficient set and sequence of motions to accomplish a given task. Their basic assumption was that there was one best way of performing any given task, and that this could be discovered through scientific analysis. Their twin objectives in motion study were an increase in efficiency coupled with a reduction in fatigue for the worker.

The work of Taylor and the Gilbreths and others resulted in the establishment of a new profession—industrial engineering—whose practitioners are still widely employed in industry today. It resulted also in the adoption of many of the mechanics of "scientific management," such as incentive systems, process control, and methods and procedures planning. However, the "mental revolution" envisioned never really took place. The reasons for this failure are varied and complex. A partial explanation lies in some of the mistaken practices advocated by Taylor and the others. More importantly, however, the principal errors are to be found in the assumptions upon which the principles and aims of "scientific management" were based. The "scientific management" movement has been referred to as "physiological organization theory" because of its emphasis on tasks that are repetitive and routine, requiring little concern with human problem-solving and decision-making abilities.[3] In that sense, the theory tended to treat workers as automatons, and there was much resistance against adoption of its work procedures because they were viewed as: (a) infringements on the worker's right to self-determination, and (b) a potential threat to job security (because of increased production). Finally, by its reliance on the "economic man" viewpoint, the theory assumed that man was, in essence, mono-motivated; that money would retain an absolute potency as a spur to higher productivity. It thus ignored the potential effects of other variables such as peer group influence on worker efforts. It was inevitable that other theories would arise in reaction to this view of man and the conceptual and practical shortcomings of the "scientific management" theory. One of the principal alternatives was the "social man" viewpoint, and it was embodied in what has come to be known as the "Human Relations" school of management theory.

THE HUMAN RELATIONS SCHOOL

Ironically enough, it was Frederick Taylor's dictum that research should replace rule-of-thumb as the determiner of managerial behavior that led to the series of experiments—called the Hawthorne studies, after the Western Electric Company plant where they were conducted during the late 1920's and early 1930's—that gave birth to the human relations movement.[4] The initial intent of the research program was to determine the relationship between working conditions and productivity. Specifically, a careful check would be kept of worker output as separate experiments were conducted in which lighting and work/rest schedules were varied.

The first set of experiments sought to determine the relationship between illumination and worker efficiency. The results were confusing to say the least. In the first test the output apparently "bobbed up and down" without direct relation to the amount of illumination. So a second test was conducted with two groups: an "experimental" group whose illumination would be varied and a "control" group that would work under constant illumination. The results of this test were even more perplexing: production increases of almost equal magnitude occurred in both groups. A third experiment followed. In this test the "control" group again had constant illumination while the "experimental" group was subjected to *decreasing* illumination. The results? Again a steady increase in efficiency for both groups (that is, until the "experimental" group complained that it had become too dark for them to see what they were doing—at which point their productivity decreased). Since further, less formal trials did nothing to dispel the perplexing nature of the results, a new experiment was planned using a different independent variable. In this study, rest periods were to be varied to determine the effects of worker fatigue on productivity. (Bear in mind that this was happening during the 1920's, when employees worked a six-day week with no breaks except for lunch.)

In an attempt to eliminate the effects of all factors other than the one being studied, five production workers (and a sixth to keep them supplied) were placed in a room by themselves (except for the observer) equipped with work stations and materials. The nature of the study had been explained to the workers and they were consulted on all the changes in procedure to be introduced as the study progressed. No experimental changes other than this shift in locale were made for a period of five weeks. Then a change was made in the incentive plan. Whereas before the workers' pay had been tied to the output of a group of about 100 employees, from this point on incentive payments were to be based on the production of the group of five. Production records for each operator had been kept, without their knowledge, for weeks prior to the start of the experiment, so that before/after comparisons could be made for each change in routine. If the workers had known that records were being kept they might have increased or decreased their productivity either intentionally or unwittingly, and thus rendered future comparisons invalid. In order to minimize the effect of the incentive plan change, no further changes were made for the next eight weeks.

Careful records were kept of all aspects of the working conditions in the test room, as well as an hourly log of test room events. Each operator was asked to report daily how many hours she had slept the night before, and was examined by a company doctor every six weeks. A further experimental condition was that there was no formal supervision in the test room. Rather, there was a "test room observer" whose job it was to keep the records, arrange the work, and maintain the workers' cooperative spirit.

The changes introduced were successively:

1. Two five-minute rest periods, one at 10 in the morning, the other at 2 in the afternoon. This lasted for five weeks.
2. Rest periods increased to ten minutes each. This continued for four weeks.
3. Six five-minute rest periods a day. This lasted for four weeks.
4. Rest periods reduced to two of ten minutes each. Workers were provided with light meals at mid-morning and afternoon. This continued for several months.
5. Work day ended at 4:30 instead of at 5 o'clock.
6. Work day ended at 4:00.
7. Work day extended back to 5:00.
8. Saturday work eliminated. This lasted twelve weeks.
9. Return to the conditions that existed prior to the experiment: rest periods, refreshments and shortened work-week were all eliminated. This lasted for twelve weeks.
10. Reintroduction of rest periods and refreshments.

Once again, the results were not as expected. Throughout the course of the experiment the output of the group kept rising, with minor fluctuations (such as during the time when there were six rest periods per day, which the workers themselves felt was too much. Even when weekly output fell off, as when Saturday work was eliminated, daily output continued to rise. And most surprisingly, when rest periods and refreshments and short work-days were eliminated and Saturday work reinstituted, output rose again. When the experiment began, the operators had been producing an average of 2,400 units a week each. Through period 9, output rose to 2,900 units—and when rest periods were reintroduced the number rose to 3,000. The unmistakable conclusion was that there had been a steady upward trend in output independent of the changes made in working conditions. Even where the conditions were the same in different test periods, the output in the later time period was higher than in the earlier, identical, period. (All the operators were experienced at their jobs at the start of the experiment, and the effect of job learning as a factor in increased production can be considered negligible, particularly since the study ran for a period of several years and the improvement was continuous.) Furthermore, the operators in the experimental group were absent only about one-third as much as regular workers on the shop floor. They seemed eager to come to work in the morning and required practically no supervision. How to account for these findings?

From the earlier illumination experiments the researchers had learned that the workers had psychological reactions as well as physiological ones. Because they were concerned with physiological factors, however, the researchers wanted to minimize the disturbing effects of the psychological factors. One of the reasons for isolating the workers in the test room was to allow the psychological reaction to disappear so that the direct effect of physical conditions on worker efficiency could be measured. But now it appeared that the physiological factors would have to be discounted and answers would have to be sought among the psychological factors. Two factors of particular significance have been identified that not only seem to "explain" the results in this particular set of experiments but also served as the basis for the theoretical underpinning of the human relations movement.

The first factor relates to what has come to be called the "Hawthorne effect." That is, the results occurred precisely because an experiment was conducted. The workers had been singled out for special treatment. They were placed in a separate room and removed from normal supervision, and they knew that the results of what they were doing could lead to the improvement of working conditions for their fellow employees. They were the focus of a great deal of attention. Their views on working conditions were constantly sought and they frequently met with a high-ranking member of the plant's management. In consequence, they felt themselves to be important and valued employees and, consciously or unconsciously, they improved their output in return for that sense of importance and worth.

The second factor relates to the group itself. During the course of the study the group went through a process of social development. Conversation between operators, normally restricted on the shop floor, was engaged in freely and they formed close friendships that extended beyond working hours. When one of the operators was feeling tired, the others would work harder to "carry" her. The operators themselves, in interviews, atributed the improvement to two factors: first, they said that "it was fun" to work in the test room; second, the absence of supervisory control—although they were under constant, minute observation —allowed them to work without anxiety. In fact, the group developed its own self-appointed leader. Finally, the group developed a common purpose—an increase in the output rate.

Elton Mayo, whose name is most closely linked with these researches, concluded that work was a group activity and that management's job was to form stable, cohesive work groups that would allow each member to experience a sense of belonging. Furthermore, recognizing the emotional needs of employees, supervisors should be interested and sympathetic rather than authoritarian. In response to these findings and conclusions, most organizations have instituted a variety of programs designed to improve human relations. These include the training of supervisors and managers in proper ways to handle people, counseling programs, and various internal communications media. All too often, however, the intent has been *manipulation*—when the studies clearly showed that it was genuine *participation* on the part of the employees that contributed to the favorable results. In addition, a common assumption based on the findings was that if employees could be kept "happy," they would be more productive. Although this was somewhat more sophisticated than the carrot-and-stick approach of "scientific management," in the sense that it set the employees emotional needs before physical conditions as a factor in productivity, the presumed connection between morale and productivity was still a simplistic one. It was not the whole answer to the problem of motivation—as many a manager with "happy" people who are producing below their capabilities has found out to his dismay. But the fundamental contribution of this research is not to be denied. Focusing attention on employee attitudes, supervisory behavior, group dynamics, and productivity as it did, it served as a "foot in the door" for the still growing symbiotic relationship between behavioral science and business management.

DOUGLAS McGREGOR AND MANAGEMENT PHILOSOPHY

Of all the behavioral scientists whose work is reviewed in this volume, the late Douglas McGregor is perhaps the best known to businessmen. In his book, "The Human Side of Enterprise," McGregor made three valuable contributions to our understanding of the motivation problem in industrial organization.[5] First, he established the point that each manager, because he is human, has a need to integrate his understanding of "the way things are" into a coherent philosophy which may or may not be consciously perceived. Second, he developed two sets of assumptions about the nature of people at work, one stemming from a common managerial philosophy, the other derived from current behavioral science knowledge. Third, he related these sets of assumptions to the problem of motivation and pointed the way toward a means of integrating individual and organizational goals.

With regard to the first point, McGregor argued that a manager's view of reality exerted a profound effect on his managerial actions, but that such actions were rarely based on a direct response to objective reality. Rather, they are a response to reality as the manager *perceives* it. For example, one's perception of the equity of a newly negotiated wage rate generally depends on whether he has been sitting on the union or the management side of the bargaining table.

Where the relationship of people to work was concerned, McGregor believed that many managers perceived reality as what he called Theory X. This theory of human nature included the following assumptions:

1. The average human being has an inherent dislike of work and will avoid it if he can.
2. Because of this human characteristic of dislike of work, most peo-

ple must be coerced, controlled, directed, threatened with punishment to get them to put forth adequate effort toward the achievement of organizational objectives.

3. The average human being prefers to be directed, wishes to avoid responsibility, has relatively little ambition, wants security above all.[6]

In contrast to this set of assumptions, McGregor postulated another set, which he called Theory Y, which he derived from recent theoretical developments in social science. Theory Y holds that:

1. The expenditure of physical and mental effort in work is as natural as play or rest.

2. External control and the threat of punishment are not the only means for bringing about effort toward organizational objectives. Man will exercise self-direction and self-control in the service of objectives to which he is committed.

3. Commitment to objectives is a function of the rewards associated with their achievement.

4. The average human being learns, under proper conditions, not only to accept but to seek responsibility.

5. The capacity to exercise a relatively high degree of imagination, ingenuity, and creativity in the solution of organizational problems is widely, not narrowly, distributed in the population.

6. Under the conditions of modern industrial life, the intellectual potentialities of the average human being are only partially utilized.[7]

Contrary to Theory X, Theory Y holds that man does not have an inherent dislike of work. It assumes that, depending on certain controllable conditions, work may be either viewed as a source of satisfaction—in which case it will be voluntarily performed—or as a source of punishment—in which case it will be avoided as much as possible. As noted earlier, that avoidance can take the form of nonillness absences, tardiness, wildcat strikes, turnover, restricted productivity, and poor quality of output.

It was McGregor's contention that Theory X neither explained nor described human nature, although that was its intent. Rather, it explained the *consequences* of management's adoption of that particular philosophy and the actions managers took on the basis of it.

McGregor differentiated between two sets of rewards and punishments: extrinsic and intrinsic. *Extrinsic* rewards exist in the environment; they include money, fringe benefits, and working conditions. *Intrinsic* rewards are inherent in the work itself. However, the reward is in the achievement of the goal. Under Theory X the assumption is made that man requires external direction, that motivation is something that you do *to* him. Most managerial activity under Theory X has been directed toward the provision of extrinsic rewards and punishments through either "tough" management, which is characterized by its use of coercion and the threat of punishment, or "soft" management, which is seen as a form of managerial abdication in which harmonious but unproductive employees continually demand more for doing less. McGregor argued that both "tough" and "soft" management were inadequate for motivation today because people are seeking to satisfy needs of a higher order, needs that can only be satisfied by intrinsic rewards.* The conditions under which these can be obtained, McGregor argued, are likely to prevail only where an organization is managed by adherents to Theory Y (or some other theory based on similarly objective findings about human nature), who assume that man is motivated from within.

McGregor asserted that the central principles of organization that derive from Theory X and Theory Y are quite different. The former relies on direction and control through the exercise of authority, while the latter requires the creation of conditions that will lead to the integration of individual and organizational goals. This does *not* mean the "bending" or manipulation of employee needs to meet company goals, but a genuine mutual coordination of goals. McGregor recognized that his concept of integration was foreign to most managers' way of thinking about the employment relationship, and that there would be a tendency either to reject it as being either anarchistic or inconsistent with human nature (as seen by Theory X), or to twist it unconsciously until it fit existing conceptions. However, he believed that if managers truly were seeking to realize the potential of their employees they were

---

* See the discussion of Maslow's theory of a hierarchy of human needs, in Chapter 3.

going to have to learn to manage in a new way: through the implementation of policies and practices, based on Theory Y, that would provide job opportunities for employees in which they could fulfill themselves *and* contribute to company success.

SUMMARY

In this chapter we have reviewed two significant early views about the
nature of man at work—"economic man" and "social man"—and the
movements that embodied those views, and Douglas McGregor's later,
more sophisticated approach to understanding the human motivation to
work. The key assumption common to both early views of man was that
the worker could be motivated by the manipulation of external factors,
be they physical working conditions, money, supervision, or such in-
tangibles as the level of morale induced by good up-and-down communications and the cohesiveness of work groups. The "scientific management" movement, based on the concept of rational "economic man,"
asserted that each worker would, if provided with a reasonable production standard and a system of pay incentives, work toward the company
interest since it would be in his own best interest to do so. The human
relations movement was based on the "social man" viewpoint, assuming
man to be essentially an emotional being, and stressed the importance of
fostering cohesive work groups in which each worker had a sense of
belonging.

Although they contributed minimally to our understanding of the
nature of motivation and its relation to productivity, both movements
did provide other benefits. By its insistence on valid research as the
basis for managerial decision-making and behavior, the "scientific management" school led to the abandonment of many ill-conceived practices
based on "rule-of-thumb" judgment and to the adoption of a more rational approach to the running of a business. There is no question that
the researches of the human relations movement have led to the existence of a much better set of relationships between managers and employees and that they opened the way for the more sophisticated behavioral science research from which much of our present knowledge
derives.

Douglas McGregor contributed a comprehensive view of the relationships between the assumptions managers hold about human nature, the way people actually behave as a result of those assumptions, and what is required if organizations are to fully utilize the capabilities of their members. To that end, he presented two different theories about the nature of man. Theory X, widely held by managers, viewed people as both requiring and wanting direction and control, and as being motivated by extrinsic rewards and punishments. Theory Y, based on behavioral science research, held that people would provide their own direction if they were given compatible environments and tasks that challenged them—toward which they would be motivated by the desire to obtain intrinsic rewards. Management's job, McGregor argued, is to bring about that integration of individual goals with company purpose. He believed that the result would be maximum organizational effectiveness.

Above all, McGregor was personally concerned with humanistic values; he emphasized the need to use knowledge to bring about the genuine participation of employees, not just manipulation of them.

REFERENCES

1. H. S. Person (ed.), *Scientific Management in American Industry*, quoted by Claude S. George, Jr., in *The History of Management Thought* (Englewood Cliffs, N.J., Prentice-Hall, 1968), p. 95.

2. Frederick W. Taylor, *Scientific Management* (New York, Harper & Row, 1947).

3. James G. March and Herbert A. Simon, *Organizations* (New York, John Wiley & Sons, 1958), pp. 13–14.

4. F. J. Roethlisberger and W. J. Dickson, *Management and the Worker* (Cambridge, Mass., Harvard University Press, 1939). See also George Homans, *The Western Electric Researchers*, in R. A. Sutermeister (ed.), *People and Productivity* (New York, McGraw-Hill, 1969), pp. 73–81.

5. Douglas McGregor, *The Human Side of Enterprise* (New York, McGraw-Hill, 1960).

6. *Ibid.*, p. 33.

7. *Ibid.*, p. 45.

Behavioral Science and Management Practice

INTRODUCTION

Bookshelves in the business section of most libraries are filled with an almost bewildering variety of approaches to the understanding of men, organizations, and the complexity of their relationships with one another. The focus of this chapter is on the nature of the interaction between human needs and the organizational environment in which their satisfaction is sought. However, it seems appropriate to begin with a definition and description of behavioral science before proceeding to an examination of some of its major theoretical contributions to our understanding of motivation. Having explored the general nature of human motivation and need satisfaction—the internal structure that the worker brings to the workplace (perhaps one could say that it is the need structure which brings the worker to the workplace)—we will turn, in the last section of the chapter, to an examination of that work environment to which our needing worker has come. We wish to see how organizations satisfy or frustrate the worker depending on their ability to provide opportunities for the fulfillment of his or her needs in conjunction with the attainment of their goals.

WHAT IS BEHAVIORAL SCIENCE?

The definition of behavioral science is reasonably straightforward. It is generally taken to be the systematic study of the full range of human behavior and its sources and causes, particularly in social settings. As such, it is concerned with the prediction of how people are apt to behave under certain conditions. It is precisely that predictive ability that is leading increasing numbers of managers to value the contribution that behavioral science can make to the running of their organizations. But the search for relevant knowledge can be confusing. There are almost as many approaches to the study of organizations as there are students of the subject. While this diversity is necessary if we are ever to fully understand the workings and effects of the institutions we have created, it does currently present some serious problems of synthesis. Methods of study are as varied as the subjects, ranging from the results of systematic thinking applied to the "soft" data of years of observation by a given investigator to full-blown computer analyses of all available quantifiable variables. Some research, primarily that which is directed toward theory-building, is desciptive; much of it is diagnostic and directed toward problem-solving applications. Some investigators, such as Rensis Likert and Robert Blake, have concentrated on the role of small groups and supervisory behavior in productivity; others, such as Warren Bennis, have devoted their attention to the problems of organizational change and the institutionalization of values in terms of the general criterion of organizational effectiveness.[1,2,3]

One reason for the generation of so many different theories and approaches is the relative newness of behavioral science itself as a professional field. Furthermore, behavioral science has developed concurrently with the growth in size and complexity of organizations and explosive changes in our society, and it is hard to develop a science for the measurement and prediction of phenomena which are continually changing. A great problem for the behavioral scientists, then, is to distinguish between the ephemeral and the substantive, and to develop methods that will permit others to verify those distinctions.

Regardless of their diversity, the various approaches share certain characteristics that permit them to be considered part of behavioral science, particularly as it relates to business applications.[4,5] First, they are concerned with the search for knowledge that is verifiable, that can be subjected to test and proof. Second, there is an orientation toward the utilization of knowledge, rather than just its accumulation. To that end, much research is directed toward the realization of various organizational criteria, including economic objectives such as productivity and profitability. Concurrent with that, behavioral science is also humanistically oriented so that it seeks knowledge and strategies to adapt organizations to the requirements of their members.

It would be impossible to do justice here to the wide range of approaches undertaken, or to the depth and progress each has attained in recent years. In general, however, they manifest a common agreement on the nature of man's need structure, and acknowledge that the higher needs of individuals, as well as the goals of the organizations that employ them, are not presently being met.

MOTIVATION AND NEED SATISFACTION

Much of the theoretical basis for Douglas McGregor's conclusions, reviewed in the previous chapter, derives from the work done by the late Abraham H. Maslow, a former president of the American Psychological Association and chairman of the Psychology Department of Brandeis University. Maslow did not agree with the common belief that motivation is something that someone does to or for someone else. He based his theoretical work on the assumption that motivation comes from within the individual and cannot be imposed on him;[6] that although it is often directed at external goals, motivation is always an internal process.

Maslow viewed humankind as perpetually wanting beings who are continually striving to find ways to satisfy their needs. A man or woman is motivated to reach a particular goal because he or she has an internally generated need to reach it. But needs are not static: *Once a need has been satisfied it can no longer serve as a motivator of behavior.* Other needs then come to the fore and behavior is directed toward their satisfaction. Maslow identified five basic sets of needs which he arranged into a hierarchy. The needs are ranked in terms of the order in which they manifest themselves ascending from the most basic survival level to self-actualization, the apogee of human existence.

The five sets of needs and the order in which they emerge are:

1. Physiological needs,
2. Safety needs,
3. Need for belongingness and love,
4. Need for esteem,
5. Need for self-actualization.

The physiological needs, the most prepotent of all, include the need for food, warmth, shelter, water, sleep, sexual fulfillment, and an almost endless list of other bodily requirements. (Maslow noted, however, that any of the physiological needs and the behavior that is directed toward their satisfaction may serve as a channel for other sets of needs as well. A person who feels hungry may actually be more interested in getting love than proteins.) By identifying the physiological needs as being most prepotent, Maslow meant that if a person were totally deprived— if all his needs were unsatisfied—he would be dominated by his physiological needs; his other needs would either become nonexistent or be pushed into the background. Once the physiological needs are satisfied, however, other "higher" needs then emerge and dominate behavior. When they are satisfied, they are replaced by other needs, which are higher in the sense of being more uniquely human, and so on. This is what Maslow meant when he conceived of human needs as being organized into a hierarchy of relative prepotency.

After the physiological needs are gratified, the safety needs emerge. Satisfaction of these requires *actual* physical safety as well as a *sense* of being safe from both physical and emotional harm.

The physiological and the safety needs are both centered on the individual. Once they are satisfied, however, the first social needs emerge: the needs for belongingness and love. At this stage the individual is motivated toward securing his or her place in a particular group and toward the development of close emotional relationships with others, including the giving and receiving of love.

Maslow called the next emerging set of needs the "esteem" needs. These not only include the need for self-respect and a high evaluation of oneself, but also for the respect or esteem of others. Maslow classified this need into two subsets. First, there is a need for independence and freedom and for a personal sense of confidence in one's competence in dealing with the world. Second, there is the need to have this competence recognized and appreciated by others.

When all other needs are satisfied, the final one to emerge is the need for self-actualization. As Maslow put it: "What a man *can* be, he *must* be." Self-actualization is not so much a state or a stage of being, like hunger, to be satisfied by periodic gratification. Rather it is a *process* of being, in which one strives to become all that one is capable of becoming.

According to Maslow, the physiological, safety, love, and esteem needs are all *deficit* needs, whereas the need for self-actualization is a *growth* need. The first four sets of needs were termed deficit because they emerge as a result of the lack of food or the lack of safety, etc. But the self-actualizing person, freed from deficit needs, is engaged in the process of realizing his capabilities, of experimenting with his concept of self. Each person is unique, and must seek his or her own way to fulfillment. It is thus an almost entirely internal process, and gratification of the need, the sense of fulfillment, comes about through the experience of doing things that fulfill one's potential. Self-actualization is a growth need because, in its essence, it is a self-perpetuating, ongoing process. Each new development of the self produces an exploration for further development.

Although Maslow held the order of his hierarchy to be generally inviolate, he did not believe that a need had to be 100 percent satisfied before the next higher need would emerge. Rather, he assumed that most people in our society are both partially satisfied and partially unsatisfied in all their basic needs at the same time. A realistic profile of average people would indicate that their lower-order needs were more likely to be near 100 percent of satisfaction than their higher-order needs. As lower order needs are satisfied, higher order needs emerge gradually; they do not suddenly pop up from nowhere.

But if the ability to gratify a lower-order need were threatened, it would exert its prepotency as a motivator and the individual would, temporarily at least, forego seeking higher-order gratification until the lower order need had been satisfied.

Maslow believed that his theory was applicable to all human beings in the sense that they had the capacity to move up the motivational hierarchy. Earlier it was noted that Maslow viewed man as a "perpetually wanting animal." This is evidenced by the fact that even a person at the top of the hierarchy continues to strive for self-actualization— and to Maslow this "reaching" was a sign of emotional maturity. He noted, however, that there were individuals who never grow beyond certain levels, who become fixated at a lower-than-possible level because of their inability to feel emotionally secure about the gratification of that deficit need. Maslow characterized such fixation as neurotic.

It will be recalled that Douglas McGregor classified rewards and punishments into two types: extrinsic and intrinsic. The former are those that derive from various aspects of the environment, while the latter inhere in the activity in which a person is engaged. Relating

Maslow to McGregor, we can see that the physiological and safety needs (potentially gratifiable by wages and fringe benefits and a feeling of security in one's earning capacity), the need for belongingness (potentially gratifiable by a cohesive work group and supportive management, as espoused by the human relations movement and its derivatives), and the need for esteem (potentially gratifiable by various forms of recognition), all lead to behavior motivated toward *external* rewards. But in McGregor's terms, the need for self-actualization is motivated by the need for intrinsic and *internal* rewards. This requires a task that will challenge the particular capabilities and imagination of a given individual, a job through which each indivdiual can realize his or her potential.

Let us assume that a person's physiological, safety, love, and esteem needs are sufficiently satisfied so that he is operating on the level of his need for self-actualization. From the extensive research done by David McClelland of Harvard University, we are able to tell a great deal about how that drive is apt to manifest itself in a work situation. McClelland refers to this source of motivation as the need for achievement, and he has been particularly concerned with its role in the behavior of businessmen. Through the use of projective tests—that is, by asking people to make up a story suggested by a picture they have just been shown and to project themselves into the picture—McClelland was able to elucidate certain traits that are characteristic of people who have a high need to achieve. It seemed that people who attributed a drive for achievement to someone in the picture exhibited a similar drive in their own daily behavior. McClelland's work has defined a great deal about the achieving personality.

A "personality" profile of the person with a high need for achievement is, according to McClelland, generally similar to the following:

He has a liking for situations in which he can take personal responsibility for finding the solutions to problems. These are situations in which the outcome is primarily dependent upon his abilities and efforts rather than on "a throw of the dice" or factors over which he has no control.

He has a tendency to set moderate goals for achieving and a preference for taking "calculated risks." He knows that if he takes on problems that are of moderate difficulty (for him), he is likely to get the achievement satisfaction he seeks. He will get little or no

satisfaction from taking on an easy task at which his success is en-
sured or an extremely difficult task at which he will most likely fail.

He has a strong need to know how well he is doing on a given task
and for this reason prefers situations in which prompt, accurate
and concrete feedback is available. He has a compelling need to
know whether his decisions and actions are right or wrong and
prefers precise appraisals to ones in which he is vaguely told that
he is "doing all right."

He is likely to choose "experts" rather than friends when he needs
help in the accomplishment of a task. Given his need for achievement he is not likely to let personal likes or dislikes stand in the
way of his reaching a goal.[7]

McClelland's research indicates that the achievement itself is of
greater importance to the person with a high need for achievement than
the money he may take away from the situation—which supports
McGregor's concept of intrinsic rewards and Maslow's definition of
self-actualization as being an internal process. Money is an important
symbol to the person with a high need for achievement, however, since
it is among the best and simplest measures of success in our society.
Thus profits are important to managers who have no direct ownership
in a firm because "bottom line results" are the measure of how good a
job they are doing in running the business. For McClelland the achievement motive encompasses the "profit motive."

In describing the hypothetical person with a high need for achievement we have related various characteristics which he or she finds desirable in work situations. The person with that need must have a job
situation that requires and rewards personal initiative and inventiveness.
Otherwise, to extrapolate from Maslow's theory, the achievement needer
will seek to actualize himself or herself outside of the work environment
and may even leave it entirely. Therefore, we turn now to a consideration of the nature of the organizational environment to which our perpetually wanting man presents himself.

THE ORGANIZATIONAL ENVIRONMENT

We have described the typically healthy, emotionally mature adult in
our society as having a variety of needs ranging from the basic biolog-

ical requirements of any animal to the quintessentially human quest for self-actualization. From the discussion in Chapter One of the kinds of personnel, production, and quality problems that managers are facing today and that are apt to characterize the future, it is apparent that in many instances our institutions are failing to provide people with opportunities to fully satisfy their needs. The problem rarely lies in the satisfaction of the basic physiological or safety needs which are provided for by wages, fringe benefits, working conditions, and the like, or with the satisfaction of love and esteem needs which tend to be gratified off the job by family and friends and on the job by fellow employees and managers who have gotten the human relations message. In our affluent society, the problem lies in the failure of organizations to provide for the satisfaction of man's highest need: the need for self-actualization, which generally results in the frustration of his drive for achievement. Behavioral scientists have been able to shed considerable light on some of the structural characteristics and managerial actions in organizations that result in such frustration with its consequent negative effects on organizational effectiveness. For it is not only the employee who is deprived when his needs are not met, but also the organization that supposedly is seeking to obtain the maximum return from its investment in its human resources. That is why McGregor stressed the practical importance of integrating the needs of the individual with those of the organization.

Chris Argyris of Harvard University has provided valuable insight into the ways in which organizations mitigate against the need satisfaction of emotionally healthy adults.[8] His understanding of the situation derives from the perspective of developmental psychology. He describes a mature adult in our society as someone who exhibits the following characteristics:

- A high level of activity
- A state of relative independence from others in terms of being able to satisfy one's needs
- A large, varied repertoire of behavior
- A deep interest in the things one does—life is seen as an endless series of challenges in which the reward comes from doing something for its own sake

- A long-time perspective in which behavior is consciously affected by considerations of the past and future as well as the present
- A position of equality and/or super-ordinacy with respect to one's peers in the society
- A high degree of self-awareness and control over one's self.

The traditional organization structure works against the realization of these developmental states by its requirement that individual's adhere to formally designated roles that rigidly define responsibilities, authorities, and lines of communication, and otherwise limit their behavior. One of the most important needs of workers is to enlarge those areas of their lives in which their own decisions determine the outcome of their efforts, but all too often they are in situations in which they have little control over what happens to them, where they are expected to be passive and dependent, have a short time perspective, and use only a few shallow, skin-surface abilities. Argyris concludes that it would appear that organizations are thus willing to pay high wages for mature adults to behave, for eight hours at a stretch, in a less than mature manner, as we have defined maturity above.

Furthermore, this incongruency increases as: the employee is of increasing maturity; one goes down the line of command in a bureaucratic organization; the jobs become more and more mechanized.

Given that motivation is an internal process, Argyris postulates that if the individual cannot meet his personal needs through the accomplishment of company goals, he will find alternative modes of satisfaction. As we have seen, this is apt to result in conflict, quitting, and a host of other costly problems for the company, as well as in frustration and a sense of failure for the individual.

The interface between the man and the organization is the job it hires him to do, and we are directly concerned with his performance on that job. The most comprehensive theory dealing with the man/job performance relationship is that of Frederick Herzberg, and it is to his Motivation-Hygiene Theory that we turn in the next chapter.

SUMMARY

In this chapter we noted that while the definition of behavioral science (the systematic study of human behavior in social settings) is relatively straightforward, the field actually encompasses a wide variety of disciplines and myriad approaches to the study of its subject matter. Regardless of which avenue to understanding is taken, however, the intent is apt to be the same: the predictability of human behavior given certain conditions. It is this capacity for prediction that makes behavioral science valuable for managers who are running complex organizations.

The motivation of people is one aspect of human behavior that particularly engages the attention of researchers and managers alike. Abraham Maslow's "hierarchy of needs" is one general theory of motivation that has gained wide acceptance. The key points of the theory are that motivation is an internal process; that once a need is satisfied it no longer serves as a motivator of behavior; that man has five basic sets of needs which can be arranged into a hierarchy in terms of their prepotency; that four of these sets of needs—the physiological, safety, love and belongingness, and esteem needs—are deficit needs in that they result from a given lack; and that the last need to emerge after the others are satisfied—the need for self-actualization—is a true growth need that involves a continual search on the part of the individual to become all that he is capable of becoming.

David McClelland has devoted considerable effort to researching what he terms the need for achievement, which is somewhat analogous to Maslow's need for self-actualization. McClelland identifies a person who has a high need for achievement as having these characteristics: a preference for situations in which he can take personal responsibility for finding the solutions to problems; a preference for situations in which he can set moderate goals and take "calculated risks"; a strong need to know precisely how well he is doing on a given task; and a disregard for personal likes and dislikes in the search for people and means to accomplish a given task. McClelland's research indicates that for the person with a high need to achieve, the achievement itself is of greater importance than the money he may earn through it, although the money has high symbolic value as a measure of his success.

While people have been reasonably successful in meeting their deficit needs in most organizations, they have generally been frustrated in their search for self-actualization. According to the research of Chris Argyris, the rigid bureaucratic structure of most large organizations forces people into roles which mitigate against their developing into fully mature adults. The consequences for the company are apt to be costly conflict, high quit rates, and a variety of other personnel problems, while the individual frequently experiences a sense of failure and seeks other means of fulfilling himself.

REFERENCES

1. Rensis Likert, *New Patterns of Management* (New York, McGraw-Hill, 1961).

2. Robert Blake and Jane S. Mouton, *The Managerial Grid* (Houston, Gulf Publishing, 1964).

3. Warren G. Bennis and Philip E. Slater, "Democracy is Inevitable," *Harvard Business Review* (March-April 1964), pp. 51–59.

4. Harold M. F. Rush, *Behavioral Science: Concepts and Management Application* (New York, National Industrial Conference Board, 1969), pp. 2–9.

5. Saul W. Gellerman, *Management by Motivation* (New York, American Management Association, 1968), p. 27.

6. Abraham H. Maslow, *Motivation and Personality* (New York, Harper & Row, 1954).

7. David McClelland, *The Achieving Society* (Princeton, N.J., Van Nostrand, 1961).

8. Chris Argyris, *Personality and Organization* (New York, Harper & Row, 1957).

chapter
FOUR
The Motivation-
Hygiene Theory

INTRODUCTION

The richness and variety of approaches in the field of behavioral science as it relates to industrial organizations accurately reflects the complex nature of the human behavior that is the object of its study. Behavioral scientists have created voluminous research literature that often seems labyrinthine to them as well as to managers who are seeking knowledge that can be put into practice. This complexity is due to a number of things. Behavioral science has evolved from several background disciplines—psychology, sociology, organization theory, and others. Varied units are selected for study, in some cases whole organizations, groups within organizations, individuals, or some combination of these. Disparate criteria are used which are not always clearly defined. Some of these are "satisfaction," "morale," "productivity," or "effectiveness."

In an attempt to clarify some of these research findings, to relate them to one another and derive some sense of their common substance, Dr. Frederick Herzberg, then at the University of Pittsburgh (now at the University of Utah), and his colleagues conducted an extensive review of the relevant literature.[1] Comprehensive as the review was, it discovered few consistently reliable relationships between the variables under study. An original research project was then undertaken in the hope of providing new ideas and information about the nature of the complex relationship between employee attitudes, factors in the work situation, and productivity.[2] It is this research which resulted in the formulation of the Motivation-Hygiene theory of work motivation that provides the main conceptual basis for Job Enrichment.

THE MOTIVATION-MAINTENANCE THEORY

The research project that gave rise to the Motivation Hygiene theory (also called Motivation-Maintenance theory) was conducted in the late 1950's. Two hundred engineers and accountants, drawn from a variety of companies in Pittsburgh, were interviewed in the study. They were asked to relate actual events they had experienced at work which had markedly affected their job attitudes. In addition to having a profound effect on job attitudes, these events had to be work-related and have identifiable beginnings and ends.

The subjects of the study were asked first to recall and relate in detail an actual time when they had felt exceptionally *good* about their jobs. The interviewer would question them further to determine the reasons for those good feelings. The engineers and accountants were also asked if those good work-related feelings had affected their performance, their personal relationships, and their well-being.

Each subject was then asked to relate a sequence of events which had resulted in his feeling exceptionally *bad* about his job. The interviewer then followed the same procedures outlined above for the "good feelings" sequences.

Analysis of the results of the interviews led to several striking findings. First, in the sequences of events that people described as resulting in exceptionally good feelings, five factors stood out as the determiners of job satisfaction: *Achievement, Recognition, Work Itself, Responsibility* and *Advancement*. Thus, people reported feeling exceptionally good about their jobs when they had accomplished some meaningful objective or had solved a challenging problem. They felt good about being recognized for that achievement. They reported feeling good when they were doing work that they found intrinsically interesting and meaningful. In line with McGregor's Theory Y assumptions, people said they had felt good about being given genuine responsibility for their work. Finally, people recalled feeling exceptionally good when they were advancd to positions of greater responsibility and/or more rewarding work. The factors of Work Itself, Responsibility and Advancement appeared to produce particularly long-lasting positive attitudes.

In the analysis of the sequences of events that resulted in people feeling exceptionally bad about their jobs, however, an entirely different set of factors emerged. The five major sources of dissatisfaction were *Company Policy and Administration, Supervision, Salary, Interpersonal Relations,* and *Working Conditions.* In most cases these feelings of dissatisfaction persisted for several weeks. People did not report feeling bad about the existence of supervisors or company rules *per se.* Rather, they reported dissatisfaction as a result of a particular policy that they felt was inherently frustrating or was appropriate in content but unfairly administered. Similarly, they reported dissatisfaction with supervisors who lacked technical expertise or who failed to support their subordinates or treated them inequitably.

The finding that salary functions primarily as a "dissatisfier" is particularly difficult for many managers to accept. People would report feelings of dissatisfaction because they had failed to receive an expected salary increase or had received less than they expected. But, generally speaking, people only mentioned salary as a source of good feelings when they received an increase that really was a form of recognition for achievement or when it accompanied advancement to a position of greater responsibility. Money is not just a medium of exchange; it also has enormous symbolic significance. A five percent cost-of-living increase that everyone in the department receives does not have the same personal value to an individual as an identical increase based on actual merit.

The second important finding emerged. Factors about which people reported feeling exceptionally bad all are part of the *work environment,* while the factors involved in exceptionally good feelings all relate to the *nature of the job* itself: the work content, the responsibility one has over one's job, the ability to achieve on the job and be recognized for that achievement, and the opportunity to advance to greater levels of responsibility and more challenging assignments. The first set of factors, those that relate to the *job context,* have been termed "dissatisfiers." They are also referred to as "Hygiene" or "Maintenance" factors.[3] The second set of factors, those that comprise the *job content,* are referred to as "satisfiers" or "motivators," hence the name "Motivation-Hygiene" or "Motivation-Maintenance" theory. The functioning of these factors will become clearer as we discuss why they are so named.

People do not come to work prepared to accept blindly whatever conditions they encounter; they come fully equipped with a complete set of expectations. People expect a company to have sensible policies, and they expect those policies to be fairly administered. They expect equitable treatment with respect to wages and they anticipate having supervisors who not only know their jobs but also behave toward them in a friendly and supportive fashion. Finally, people expect to have working conditions that are safe, comfortable, and conducive to getting their work done. When these expectations are not met, people become dissatisfied. Thus, if a company is to prevent dissatisfaction, it must provide a "hygienic" environment which is relatively free of factors that dissatisfy people. It must *maintain* each of these factors at a level consistent with people's expectations. Then people will produce what is needed to ensure continual replenishment of those Hygiene needs. In this way, the Hygiene factors are very much like Maslow's "deficit needs," described in the preceding chapter.

But few companies or managers would be willing to settle for this minimum level of performance when they know that people possess the potential for much more. To tap that potential they must provide work that will prove satisfying to the employee; work that he or she finds intrinsically rewarding to do, whose content is inherently interesting and challenging; work for which the employee feels responsible, at which he or she can achieve, and which affords the potential for growth and advancement. Such work the employee will be motivated to perform well above the required minimum, and it is for this reason that the "satisfiers" are termed the "motivator" factors.

In summary, the study produced three significant findings. First, the factors that produce job satisfaction are separate and distinct from those that produce job dissatisfaction. Second, it follows that since job satisfaction and job dissatisfaction arise from different sources, they must be conceptualized as two separate attitude "sets" rather than as the opposing extremes of a single attitudinal continuum. This can be depicted graphically as follows:

Job Satisfaction

None   High

Job Dissatisfaction

High   None

Thus, the opposite of job satisfaction is *no* job satisfaction and the opposite of job dissatisfaction is, simply no dissatisfaction. (To state the rule generally, the absence of a negative does not necessarily indicate the presence of a positive, and vice versa.)

The third important finding was that the factors that are associated with job dissatisfaction all relate to the work environment, or job context, while the factors that are involved in job satisfaction all relate to the job content, as shown here:

Job Dissatisfaction	Job Satisfaction
Hygiene/Maintenance Factors	*Motivation Factors*
Company Policy and Administration	Achievement
Supervision	Recognition
Interpersonal Relations	Responsibility
Salary and Benefits	Work Itself
Working Conditions	Advancement

Because of the significance of these findings, the theory has been subjected to numerous tests by other behavioral scientists. Using people from a wide variety of occupations as subjects, these investigators have produced an impressive verification of the theory.[4] It had been contended by some critics that the motivators would have appeal for engineers and accountants (the original people studied) and other professionals, but not for people in low-skill or relatively low-paying occupations. These later studies show that what motivates the manager also motivates the man or woman on the production line. As we will see in later chapters, the theory has been verified not only through repeated interview and questionnaire studies, but, most importantly, through its application to actual work situations.

It is unfortunately true, however, that not everyone will respond to the motivators. There are some people whose experience in growing up has not included any opportunity to learn the satisfaction that can be derived through the sheer doing of something meaningful. These are people who, in Maslow's terms, have been fixated at some developmental level where they are bound by their deficit needs. Herzberg has termed such people "Hygiene seekers," people who are solely concerned with doing whatever minimum is necessary to ensure their creature comforts. At the other extreme are "pure" motivator seekers: artists who survive in garrets, happy only as long as they are painting; monks who live only to pray and to work, having renounced all earthly pleasures and any but the barest minimum of comforts. We have already encountered this type in less extreme form—the individual with a high need for achievement whose personality has been so extensively researched by David McClelland. The "average" person, however, exists with both sets of needs. He desires his Hygiene (his creature comforts) and as much as he can get of them; but he also needs to fulfill his uniquely human needs through his work.

Given that the traditional labor-management battlefield has been the area of wages and benefits and, to a lesser degree, working conditions, it is not surprising that many managers have been taken aback by the research findings represented by the Motivation-Hygiene theory. Yet, a moment's reflection indicates that such surprise is perhaps unwarranted. For after the often bitter wage negotiations have been concluded, after the supervisors have been put through another human relations training program, after a new two-way communications program has been installed and the softball league has been organized and supported by the company, and after the cafeteria is serving better soup and the walls are a nice new shade of blue, the managers have then waited year after year for their grateful employees to respond with new bursts of productivity and loyalty. Assuming the correctness of the Motivation-Hygiene theory, they still have a lot of waiting to do . . .

This is not to depreciate the importance of doing these things, however. One of the most crucial errors of understanding that managers have made after first encountering the Motivation-Hygiene theory is to think that they can afford to neglect the maintenance items because they cannot, in the long run, really serve as sources of satisfaction. But the Hygiene items require continual replenishment. If people's expectations are not met, their dissatisfaction will be immediate and often vocal, especially in this era of militancy.

Reflecting on Maslow's need hierarchy, it can be seen that the Hygiene factors of Herzberg's theory correspond to the deficit needs that Maslow identified. Thus it is through wages and benefits that a person is able to provide for the satisfaction of his physiological and safety needs (the latter also being provided for by adequate working conditions), and through the proper management of human relations that the individual's needs for belongingness and esteem can be satisfied. Maslow's theory also held that if any of these needs is unmet at any time it will reassert its potency at the expense of the "higher" needs. The Motivation-Hygiene and the need hierarchy theories thus confirm each other with respect to the necessity for providing adequate maintenance factors.

They are also mutually confirming with respect to what Maslow termed the need for self-actualization and Herzberg called the "Motivators." Maslow regarded the need for self-actualization as the only real "growth" need, and it is evident from Herzberg's research that one can grow at work only when the Motivators are present in the work. Indeed, people reported the opportunity for growth as a source of motivation. Herzberg has defined psychological growth as: (1) continuing to know more, (2) seeing more relationships among what is known, (3) being creative, (4) being effective in ambiguous situations, (5) developing one's individuality, (6) attaining "real" growth; that is growing absolutely oneself, not just seeming to grow through the downgrading of others.[5]

Providing the means for employees to become motivated toward their work is no substitute for providing good Hygiene, and vice versa. To make use of this new understanding about motivation requires that managers assume a new and broader role, one that includes the responsibility for providing employees with jobs that challenge their interests and abilities, that provides them with the opportunity to achieve and to be recognized for that achievement, and that lets them grow psychologically. The acceptance of this new responsibility by a manager almost always results in his viewing *his* job as being more intrinsically rewarding. The process through which this change in the nature of work is brought about is called *Job Enrichment*. We shall fully explore the concepts involved in that process in the next chapter.

SUMMARY

The Motivation-Hygiene theory developed by Dr. Frederick Herzberg holds that the factors that lead to job satisfaction are separate and distinct from those that produce job dissatisfaction. The latter factors, termed Hygiene or Maintenance factors, include Company Policy and Administration, Supervision, Interpersonal Relations, Salary, and Working Conditions; that is, they include all the elements that comprise the job *context*. The factors that lead to job satisfaction, however, all relate to the job *content*. These factors, called Motivators, include Achievement, Recognition, the Work Itself, Responsibility, and Advancement and the Opportunity for Growth. The theory holds that if job dissatisfaction is to be avoided *and* individuals are to be motivated to improved performance, then organizations must continue to replenish people's Hygiene needs at the same time that they seek to provide them with jobs that are intrinsically rewarding. The process for changing jobs so that they incorporate the Motivators is known as "Job Enrichment."

REFERENCES

1. F. Herzberg, B. Mausner, R. Peterson and D. Capwell, *Job Attitudes: Research and Opinion* (Pittsburgh, Psychological Service of Pittsburgh, 1957).

2. F. Herzberg, B. Mausner, and B. Synderman, *The Motivation to Work* (New York, John Wiley & Sons, 1959).

3. Attributed to Dr. Robert N. Ford, formerly of American Telephone and Telegraph Company, now retired.

4. F. Herzberg, "Work and the Nature of Man" (New York, World, 1966).

5. F. Herzberg, *op. cit.*, p. 70.

chapter FIVE

From Motivation Theory to Principles of Job Design

INTRODUCTION

From the previous chapters' review of recent research in the behavioral sciences we have seen compelling evidence that lasting worker self-motivation is generated by the experience of work itself. This is not to deny the importance or necessity of the improvements that companies have made and must continue to make in the environmental factors that surround the work. However, managers should not expect such efforts to solve the complex behavior problems that are commonly arising now that increasing numbers of people are attempting to fulfill their growth and achievement needs at work. Further applications of good hygiene, such as pay increases and improved supervisor-subordinate relationships, will be eagerly accepted, but these things can offer little or nothing toward the fulfillment of growth needs for most people. The case of the four-day week is interesting in this context: if people had jobs that engaged their interests and challenged their capabilities we would expect them to be demanding the right to spend time at them, rather than less. So long as those growth needs, which are becoming more dominant, remain unfulfilled, people will continue to give less than their best, absent themselves, and quit when they can.

The cumulative thrust of motivation theory as developed by the leaders in the field directs us to the conclusion that the work itself must be changed so that people can feel good about themselves and what they are producing. Only in this way will we see motivated behavior on the job that leads to sustained high performance. The new findings, however, provide little more than a foundation for understanding what causes the difference between high and low (or "negative") motivation on the job. We have discovered that most people become motivated to the extent that they find opportunities for real responsibility, personal achievements, individual recognition, a sense of professional growth, and advancement in the job. Isolating these requirements as motivators, however, establishes only the objectives for restructuring jobs; it does not tell us in specific terms how to provide them. We must translate these general terms into more concrete principles that will tell us how to change the content of work to gain positive responses.

It is a long step from understanding motivation theory to making specific changes in the design of jobs. Lynda King Taylor, a British author, in her recent book about Job Enrichment entitled *Not For Bread Alone,* offered a quote from Sir Winston Churchill that relates to that step: "I pass with relief from the tossing sea of Cause and Theory to the firm ground of Result and Fact." [1] Our purpose in this chapter, then, is to pass from the discussion of Cause and Theory to some firmer ground where we may discover how to structure jobs so as to give people tasks and responsibilities that are personally rewarding.

Two perspectives on job structure will be presented: (1) the characteristics of poor jobs that do not motivate, and (2) a discussion of two sets of principles for redesigning jobs to make them more motivational.

WHAT'S HAPPENED TO JOBS?

There have been a number of negative influences on job structure in many companies. These influences have resulted in emasculation of the work to the point that very few people can find it interesting or meaningful. Bob Ford, retired from A.T.&T., has said "The natural history of most jobs is to get worse." As we look at what has commonly happened to jobs, the basic truth of Ford's remark becomes clear. The most common influences on this worsening trend are technological advances and job fragmentation.

Technological Advances

The normal tendency is to regard technological advancement in industry as an unquestionable good, and certainly it has been at the core of economic supremacy in industrial nations. However, from the perspective of good, motivational job design, technological advancement is sometimes a mixed blessing. Many jobs have undergone drastic surgery as parts of them have been either altered or made obsolete by improvements in technology. Some jobs that once provided great challenge for a worker who performed the complete job have been eroded away to the point where there is little left to do that tests any of the worker's abilities, let alone judgment or skill. Many jobs have lost so much of their original substance that there is no way for a person to avoid numbing boredom if he or she continues in that job. Since awareness of the behavioral impact of such changes is relatively new, this gradual erosion has not been commonly recognized as a costly process. It is entirely possible that technological improvements may have made some jobs so boring that their expected savings could be cancelled out by increased costs of poor work, employee turnover, rehiring, and training—in other words, that the net gain of those improvements might be zero.

An example is the elevator operator's job. When elevators were primitive they were quite complex to operate. A man could feel that a good deal of mechanical skill was required, and that people depended on him for transport. Elevator operation has become increasingly automated to the point where human services are rarely needed any longer. In those cases where operators are still on the job there is very little job substance left for them and no way they can become motivated in their work. There is probably no way to keep people with any ambition or needs to find self-worth on such jobs. This example may seem extreme but countless other jobs are undergoing the same process as technological advancement through electricity gives way to advancement in electronics. Such advances are leaving many workers in a half-automated limbo in which it is unusual to find anything like motivated work behavior.

The fact that technological advancement makes many jobs paralyzingly dull does not mean that we should cease automation and technological improvement. The wise manager, however, will assess the effects of such improvement on the job content and make decisions that will result in a true net gain. It may be wise to go all the way with automation, get the worker out of the job and find a more useful place for him or her in the organization; or it may be better to accept what is left of the job and combine it with some other related tasks in order to construct an operation that would have meaning for the worker performing it.

Fragmentation of the Job

Perhaps the most common cause of job ruination is the fragmentation of a meaningful whole into meaningless parts. Many jobs are now set up in assembly line fashion with each person doing only a small portion of the work. This makes it difficult for the worker to perceive the whole process or to know what he or she has contributed to the product. Several different rationales are offered to justify such fragmentation of jobs, and it is true that they all make some sense in one way or another. Here are some of the most common:

1. *Efficiency*

The industrial engineering approach to job design has been used frequently to break jobs down into their simplest components in an attempt to establish perfect work procedures. This approach to job design rests on the assumption that workers will be able to completely master their small fragment of the total job and be very happy in that mastery. Henry Ford, father of the assembly line approach to job design in the automobile business, showed the way in this direction. The principles have been used not only in manufacturing situations and heavy industry but to some extent in many clerical operations as well. In some situations fragmentation of work for more efficient operation may be economically wise. But the behavioral consequences of such a breakdown of the work can be very costly, and the significance of these behavioral consequences has not been generally recognized. In many cases, while fragmented work operations have achieved a higher degree of efficiency in terms of time and motion, overall work may have been reduced. This has become an abiding principle in the newer approach to job design which acknowledges behavioral realities—the object of wise job design should be an increase in total *effectiveness* rather than simple efficiency alone. This is an entirely different concept.

2. *Reduction of Training Time and Training Costs*

Many companies have sought to reduce the amount of training time and the attendant costs by breaking jobs into component parts which are less complex and easier to teach the new employee. Once again we are learning that going too far in this direction can leave so little to be mastered in the fragments of the job that workers quickly become bored, cease to grow in the work, and find no opportunity to discover their own worth through their work. Couple this with the fact that educational levels are generally increasing and we find ourselves educating more and more while having people do less and less. Many times the savings realized through reduction of training time on simpler jobs are more than offset by the losses in productivity due to the poor work behavior that results from assigning people to tasks which are too easy to master and tasks that negate growth.

3. *Increasing Management Control*

More and more commonly, and for a variety of reasons, control over the work process, over rates of production to meet quotas and deadlines, and over product quality is being taken out of the hands of people doing the work. Rules, procedures, standards, and regulations proliferate to the point where people are bound into jobs that allow them neither autonomy nor latitude for judgment. Decision-making and control over their own work process is gone. The result in most cases is a sense of alienation from the work, a very low sense of self-worth, and the feeling of being accountable for very little. Should it be surprising that workers perform poorly in such situations, in which everything about the job convinces them either that someone else has the responsibility for the end product or that the system is so highly organized that no one is allowed any decisions or authority that could materially effect the final outcome?

4. *Work Specialization*

Work specialization has been worshipped in industry as a creed or an article of faith in recent years. The trend toward specialization is all around us in diverse fields. It has become common in many professions, in the sciences and the trades. As technological knowledge expands, specialization for heightened expertise has been somewhat unavoidable. Here again it is necessary for the manager to keep both eyes open when making decisions about further specialization and about the present state of jobs as a result of specialization. Too many people have become so far removed from doing a whole job—or any part of it big enough to have meaning and significance—that they cannot avoid placing a low value on their contribution to the work process. A wise manager will

look back at what the jobs in his operations once were like, assess carefully what they have become, and determine what has been the true net
gain of all the specialization and fragmentation of the work that has
occurred.

There are two principle consequences of fragmenting and specializing jobs: The first is that people who perform only a small part of a job
cannot see that they are making a valuable contribution to the whole.
They cannot see that they have achieved much, so their work gives them
little sense of self-worth. Neither errors nor successes can be clearly
identified with one person. Feedback on performance, both positive and
negative, is delivered on a group basis which reduces its effectiveness.
The second consequence of job fragmentation is that it produces a situation in which one's own contribution doesn't seem to matter. Thus it
becomes tempting to coast, to disappear into the maw of the great corporation and be carried along with little effort throughout a working
career. The anonymity of group endeavor in a work process is a great
depressant upon individual effort. In business after business, in office
and in factory, one of the most constantly heard remarks is: "This
wouldn't be a bad place to work if they get some of the slackers off
their butts and get them to do their share." A kind of reverse synergy
sets in so that the total effect of the group is less than their total potential capacity.

5. *Tightening Up*

No one should quarrel with the manager who decides that his or her
operation needs a clean sweep and some old fashioned tightening up.
During times of relative corporate prosperity many work operations are
found to be overstaffed, wasteful, inefficient, and more costly to run than
they should be. The astute manager, taking over such an operation or
pressed by his boss to devote renewed energy to running a more taut
operation, will decide on various methods of tightening up. But caution
is necessary, for when these methods are overdone or abused they also
reduce the worker's satisfaction and further ruin the job.

Work Measurement.   Let there be no doubt that sound and well-organ-
ized methods of work measurement can be highly beneficial to a relatively disorganized and unstandardized work process. Work measurement, briefly described, is the process of timing the various moves, tasks,

and processes in each job contained in a work process, affixing unit time values to each of these work functions and establishing standard times for the performance of each function. This makes it possible to translate the work performed into unit time values which can then be compared with the number of man hours required to do a given piece of work. Standard or desired unit time values for the performance of work can then be used by management to set objectives and controls. Many work operations have no such framework for establishing standards and are consequently highly wasteful of time and effort. The work measurement process can often identify areas of ineffectiveness, wasted motion, and flagrant underproduction.

While the establishment of a work measurement system can often bring about positive advantages, the process often contributes to either fragmentation of the work or excessive external control over workers. Fragmentation often results because detailed examination of the work process suggests changes in job design to break down the work into smaller component parts for more effective measurement. Excessive external control often results from a heavy-handed misuse of work measurement productivity objectives to force higher rates of production. This is often understood to be motivational activity. Abused work measurement principles can drastically alter the nature of the work and serve not as a stimulus to improve productivity but as a distinct depressant on motivation. And this usually results in a *reduction* of productivity.

Pulling responsibility and accountability higher and higher up the supervisory pyramid. In a slack work operation in which productivity is poor or where errors, defects, and breakdowns are rampant, management will often decide that less and less responsibility can be entrusted to the people doing the work; that instead the work be reviewed, verified, double-checked or examined by supervisory people at levels above where the work is being done. In instances where a major error has occurred, managers may tighten up by ordering that verification must take place at even higher levels. This form of tightening up often removes all responsibility for the work from the people who do it, leaving them with the feeling that they are no longer accountable or truly responsible for anything. This feeling is known to be a major depressant on motivation, since one of the key work experiences that fosters motivation is the sense of being individually responsible. The result is often a great laxity and disregard for standards, work quality, or organizational objectives as a whole.

On discovery of any kind of repeated error, many managers will establish instant rules, requiring double checking, verification, or inspection to control that particular type of error. In some cases a completely new job related to quality control, inspection, or verification, will be layered into the job hierarchy where no such job previously existed. Establishment of such new job layers often results in a kind of double jeopardy in terms of reducing motivation. People placed in the verification or checking jobs are often found to have little enthusiasm for the work, since it is very much removed from the actual work process and the true significance of the task. At the same time their presence encourages a lessening of concern and application by the people who are doing the work. This situation is analogous to having two shortstops on a baseball team. The forward shortstop (the first checker) is not likely to put out a maximum effort to handle every ball hit to him; after all, let the backup shortstop (the second checker) do a little work. And the backup shortstop isn't going to go all out either; it's the forward shortstop's job to stop the balls, isn't it? Setting up jobs in this fashion distinctly reduces the effort toward error-free work. The individual who examines jobs for their motivating potential would do well to look very closely at job situations in which there are doers and checkers or verifiers in the same work operation. Wherever some people are on the job solely to catch other people's errors, there are liable to be motivation problems on both sides of the fence.

There is a valuable maxim related to this kind of tightening up: "If you want to *catch* errors, check and double-check the work. If you want to *prevent* errors, place responsibility on those who do the work." The establishment of instant rules for checks and double-checks and verification by supervisors, or the establishment of layers of people for verification of work reduces the job to the very lowest common denominator of performance; it tars everyone with the same brush and makes no distinctions for those who do excel. If management makes no distinction between the competent and the incompetent; if the former have no immunity from checks and double checks set up for the latter, then usually the highly competent soon cease to excel. Such organizations seem to be saying to everyone alike—"You can't be trusted; sooner or later we know you're going to flop." In such a situation it's too easy for the good worker to give in and coast with the pack.

For apparently good and cogent management reasons jobs tend to get worse over time. Job ruination has been occurring as a distressing counterpoint to the increasing demands from workers for work which is more fulfilling. Let us turn now to a consideration of the best principles so far developed for rebuilding job content. There *are* effective ways to make work more of a rewarding pursuit and less of a numbing daily exercise in drudgery.

JOB DESIGN PRINCIPLES

There are currently two sets of job design principles or job criteria that have evolved independently and that will be of value to any practitioner of Job Enrichment. The first set evolved out of job redesign techniques pioneered by researchers at the American Telephone and Telegraph Company.[2] They have been further developed and refined into a set of Implementing Concepts through the practical consulting work of Roy W. Walters and Associates in numerous Job Enrichment projects that have yielded significant results. These principles have been labeled Implementing Concepts, since they are the conceptual tools used in the process of implementing Job Enrichment theory in actual job situations. The second set of criteria, called the four Core Dimensions, were developed by two researchers, Dr. Edward E. Lawler III and Dr. J. Richard Hackman, at the Administrative Sciences Department of Yale University.[3] The four Core Dimensions have been tested by Lawler and Hackman in their work with outside companies and have been found to be accurate definitions of job elements that produce highly positive responses from workers.

These sets of concepts can be used in two ways. First, in jobs characterized by poor work behavior, they are an invaluable aid in determining existing motivational strengths and weaknesses. Second, they are also used in redesigning the jobs to focus on the detailed changes needed to make the work more engrossing and motivational.

It should be pointed out that these job design principles are still evolving, as is true of the entire field of job design. In years to come these job design principles will undergo more intensive definition and testing and others may be added. From experience and results so far, however, it may be safely stated that these are reliable guideposts for the complex and demanding process of reshaping work. They have been developed out of numerous studies of the features that make good jobs highly motivating and the features that make bad jobs dull and unrewarding. They have been hardened by the practical experience of finding out what kinds of job changes have caused large numbers of people to become both more satisfied and more productive at their jobs.

THE IMPLEMENTING CONCEPTS

The Implementing Concepts consist of six principles for good job design. All six are used to evaluate existing job designs to determine motivational strengths and weaknesses. The six concepts are:

1. Natural Units of Work: a way of distributing work items,

2. Client Relationships: a way of establishing contact with people who receive completed work items or service,

3. Task Combination: a way of gathering the tasks done for a client into one job,

4. Vertical Loading: a way of pushing responsibilities downward into lower-level jobs,

5. Task Feedback: ways of informing workers how well they are performing their tasks and responsibilities,

6. Task Advancement: increasing levels of responsibilities and proficiency in the job which allow a person to continue to grow within the same job by requiring him or her to learn new things and meet new challenges.

The first five concepts are used as building blocks in the process of job redesign. They are also used as criteria for evaluation of the motivational status of jobs as they exist before any change. They point to various aspects of the job structure to be analyzed and changed as necessary. The sixth concept, task advancement, is an effective measure of the present status of a job but is not normally used as a guide to specific job changes. Opportunities for task advancement occur naturally as a result of effective changes made by using the other five principles.

Before a more detailed description of the Implementing Concepts is presented, a word about their use in redesigning jobs may be helpful. While actual examples of all of these concepts are usually found in the best jobs that are highly motivational, we have found that it is not always possible to work all of them into every job that is to be enriched. There may be operational restrictions, for example, that will prevent setting up of natural units of work for each individual. There may be limited opportunities for establishing meaningful client relationships for each worker, and other limitations may curtail the amount of task combination that can be accomplished. It is important to realize that these concepts present the ideal set of features that make jobs highly motivational. They should be looked on as goals to strive for in designing the optimum job in any situation. In cases where the ultimate in any of these concepts is not feasible, it may still be possible to enrich the job significantly by designing it as close to the ideal as possible or by emphasizing other Implementing Concepts to a greater extent. The fact that not all of these job design principles may be applied to a given job does not mean that the job cannot be measureably enriched. For example, many jobs have been greatly improved with impressive results using only the Vertical Loading and Task Feedback concepts.

Natural Units of Work

One of the most effective ways of affixing responsibility for the work at hand is to distribute work items—the things on which workers perform their assigned tasks—in groups or batches that have some continuing identity. These continuing assignments are called *natural units of work*. Work items are typically distributed among workers with regard only for current workload or worker experience. Thus, if there are 10 supply clerks in a section the assignment clerk or supervisor will randomly divide the day's workload into 10 batches and distribute them among the clerks. It is only through chance that a clerk would get to process

supply requests for the same group over a period of time. As a consequence, the job with random distribution has no real meaning or personal value for the clerk; there is nothing in it with which he can
identify.

Distributing work items by natural units is different in that logical
groups of work items are set up and each worker is given continuing
responsibility for his own group of work items. In the case of the supply
clerks, each clerk would be given the job of processing supply requests
from a particular group of requesters on a continuing basis.

The Principle of Ownership

Setting up natural units of work is the foundation on which a worker
can develop a sense of ownership for a particular portion of the work.
Feeling ownership for one's work can be the key difference between
work that has meaning and relevance and work that seems detached,
empty, and boring. The sense of ownership is a major ingredient in the
building of a satisfying sense of self worth for a person through what
he accomplishes at work. Without ownership true responsibility and
accountability cannot take root.

The creation of natural units of work is a two-step process. First,
the primary work items must be identified. They may consist of tele-
phones to be installed, roads that must be sanded and plowed, or forms
that must be processed. Second, the work items must be grouped logi-
cally. While work items can probably be divided in many different ways,
depending on the nature of the job, the most common categories are:
geographical, organizational, alphabetical or numerical, customer-re-
lated, type of business. Some examples of logical divisions are:

Geographical:	City policemen are assigned a particular city block or group of blocks to patrol.
Organizational:	File clerks can be assigned to handle reports from a particular company or department.
Alphabetical or Numerical:	Three claim processors handling extensive Medicare claims can be assigned to claims according to alphabetical division of the claim-aint's name: A-G, H-Q, and R-Z, or cases #0000–0999; 1000–1999, etc.

Customer-Related:	Members of a bank's credit research unit can be assigned to their own corporate account.
Type of Business:	Securities analysts can be assigned to particular business areas: Utilities, Transportation, Communications, etc.

Because work items can vary considerably in volume or complexity, natural work units need not always be simple and even divisions of work items. For example, suppose that the natural division of work in a given job is by customer accounts. Typically, this would include a number of large complex accounts and many small accounts. To divide the work, the large accounts could be broken down into subsidiaries and departments and the small accounts could be batched. Thus, one employee might be responsible for a subdivision of a corporate giant, another for a large manufacturing company, another for three small firms, and so on.* The point is that each employee would have continuing responsibility for that part of the work.

Client Relationships

For every business there are "recipients," people or organizations who receive a product or a service from workers. These recipients may be internal or external. When an interviewer in the Personnel Department of a company hires a new employee for the Manufacturing Division, he or she is providing a service for an internal recipient. When a telephone operator satisfies a caller's need for assistance, he or she is providing a service to an external recipient.

Few workers, however, have the opportunity to provide a product or service to the same recipient on a regular basis. When the recipient is always different, the worker usually lacks a sense of identity with, or commitment to, desired quality criteria.

In order for workers to build client relationships they must first be given continuing responsibility for a particular recipient or group of recipients. Once a continuing client is established for a worker, a rela-

---

* Given a geographical division, one unit of work might be a section of a large city while another might be a group of small states.

tionship can form analogous to that between lawyers or accountants and their clients. Such a relationship can develop when a worker:

1. contacts and is contacted by clients directly,
2. personally deals with clients to solve problems,
3. commits self to good performance for a client,
4. feels responsible in the case of error or poor service,
5. identifies with a client,
6. feels that the client "belongs" to him or her.

The creation of client relationships is a three-step process. First, the client must be identified. Second, direct contact should be established between the worker and the client where possible. Third, ways should be found for the client to judge service or product quality and give feedback where possible.

Particular clients for each worker are often established right away when natural units of work are identified and assigned. For example, an order clerk's clients could be the recipients in a particular geographical area, a keypunch operator's clients could be particular departments, and a credit researcher's clients could be particular business organizations.

A worker should have as much direct contact with the client as is necessary and possible. Face-to-face contact is best; where that is impossible, telephone or mail contact can be used. Establishing such direct contact is not as easy as it may seem, however. Client contact commonly occurs at the managerial level and business etiquette often calls for managers to talk to their counterparts in the client organization even if the problem might be more readily dealt with at a lower level. One solution is to arrange direct contact for the worker in day-to-day practical matters and to leave managerial contact for larger and long-range matters.

Finding ways for a client to measure the quality of the service being received involves listing the tasks, then determining what to measure, how to measure, and how often to measure.

The things a worker does for a client can be seen as a number of distinct tasks. For example, a supply clerk may perform three tasks for clients:

1. Process computerized requisition cards.

2. Process manual requisitions in case of emergency or special handling.

3. Follow up on delays and errors in shipment.

It is important for both the client and the worker to clearly understand and agree on each task performed, for only then can reliable measures of performance be identified. These might include productivity, error rate, deadlines missed or met, and product quality. In the case of the supply clerk, for example, shipment error rates could be a useful way for a client to measure performance.

There are many different ways of making such measurements. These include computer printouts, the client's informal comments on performance, customer service surveys, and direct client comments.

The frequency of evaluation will also vary from job to job. The point is that it must be frequent and regular enough to be relevant.

Task Combination

One of the chief consequences of the widespread application of "scientific management" principles was what we have previously referred to as the fractionalization of jobs. Instead of one individual putting together 10 components to form a complete product, 10 different people may each add one component over and over. The assumption was that breaking jobs down in such a fashion would result in maximum efficiency and minimum errors since workers would be satified to work at one task they could completely master.

The Job Module

This term has become a useful descriptive label for the type of job assignment that results from imaginative task combinations. It deserves some further clarification.

A job module is a job structured in such a way that all (or nearly all) the tasks required to process a given piece of work or a service function are performed by one individual, as opposed to the fragmented setup of work so commonly found today. A job module is normally established through the process of assigning individuals to be accountable for a whole natural unit of work, setting up clear and individual client relationships, and combining tasks so that each person can clearly see the effect of his or her own contributions separate and distinct from the contributions of others. A job module assignment affords the best opportunities for an individual to see and measure his or her own achievements and better assess individual worth and growth in the job.

At times it is not feasible to set up fully individual job modules due to various mechanical or technical limitations in the work flow. In such situations it may be possible to set up team modules, in which a small team of two or three individuals complete all the tasks related to a given natural unit of work. Though not quite as effective as an individual job module, the team module may prove to be a very effective improvement on a heavily fragmented job.

The concept of the job module based on the task combination principle is shown in Fig. 5.1.

Look at the Workflow.   The entire flow of work should be analyzed for ways to combine fragmented tasks into whole jobs. Ask: Where does work come from to a given station and where does it go afterward? Can tasks be pulled into the station being analyzed from either direction to form a meaningful and complete job module? For task combination the workflow is analyzed for related tasks which may or may not occur sequentially. For example, the job of sorting incoming office correspondence is often part of a sequence that begins with receipt and logging of the correspondence, then sorting, processing, and preparing a reply. In order to create a job with greater variety, challenge, and responsibility, the handling of correspondence from start to finish would be placed in one complete job module with one individual doing the whole job for a given unit of work.

Some tasks are simultaneous in the workflow rather than sequential. For example, the work in a given section might involve the processing of three different forms with different people responsible for each one. If the forms were related, it may be possible to combine the processing and checking of all three forms into one complete job, and then the workload would be assigned according to some natural unit.

A Caution About Task Combination.   To provide true enrichment of the work, any task added to the job must make the work more inter-

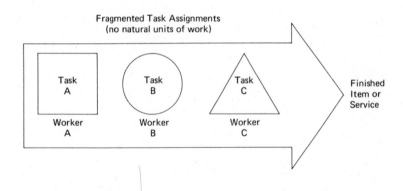

Fragmented Task Assignments
(no natural units of work)

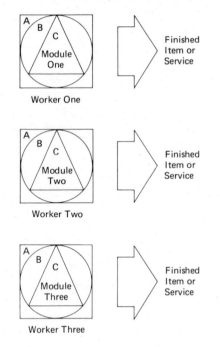

Job Modules (each worker performs tasks A, B, and C)

FIGURE 5.1

esting and challenging. The mere addition of a task may add nothing in itself—zero plus zero equals zero. The added task must be meaningful as a net result. Many an unwary Job Enrichment practitioner has been fooled this way.

Vertical Loading

Vertical loading describes the process of pushing responsibilities down from above and expanding the scope of authority to give workers more control over their own work.

In most work situations, the worker usually does the work while the supervisor or manager has the responsibility for planning, directing, and controlling the work. A common result is that workers often do not feel the need to meet the production schedules and goals set for them by someone else. In marked contrast to this, able workers who are given the responsibility for planning, directing, and controlling their own jobs often develop an internal need to meet schedules, goals, and standards they set themselves. They can gain positive satisfaction from managing their own jobs.

If there is a conceptual crux in the process of Job Enrichment, it is surely the principle of vertical loading of the job. The term "vertical loading" is used since most responsibilities, controls, and elements of autonomy to be loaded back into the job will be found at levels above the job in question. In a schematic view, such loading will occur in a vertical direction. Using the vertical loading concept on a job means, in many cases, replacing controls and responsibilities that formerly were part of the job before the process of erosion extracted the real essence from it. In other cases it will result in building the job into a much more demanding assignment, for some workers, than it ever had been before. Vertical loading of new responsibility will be found to have taken place in every job redesign that results in significant enrichment of the work. It is the process that truly extends the boundaries of job experience to include a broad range of chances for new personal achievements.

There are several sources to examine for new motivational substance to load into a job:

1. *Removal or Reduction of External Controls.* The job should be examined for the erosion of responsibility outlined in the earlier section

on What's Happened to Jobs. There may be evidences of erosion due to technological advance, training cost reduction, specialization, or tightening up which have taken control of the work out of the worker's hands. Quality checks should be examined; authorization and signature levels may be too high; all scheduling and planning may be part of another job; supervisors may be trying to do all the more challenging things in the job, failing to use the talents of even their best subordinates. Look at all the controls established to ensure the meeting of objectives. The chances are that many of them will be outdated, unnecessary, duplicated, or just plain ineffective. Such controls can stifle initiative and make work a depressing bore. The object should be to load back into the job as many of these controls as possible; to require the exercise of self-control by workers. Remove or reduce controls on work on a selective and individual basis. It may be unwise to allow complete freedom to everyone at once. Having to evaluate matters and decide how much freedom to allow individuals creates a new and crucial role for the supervisor in the enrichment process. More discussion of this supervisory role is included in Chapter Ten.

2. *Addition of Management or Supervisory Functions.* The job to be enriched should be examined by supervisory or management personnel who are one or two levels higher. This may disclose some planning or organizing functions that should be made part of the job. Tasks that have become somewhat routine in a given job level may provide a challenge for people at lower job levels. The competence of experienced workers can sometimes be recognized and utilized by having them give on-the-job training or on-the-spot advice to the less experienced.

3. *Addition of New Technical Tasks.* Often technical parts of the job that are performed by people above the worker (other than his direct supervisor) can be loaded into the lower-level job for enrichment. Once again, it is the principle that routine things in a higher job can present a challenge at a lower level.

4. *Granting New Authority.* This, of course, is the essence of vertical loading. The process can be made clearer by considering three different levels of new authority, which can be used to determine just how much authority should be granted to each individual:

a) *Total authority:* A worker can be granted freedom of judgment and decision-making in a given area.

b) *Reviewed authority:* The subordinate may decide and take action
   in a given area but is required to advise his superior of the action
   afterward for review.

c) *Restricted authority:* This is hardly different from none at all. The
   subordinate can develop a decision or course of action but must
   obtain clearance before proceeding.

Each individual can be placed at the level of responsibility appropriate
to his or her competence. The challenge to the supervisor is to bring
about the advancement of his or her subordinates to the level of total
authority.

5. *Time Management.*   Examination of a job can determine how free
the job holder is to make decisions about use of his own time; when to
work and when to break; when to start and when to stop; and assignment of priorities to items of work. Time management is a challenge
and a freedom in most management jobs. It can provide a way for
people to heighten their sense of self worth through more complete
mastery of work life. Time management is a key to autonomy.

6. *Trouble and Crisis Decision-Making.*   Vertical loading opportunities can be found by asking who makes decisions and solves problems
when troubles, breakdowns, or crises arise. Could the functions of this
"troubleshooter" be loaded into the job to be enriched?

7. *Financial Controls.*   Responsibilities involving expenditures, budgets, and profit concerns are often completely denied to individuals for
whom such concerns could be highly motivational. Control of the purse
strings in any job situation can be a fertile area for vertical loading.
Involving a person in control over profit (or at least expenditures) related to his job can make all the difference for motivation. Just as the
profit-center concept often brings vitality to large conglomerate enterprises, so can it enliven work life for individuals.

8. *Demands for Creativity.*   Find ways to involve the job holder in
situations that call for innovation and creativity. Allow him or her to
develop a solution, obtain advice where necessary, and implement the
change.

A Caution About Vertical Loading

The same bit of advice offered for task combination is equally appropriate for vertical loading. Be certain the new responsibilities loaded into the job add something meaningful. There are often many meaningless things added to jobs in misguided attempts at vertical loading. Vertical loading is worthless when it involves trivia.

Dr. M. Scott Myers has neatly captured the essence of vertical loading in the title of his recent book "Every Employee A Manager." [4]

Task Feedback

Task feedback refers to the data about a worker's personal performance which he can receive from all sources. Such feedback might be expressed in some measurement of customer satisfaction, productivity rates, or product quality. Most people want to know how well they are working and what their progress has been; indeed, such knowledge is necessary if they are to improve in any way. But many workers rarely see any *trend* of data about how well they are doing. This occurs for a variety of reasons:

1. There are often no standards of good performance.
2. Performance records are kept at higher levels.
3. Supervisors may discuss performance only when it is poor.
4. Supervisors may check and correct errors themselves.
5. Errors may be sent to special units for correction.
6. Quality inspection is done by other workers.
7. Records are kept by section or department but not by individual performance.

Effective feedback received directly during an activity is a powerful factor in getting people engrossed in what they do. There is a fascination for most people in being able to find out how they personally measure up to some standard. The key factor is feedback on *personal* performance, rather than group or team performance. This is readily apparent in the field of individual sports. Bowling has been cited by Dr. M. Scott Myers[4] as feedback-filled experience. Feedback comes directly and immediately to the bowler at every stage of the game. Every time bowlers bowl a ball they know right away whether they crossed the foul line, lofted the ball, or aimed correctly. They find out immediately how many pins were downed. After each game they know exactly how well they did on their own. They can compare that to the perfect game of 300 to judge how well they play. They can compare themselves to those they bowl with and to the pros. They can determine the trend of their own established average and that of their team. Bowling is a constant series of personal tests and challenges to one's competence. The constant feedback is what sustains the fascination and makes a bowler eager to get out there every Monday night. They want to see how well they can do this time even if they had a poor showing the previous week.

Now imagine what would happen if the feedback situation was drastically changed so that the immediate, direct feedback was stopped and information was provided in another form. Suppose a large soundproof barrier was erected across the middle of the alley so that the bowler could neither see nor hear how many pins were knocked down with each ball. Suppose further that a bowling foreman was standing up at the pin end of the alley to keep score for everyone, but that instead of giving the talley at the end of each frame or game—or even at the end of the night—the foreman just kept everyone's score for three months at a time. The players would be told to keep quiet and bowl for three months and then they would get a complete record on the score of each game, each person's average and the team average, and the standing of the teams. Under those circumstances it's hard to imagine that bowling would have anywhere near the fascination that it now does for so many people. Yet, is this not exactly the situation in which many people find themselves at work with regard to data on their own performance?

Regular, personal, immediate feedback on performance is surely the element that makes bowling so engrossing. Equivalent forms of feedback on personal performance and competence are possible in many jobs, but few have them because the personal value of feedback has not been understood by many people in management. Most work situations are like the altered bowling situation described above, in which feedback is either absent or delivered in such a way that the data has lost most of its immediacy and meaning. With some effort and imagination, however, the fascination of feedback can be captured in most work situations.

To create effective task feedback requires that the desired results of job performance be identified and that a procedure be set up for giving the data on results regularly. The desired results of job performance might be any or all of the following:

- Customer satisfaction
- Product quality
- Product completeness
- Worker accuracy
- Worker productivity
- Worker efficiency
- Worker effectiveness

There is an almost endless number of forms for providing data on results. Among the most common categories are computer printouts or display screens, manual record-keeping, and customer service surveys. Computer or other data printouts are usually connected with high-volume tasks such as keypunching, textiles, or chemicals production. They usually provide feedback for productivity, accuracy, and efficiency. In other situations computer display screens often give a worker immediate data on performance as he or she uses a system component.

Manual records are useful for small amounts of data and can be kept by a worker or the worker's client. They commonly provide feedback for worker effectiveness and efficiency, product quality, and product completeness.

Customer service surveys offer a means for clients to tell a worker how well his or her performance satisfies them.

Task Advancement

In this case task advancement does not mean upward mobility, i.e., promotion to successively higher levels of jobs. Rather it means the redesign of current tasks so that those who perform them have some measure of their increasing net worth, both to themselves and to the organization.

Statistically it is unreasonable to hold out the promise of promotion to workers who are in mind-numbing jobs. There simply are just not that many opportunities. A more sensible approach is to work at redesigning the present job so that the worker knows that he or she is growing, and is more capable today than yesterday.

An example of task advancement would be for a secretary who has demonstrated proficiency in shorthand, typing, filing and telephone answering to be gradually given the following:

- Composition of letters on the basis of key information given by the supervisor
- Management of the supervisor's appointment schedule
- Management of the supervisor's travel schedule, including transportation, lodging, etc.
- Management of details for conferences, i.e., space arrangement, hotel arrangements for conferees, audiovisual equipment details, procedures record keeping, etc.

Note that the worker is still a secretary; the title has not changed.

Another example would be that of a design engineer who has been designing electrical systems for buildings to gradually be given the following:

- Design of heating systems
- Design of ventilating systems
- Design of building foundations
- Design of walls and roofs
- Direct dealing with suppliers

Task advancement always includes new learning. This concept is difficult to implement in those organizations that are locked in to rigid, inflexible, job classification systems.

The reader will quickly recognize that these changes involve several of the implementing concepts. They are not clearly defined or isolated but do overlap and are often interrelated.

THE FOUR CORE DIMENSIONS

Over a period of several years Professors Edward E. Lawler III and Richard J. Hackman of Yale University conducted a number of studies to determine those job characteristics that play a significant role in employee motivation, satisfaction, performance, and effectiveness. They identified four such factors, which they termed "Core Dimensions":

1. Variety: the extreme to which a job requires employees to perform a wide range of operations in their work or to use a variety of equipment and procedures.

2. Autonomy: the extent to which employees have the authority to schedule their work, select the equipment to be used, and determine the procedures they will follow.

3. Task Identity: the extent to which employees do an entire piece of work or a "whole" job and can clearly identify the results of their efforts.

4. Feedback: the information employees receive about their performance while they are working.

When those Core Dimensions are present to a high degree in a job, three important conditions for worker satisfaction have been met. First, workers will know that what they have accomplished has been through their own efforts. Employees who have a high degree of autonomy in the job know that they are personally responsible for whatever successes or failures occur, and this is a powerful and positive influence on the development of internal motivation. In jobs of low autonomy, however, where procedures are completely spelled out in advance and the supervisor constantly hovers in the background to deal with anything out of the ordinary, it is hard to imagine employees feeling any personal stake in accomplishing the work.

Second, the accomplishment will be meaningful to the individual. It is hard to think of a person being concerned with doing a job well if he feels that the work has little importance for anyone, including himself. But work will be experienced as meaningful by an employee if it has a high degree of task identity and/or variety. A job in which a worker does an entire or "whole" piece of work, and in which there is a requirement to develop and use a repertoire of skills and abilities is one that will contain intrinsic importance for the worker.

The final condition is that the individuals will be able to determine how well they are performing as they work. Without feedback there is no opportunity for the self-recognition of achievement that is the corner-stone of internal motivation. The feedback may come directly from the task, from a supervisor, or from a client. But it *must* come.

Lawler and Hackman also address the question of how to change jobs to make them high in the Core Dimensions. They propose that we think of jobs as being on an automation continuum, running from unit production performed by individual craftsmen at one end to the completely automated production facility, where the worker controls highly sophisticated automated equipment, at the other end. Mass production assembly line jobs fall at the middle of the continuum.

Both unit production jobs and jobs in automated plants can be satisfying and motivating, the former because they provide the worker with the responsibility for the production of an entire product, and the latter because they require high skill levels and because workers feel that they are controlling the production process.

The closer one approaches to the center of the continuum, however, the lower on the Core Dimensions a job seems to become. The assembly line has simplified work that provides no variety or challenge and the machine controls the worker rather than the other way around. To improve jobs, then, requires that we move away from the center of the continuum toward either end. The specific direction in any given instance would, of course, be determined by the nature of the product or service and the work force. In general, however, moving from the center of the continuum toward the unit production end would appear to be advisable when: (1) current capital investment in machinery is low; (2) employees are overqualified for their jobs as presently designed and they desire more challenging work; and (3) there are problems of low job satisfaction, high absenteeism, and poor work quality.

From the foregoing presentation of the Implementing Concepts and the four Core Dimensions it should be evident that there is a remarkable convergence between job design criteria that are developed through extensive consulting experience with enriching jobs and those that are developed through controlled research programs. Thus, the task identity and variety dimensions of Lawler and Hackman are very similar to natural units of work and task combination in the Implementing Concepts. They point to the same thing: the importance of giving a worker a part of the work that is defined as his own; one in which the worker can perform a variety of task functions and turn out as nearly a whole piece of work or service function as possible. This forms the basis for individual achievements which allow workers to clearly see what they have contributed—things they can take pride in and for which they can gain recognition. The autonomy dimension is the direct equivalent of vertical loading in the Implementing Concepts. They both represent the fact that most adults at work find greater satisfaction in having control over what they do and how they do it than in being closely followed up and controlled by others. Being held accountable for an operation with autonomy and authority in the bargain can be a powerful internal motivating experience. Feedback is equivalent in both sets of principles. The Implementing Concepts offer client relationship and task advancement as additional measures of the motivating potential of a job. We suggest to the Job Enrichment practitioner that a combination of the two sets of principles will yield an effective set of criteria both for evaluation of existing job designs and as a guide for restructuring work.

SUMMARY

For this chapter we have reviewed the primary causes of job technological advances, fragmentation of jobs in its many forms, and the denial of responsibility to the worker. We have presented two complementary sets of principles for job design (independently evolved) that are valuable in bridging the gap from motivation theory to the actual restructuring of jobs to make them motivating, satisfying experiences for employees. One set, termed the Implementing Concepts, was developed by Roy W. Walters and Associates through their consulting experience in Job Enrichment, and comprises six factors: natural units of work, client relationships, task combination, vertical loading, task feedback, and task advancement. The second set, called the Core Dimensions, developed through the research of Drs. Edward E. Lawler III and J. Richard Hackman of Yale University, contains four factors: variety, task identity, autonomy, and feedback. Jobs that are organized around these sets of principles will provide most people with the opportunities for real responsibility, personal achievement, individual recognition, and a sense of professional growth and development in the job that are the motivators of sustained high performance.

REFERENCES

1. Lynda King Taylor, *Not For Bread Alone* (London, Business Books, Ltd. 1972).

2. For a description of the A.T.&T. research see R.N. Ford, *Motivation Through The Work Itself* (New York, American Management Association, 1968).

3. Edward E. Lawler, III, and J. Richard Hackman, "Corporate Profits and Employee Satisfaction: Must They Be In Conflict?" *California Management Review* (Fall 1971,) pp. 46–55.

4. Dr. M. Scott, Myers, *Every Employee A Manager* (New York, McGraw-Hill, 1970).

5. *Ibid.*

chapter
SIX
Preparing for
Job Enrichment

INTRODUCTION

This chapter will deal with the various problems of preparing for a Job Enrichment application. These range from gaining initial commitment from the organization to selecting a work group, planning a model of the application, and developing a staff. How well these concerns are handled will determine the eventual success or failure of a project and thus the probable future of Job Enrichment in the organization.

GAINING INITIAL COMMITMENT

The key problem in gaining initial commitment is convincing key executives that Job Enrichment offers something more than a way to establish better human relations and worker attitudes. To persuade most executives to invest a substantial amount of time, money, and effort to improve the quality of corporate life or to improve human relations in the organization is a difficult sell. Many of these executives got where they are during a different era, when there was less concern about these matters. Some, of course, will tune into this kind of approach rather quickly. They may be further ahead in developing a concern for a people-centered organization. Most managers, however, are instinctively suspicious of proposals for investment in programs designed to make workers feel better. They have been conditioned to feel that these are less important concerns that have little to do with profitability. On the other hand, an executive charged with operating responsibilities will always take the time to listen to a proposal that suggests a way to reduce the cost of doing business and to improve bottom-line results.

Therein lies the essence of the most effective approach to top executives on the subject of Job Enrichment. Job Enrichment programs *do* beneficially affect profitability and bottom-line results. Abundant evidence can be marshalled to make a good case for an investment in a Job Enrichment application for purely economic reasons, a good case based solely on a strategy for more effective management.

In an article in the Harvard Business Review, Raymond Miles of the University of California set down some key ideas that would be very helpful in preparing a case for Job Enrichment.[1] Miles presented a compelling case for the need for better management of the human resources or human assets of organizations. The point of key interest for line managers is that finding ways to more effectively manage human resources represents far more than a concern for the welfare of the workers in the organization. It is very much an economic concern that involves improved handling of a crucial set of assets under a manager's control. Miles sets up a challenge for managers to handle their human resources with the same meticulous care they devote to their other resources, such as capital assets, financial assets, and raw materials. In most organizations a manager is not allowed to get very far out of line in mismanaging those assets. But not many managers are held accountable for their handling of the human assets available to them. In many, many cases today, human assets are underutilized, wasted, or even liquidated. A manager would soon be taken to task if he handled his other assets in similar fashion. Although Job Enrichment is not specified in the article, it is a strategy for managing that is directed exactly to the need for better management of human resources. Although improvement of organization life is certainly one of the effects of a successful Job Enrichment application, it can make a lot more sense to line executives when presented as a call to them to be completely professional and effective in their handling of all forms of assets. The point should be made that Job Enrichment delivers measured results in terms for which managers are accustomed to being held accountable. It is based on the premise that most people at work today could deliver far more (and far better) work than they presently do if their jobs required more of them and gave them the opportunity and freedom to achieve on their own.

Better management of human resources through strategies like Job Enrichment represents a happy combination of good for the organization and good for the worker. It is difficult to think of another management strategy that serves the objectives of the organization and the individual in quite this way.

Efforts to persuade top management to begin the process of Job Enrichment must be highly results-oriented. This is the only language that most line executives understand or will respond to when crucial decisions must be made. Producing results and delivering on responsibilities constitute the name of the game for line managers. The case for Job Enrichment must relate to that results-oriented tradition. It will be important to avoid an overly theoretical approach. Avoid overemphasis on research, behavioral science and motivation theory. For many managers, at this point, such concerns are quite foreign and seem to have little to do with the hard-nosed business of managing. Their response to academic and theoretical presentations is likely to range anywhere from polite skepticism to vociferous rejection. Emphasize the fact that results of Job Enrichment applications can and have been successfully measured. This is a crucial question for most executives considering the application of any new system or method of management. They want to know: How much can I save? How much more can I produce? What will it deliver? Measurements of results can be devised in terms that are most meaningful to the manager who becomes involved in Job Enrichment.

In most cases, Job Enrichment is initially presented to an organization by someone in a staff position. It is most often people in personnel or training functions who take up the task of gaining initial commitment. While it is painful for such staff people to realize or admit, they and their proposals are often regarded by executives in operating positions with some degree of suspicion. At the least they are accorded a lesser degree of respect than are those in line positions. Whether such attitudes are justified or not, they commonly exist and therefore must be borne in mind in the interest of gaining commitments for a job enrichment project. It will be difficult to build a bridge of understanding to those with line operating responsibilities, but doing so offers a significant opportunity to people in personnel and training. Job Enrichment, with its structured and pragmatic approach to delivering operating results, can provide a foundation of respect and credibility for the staff individuals who establish the beachhead. This foundation can have significance and value as a stepping stone to other applications.

The pattern of most likely opposition in organizations is worth examining. Typically, individuals in executive management are often quite receptive to proposals for improving the management of human resources. Their perspective is more long-range, they are less concerned with the day-to-day details of producing results, and they are less subject to short-term pressure for results than are the middle levels of management. In our experience cooperation of the lower-level managers and first-line supervisors can be gained after a brief period of education and experience. In most cases they become active supporters and very excited about the effort. The opposition problem lies mainly among managers at the middle levels. These are the individuals for whom risk poses the greatest threat. Their orientation tends to be short-term and narrowly focused on producing results during a relatively short tenure in a job. They tend to be highly aware that their progress toward the top is threatened by innovation and risks taken. They are likely to present the most formidable opposition and to respond only to approaches which emphasize results measurable in terms of profitability. It may be useful to list some of the common initial responses of managers to Job Enrichment proposals. Keith Robinson, a successful Job Enrichment practitioner with Imperial Chemical Industries, Ltd., of Great Britain, presented the following list of common initial responses some time ago. They are still frequently encountered:

1. "This is a sound approach but my department is different." All sorts of reasons are given as to why a department is different or why changes in methods, production schedules, new employees, etc., make it an inopportune time to begin. There is no single answer to that objection but such a response should be anticipated and plans made to deal with it.

2. "We have already designed all our jobs as enriched jobs." This too is a common response and in our experience it is very unlikely. The manager who makes this claim should have no objection to an examination of those jobs and verification of the enrichment of the employees in the job. It is invariably found in such situations that the jobs are far short of being rich.

3. "The risk is too great." The tactic here should be to shift from the general to the particular, requiring those who are afraid of risks to be very specific about which risks, their reality, and how can they be controlled.

4. "We cannot afford to make the initial investment required." This should be countered by enumeration of all the hidden costs of things like underproduction, turnover costs, retraining costs, correction of defects in work, and absence. A case can be made that, in view of all these kinds of costs, an organized effort to reduce them is certainly worth consideration.

5. "I'm under pressure from above. I haven't got time to change methods." This is a very valid concern for a manager and there is really no sure way to deal with it unless supportive signals from above can be generated to indicate that there is also pressure from above to undertake this kind of a strategy.

6. "This concept would work fine on the assembly line or the accounting department or the quality control division." Really in any other department but mine, is what the speaker means.

There is another key point to be made on the subject of opposition: Job Enrichment cannot be forced down unwilling throats. It cannot work in the hands of people who are actively opposed to it, unwilling to devote effort to it, or generally ill-disposed toward changing their style of management. There are just too many ways to make sure it does not work in the course of a project. The project will pose many difficult decisions and strains for such individuals which they will be unwilling to accept. It is not necessary, however, to conclude that all-out active commitment at the top is necessary in order to begin a project. The minimum requirement is a neutral "Show me" attitude. If that much of a commitment can be gained it is worth proceeding.

Here are some suggestions for gaining commitment:

1. Depending on one's position in the organization, discussions of Job Enrichment can be started at either middle levels or top levels of the organization. However, an open and receptive channel of communication to the top will be necessary to gain either full commitment or the willingness to undertake the trial application. This kind of initial support can obviously be the answer to almost all of the opposition likely to develop later at middle levels. The more common approach is to hold a gathering of midle-level executives who have their own budgets and decision-making power about such programs to describe the Job En-

richment procedure and objectives and to attempt to identify potential clients for such an application. This is done either in the form of a seminar to identify initial interest or in one-to-one meetings with key line executives. Probably most successful is the strategy of working assiduously to gain the commitment of one line executive who wants to try. In many cases his support and interest almost assures approval at the top. To identify whom to talk to in one-on-one discussions about Job Enrichment, look around the organiaztion and find the executives who have problems with quality, production, service, or turnover. They are most likely engaged in a painful soul-searching about their management style and effectiveness and are most likely to respond favorably.

2. Do not identify the proposed application as the latest personnel gimmick or the specialty campaign of the year. Nothing could be worse for the long-term future of Job Enrichment than to have it so identified.

3. Contacts and data gathering with other organizations involved in job enrichment can provide very useful material for internal discussion about job enrichment.

4. Many organizations have found it worth while to have a professional Job Enrichment practitioner help soften up top management by describing the process and its objectives and relating the experiences of others.

To say the least, gaining initial commitment for Job Enrichment or any behavioral science application among managers is a difficult proposition. As things stand today, however, the effort to gain initial commitment will succeed to the degree that the activist who introduces job enrichment adopts a highly results oriented and profit oriented approach couched in language that line managers under great pressure understand and respond to. Frederick Herzberg summed up the argument for job enrichment quite succinctly.[2] Herzberg set down three options in facing a manager in terms of the use of human resources:

1. If you have someone on a job—use him.

2. If you can't use him on the job—get rid of him either by automation or by selecting someone with lesser ability.

3. If you won't use him well and you can't get rid of him, you will have a motivation problem.

IS JOB DESIGN THE PROBLEM? DIAGNOSIS/ FEASIBILITY STUDY

Although inadequacies of job design are virtually a common denominator among work groups with performance problems, there can be other sources of trouble as well. Among such factors are the following:

- Poor employee selection
- Poor training
- Absence of operating controls and work standards
- Poor superior-subordinate relationships[3]
- Equipment or material problems
- Ineffective work procedures
- Lack of management training and development
- Poor communications
- Inadequate pay or other Hygiene problems

It is possible for some of these problems, or combinations of them, to cause poor performance even when the content and structure of the work are basically sound according to motivational principles. In our experience, this is a rare situation. The reasons have been touched on earlier, but the two major ones can be briefly recapitulated here: First, most companies have devoted more effort to dealing with the "laundry list" of problems above than they have to motivational factors. Second, several trends in technology, industrial engineering, and management have caused or accelerated the deterioration of many jobs in motivational terms.

As a result, job design plays a large part in many cases of poor performance. It is important, however, not to decide that job design, or any one of the other possible factors, is *the* sole or major problem area without thorough diagnosis.

Poor diagnosis, or none at all, is probably the biggest single cause of "Job Enrichment failure." There are three basic patterns of misuse of Job Enrichment:

1. Job design is identified as the root problem, and jobs are redesigned, when the real reason lies elsewhere.

2. Other problems are identified as the root causes (for example, pay or technology) and job design is wrongly left alone.

3. Job design is identified as the sole cause, and jobs are soundly re-designed; but other problems are overlooked, and continuing problems undermine the effects of enrichment.

The purpose of diagnosis and feasibility study, in a Job Enrichment context, is to prevent these kinds of misuse. To do so, the study must gather many different kinds of information by many methods. Some of the objectives and methods will be discussed here.

Chapter 5 dealt with the Core Dimensions of jobs, as described by Lawler and Hackman of Yale. It also dealt with the Implementing Concepts of job design, as practiced by Roy W. Walters & Associates. The ideal tool for job design diagnosis should be able to evaluate a given job in terms of the Core Dimensions. If the job is inadequate in those terms, the tool should be able to pinpoint the inadequacies and indicate changes to be made in job design through use of the Implementing Concepts.

Such a tool has been developed recently, through joint effort of a Yale University team headed by Prof. J. Richard Hackman and Roy W. Walters & Associates. Called the Job Diagnosis Survey, it has proven valuable in comprehensive diagnostic studies in a variety of industries.

The inventory is a multipurpose questionnaire divided into eight parts. Workers in the jobs where enrichment is contemplated are asked to complete the questionnaire, applying seven-point rating scales to a variety of statements about their jobs.

Some of the sections concern subjective attitudes of the employees toward their jobs. Others ask them specifically to be as objective and factual as possible in describing actual characteristics of the job. The questions are chosen and organized in such a way that the instrument, taken as a whole, provides data in several categories:

- The degree to which the job possesses five Core Dimensions—skill variety, task identity, task significance, autonomy, and feedback.

- The degree to which the job holders experience three psychological states associated with job satisfaction—Meaningfulness, Responsibility, and Knowledge of Results.

- The strength of individual workers' needs for personal growth, which can affect their response to the job in terms of satisfaction and internal motivation.

The inventory provides several useful statistics. First there is an overall Motivation Potential Score, a summary measure of the strength or weakness of the job in characteristics that should cause high motivation. Second, each Core Dimension can be scored separately to give a profile indicating what particular aspects of the job should be strengthened and which Implementing Concepts should be applied. Third, the strength of the workers' growth needs can be analyzed to indicate whether they are likely to respond to job design changes that seem sound in themselves.

A Job Diagnosis Survey or similar instrument should be the basic step in a diagnosis/feasibility study. (Another instrument that has been used frequently is the Borgatta Job Reaction Survey. Developed by Dr. Edgar Borgatta, formerly of the University of Wisconsin, the questionnaire measures employees' attitudes toward the content of their work in terms of nine criteria.)

Although valuable and central to the study, these instruments alone cannot quite complete the diagnostic phase. Other kinds of data are needed—for example:

1. *Demographic profile.* Pertinent data are collected about age, sex, education, time in job, etc. The Job Diagnosis Survey, like many other surveys, includes basic questions about these facts. Any data that may not be elicited by such an instrument are usually available from personnel records.

2. *Interviews with supervisors.* All levels of management and supervision are interviewed to gain information about the main forces at work in the group, such as work volume, work force, projected systems changes, staff competence, key problems and troubles, goal setting, performance appraisal and reward systems, work flow patterns, leadership style, and key pressure points from higher management. The discussions with employees at each level are compared by the interviewers with those at other levels to determine conflicts and differences of view.

3. *Interviews with employees.* A substantial sample of the work force is interviewed individually (in pairs if they desire it) to gain informa-

tion about personal responses to work content. Called "critical incident interviewing," the intent of the interview format is to get a person to talk freely about work experiences he has had that he remembers as having been either particularly good or particularly bad. The real effectiveness in this tool lies in the interviewer's adroitness at probing for relevant information. Interviews are tape-recorded whenever possible. This not only allows the interviewer to concentrate on creative probing for information rather than on note-taking, but also provides an opportunity for the material to be anonymously excerpted for reports.

4. *Supervisory Time Apportionment Survey*. The object of this form, which is filled out by supervisors, is to determine the ratio of production-related work done by supervisors to the work they do developing subordinates. It is intended to indicate the level of awareness among supervisors of their responsibility for subordinate development and the extent to which they are allowed to pursue it.

5. *System Four survey*. This survey, designed by Rensis Likert of the University of Michigan, measures the characteristics of an organization's managerial system and the style of leadership most commonly used. The survey is useful in identifying conditions which can affect Job Enrichment progress.

6. *Hygiene evaluation*. In Job Enrichment applications the focus of attention is on reshaping the work itself. However, workers are affected by a variety of factors surrounding the work, such as physical environment, boss/subordinate relationships, pay, and other hygiene factors. The condition of these factors must be known if we are to know how strong the sources of dissatisfaction are, how hard they will be to overcome, and what effect they will have on the enrichment process. In some cases bad hygiene must be corrected before Job Enrichment can proceed.

7. *Work flow diagrams*. When the work flow is relatively simple, it is often useful to diagram it. This can be done with the aid of a worker or supervisor. In addition to helping one learn quickly what the job structure is like, such a diagram can be used in analyzing possible sources of enrichment.

A typical feasibility study need not use all these tools. The exact choice will be determined partly by the clarity of the central findings of the survey, partly by the strength or weakness of other kinds of information, and partly by the intuition of the specialist, internal or external, about the nature of the problem.

As mentioned before, job design is a problem common to a good many poor-performance situations. A diagnosis carried out by the principles outlined here should indicate whether Job Enrichment is a likely remedy, and how it should be focused.

The diagnostic procedure is sufficiently open-ended, however, to indicate other courses of action in place of, or in addition to, Job Enrichment. There are many situations in which poor performance is due both to job design and to some of the other problems mentioned. In such cases, Job Enrichment often has a catalytic effect in mobilizing management for a broader campaign of organizational change. This valuable effect of Job Enrichment will be discussed fully in a later chapter.

The data gathered by the feasibility study are developed into a set of findings and recommendations. These are then presented to key executives to give them a complete picture of: (1) the existing state of the job design, (2) the need for enrichment, and (3) the areas of opportunity for job changes. Where appropriate, this presentation should also include an implementation model or plan for the project.

The feasibility study is a key component in the strategy for gaining initial commitment to a project. The organization must develop a team of people who can conduct such studies and develop convincing data for presentation to lower- and middle-level management. Properly executed, the feasibility study can be an eye-opening experience for management as it quantifies the underlying causes of problems they have sought for years to solve.

MORE ON THE SELECTION OF THE WORK GROUP

In our preceding discussion we showed how the feasibility study shows whether job design is really the cause of the work group's problems. It will also show whether the selected job can be enriched—and whether it should be enriched instead of being automated out of existence. When these three questions have been decided in the affirmative there are others that must be considered before the final choice of work group is made.

These criteria should not be regarded as inflexible—enrichment can be successfully accomplished in a variety of situations—but it is very helpful to be aware of all the factors that are likely to make an application successful. This is particularly true when the work group being selected is to receive the initial application.

There are 10 points that must be considered in selecting work groups for Job Enrichment when the project is not an initial one, and there are five others that must be considered when selecting a work group for an initial project.

When Selecting a Work Group for Enrichment Application

1. A major consideration is the receptiveness of the management team to the basic approach of Job Enrichment. If the preliminary analysis shows that the local management of the work group shows opposition or even low receptivity to the enrichment of the jobs, there is little point in undertaking the effort. Success is highly dependent on being able to develop a rather deep commitment on the part of the managers and supervisors in the work group who must bear the major burden of the enrichment process. It was said earlier that a neutral "show me" attitude on the part of upper management is all that is required for the beginning of an enrichment project. However, the local management team should have somewhat better than a neutral attitude. It is not necessary that they be wildly enthusiastic about a project, or that they evidence a complete prior commitment to it, but they should show a potential for change in their approach to management and considerable willingness to experiment.

2. The size of the employee population in the work group under consideration is also important. The selected work group should be of sufficient size to allow for differences in individual response to the enrichment process. It cannot be assumed that everyone in the work group will respond with equal enthusiasm to enrichment of the jobs. Therefore, if the employee population is too small, reluctance on the part of even a portion of the work group may make it very difficult to achieve any substantial success. Furthermore, the employee population should be large enough to establish significant results that will make an impression on the rest of the organization. In general, work groups numbering between

50 and 200 employees are most desirable for enrichment applications. This criterion, however, should not be applied with great rigidity. If there is a work group of small size or even of very large size which is crucial to the organization and badly in need of enrichment, other factors may make it well worth the effort to work with that group despite its size.

3. The size of the supervisory population in the work group can be a critical factor. In fact, the number of supervisors in the work group can be a more critical factor than the number of employees. This is because most of the planning and problem-solving activities in the process of redesigning the jobs are carried on by the first line supervisory team. If that group is too large, it becomes unwieldy to work with and too little time can be spent with each team of supervisors. In this situation the activity often becomes diluted and it's difficult to maintain momentum. Generally speaking, a supervisory team of from 15 to 18 members is optimal for an enrichment application. It becomes difficult to handle more than 18 supervisors during the process. Once again, however, this criterion need not be applied too rigidly, for there are ways to handle larger groups of supervisors. If there are enough Job Enrichment specialists to give continuing guidance to a larger group of supervisors, then a supervisory team exceeding 18 may well be acceptable by having them work in separate groups.

4. Geographic location of the selected work group can be an important consideration. It should be borne in mind that the Job Enrichment specialist should have frequent contact with the members of the work group during the project. Therefore, if the latter is located too great a distance from the specialist who must serve them, communication becomes difficult, contact is not frequent enough, and momentum can be lost. This does not mean that the work group must be located near the specialist, but when they are a great distance away, the problems of application are compounded.

5. No major changes in systems, equipment, or work flow should be contemplated for the selected work group during the period of the enrichment project or shortly thereafter. The importance of this point should be readily obvious. A great deal of time and effort may be devoted to redesigning the jobs to reach optimum motivational effective-

ness during the project. Major (or too many) changes introduced too soon could negate much or all of the enrichment project's efforts.

6. A work group should be selected in which no more than a normal turnover of supervision is expected during the period of the enrichment project. If there is an abnormal amount of turnover in supervision, it becomes difficult to sustain the activity because of the need to orient new members of the supervisory team and gain their commitment in the midst of the project.

7. If the group under consideration has been subjected to regular and frequent transfer or rotation of employees, and if that pattern cannot be reversed, it may be wise to select another group. It stands to reason that if the full effect of Job Enrichment is to be realized, the workers in the enriched jobs must remain there long enough to experience the personal achievement possibilities.

8. It is often an advantage to select a work group in which changes or restructuring of the job have already been contemplated for other reasons, such as improving the work flow. This is often a good time to bring up the behavioral point of view. It's much better to redesign a job once, with behavioral enrichment, than to do it once for work flow and later for enrichment. And of course management would much prefer a one-shot redesign to two separate redesigns at different times. There is one potential disadvantage to a redesign that combines enrichment with another objective: the possible difficulty of separating the improvements attributable to job enrichment from those stemming from procedural changes.

9. It is often a good idea to make a Job Enrichment application at the time that a work group is moving to new quarters. A physical move often generates an atmosphere of receptiveness to change, and this can mean a responsive and cooperative attitude toward the enrichment project. (See paragraph 5 under heading "When Selecting a Work Group for an Initial Project.")

10. Sometimes the work group selected for Job Enrichment is to serve as a pilot group, and the completed program is to be applied to other groups of similar type. In such cases it is important that the selected work group be a truly representative sample. If it is not, the other work groups can raise the objection (which may very well be legitimate) that

the enrichment program is not suited to them. Moreover, it stands to reason that the more similar the groups, the less time, money, and effort it will take to apply the program to all of them.

When Selecting a Work Group for an Initial Project

1. It is wise to avoid a work group in a newly established job or with a highly inexperienced work force. For one thing, it is more difficult to introduce enrichment changes at a time when people are struggling to learn the basic work process itself. Beyond that, one can't be at all sure that any improvements in productivity or quality are not just normal results of maturation and experience, rather than results of the Job Enrichment program.

2. The work group selected for an initial trial project should be doing a "core job"—that is, a job that is crucial to the organization and a work group in which Significant results with a core-job work group would make a real impression on key individuals in the organization. Jobs involving service functions are often highly desirable places at which to introduce the initial enrichment project in an organization. This is due to the fact that enrichment possibilities and opportunities for individual responsibility for innovation and improvement on services are nearly limitless in service jobs, whereas there may be some limitations to the number of changes that can be made in machine-bound or manufacturing jobs.

3. There should be sound and valid measures of productivity and work quality in the selected work group in order that there be as little question as possible about the results of the enrichment application.

4. For an initial trial project, it is wise to choose a job which is not too closely bound up with either a machine process that is difficult to change or rigidly established work procedures which will present obstacles to change. This is not to say that such jobs should be avoided entirely. The point is that the job selected for the initial project should offer the most opportunity for change with the least number of obvious restrictions at the start. This will permit maximum freedom for the redesign of the job.

5. If the results of an initial trial project are to be as unassailable as possible, it is wise to avoid selecting a work group which is about to

receive major changes in hygiene. In other words, do not choose a work group which is about to receive new air conditioning, new quarters, carpeted work areas, a new face lift, a drastic increase in pay or other very attractive hygiene improvements. Opponents of Job Enrichment can always claim that it was these changes that brought about a short term improvement in performance rather than the changes made in job design alone. Coincident hygiene changes, if they are significant, can diminish the impact of results gained through changing job design.

DECISIONS ABOUT THE PROJECT MODEL

The project model is the plan of activity intended for the application. The initial Job Enrichment effort for an organization can take various forms. The most appropriate project model is determined by organization needs and the Job Enrichment objective. There are three basic project models: the Pilot Project, the Full Scale Program, and the Proving Project with experimental controls.

1. *The pilot project* consists of selecting one work group in which to make a Job Enrichment application. All of the job redesign effort is concentrated on this one work group with the object of producing convincing measured results which may be used to demonstrate to other executives the impact of redesigning jobs.

2. *A full-scale program* involves either the education of many managers throughout the organization, with the intent of having them make their own enrichment applications, or the conducting of simultaneous guided enrichment applications with specialists assigned to multiple work groups. The object here is to gain the greatest possible impact at the outset of the program.

3. *A proving project* is a testing project with experimental controls. Its purpose is to: (1) isolate the specific job changes made in an experimental group, (2) measure the impact of those changes, and (3) compare the results in the experimental group with any number of control groups in which either different changes have been made or in which conditions have been maintained as constant as possible. The point is to prove that it was the job changes made in the experimental group that produced the results measured. The purpose of the proving

project with experimental controls is, of course, to present unassailable evidence to a skeptical organization that it was the changes in the content of work that brought about the results.

Consulting experience leads us to recommend the pilot project over the other two project models for a number of reasons. Undertaking Job Enrichment is a difficult decision for an organization to make. There are many strains and problems involved and, in most cases, it is necessary to provide some convincing demonstration that it is worth the effort and that profitable results can be produced. In most organizations it is difficult to gain commitment for anything more than a demonstration trial of some type. A pilot project can show the effectiveness of Job Enrichment without requiring a heavy initial commitment from the organization.

Perhaps some discussion of the other project models may demonstrate the value of the recommended pilot project. In some situations, it is difficult to avoid setting up a proving project with experimental controls. There may be such a level of skepticism among managers and executives that some irrefutable proof of the effectiveness of changing job design must be presented. However, we recommend avoiding the proving project, with its complicated controls, if at all possible. There are a number of reasons for this:

1. It is often difficult to find exactly similar groups for comparison in which no factors would vary other than the changes in job design.

2. Where similar groups have been found, it has been discovered that maintaining constant conditions in the control groups is a very trying task. In most control groups, for one reason or another, conditions do not remain constant. In live operating work groups, managers and supervisors are sometimes unwilling and often unable to act as if they were running a laboratory experiment. Often events beyond their control cause them to alter conditions, and this tends to open the results to question.

3. It's often found that as things begin to go well in the experimental group, management in the control groups does not want to wait to make similar changes with their own work force. Or, if they do not undertake the same changes in work content, they may make other changes or exert other pressures to improve their own results so they will not look bad.

4. Perhaps the most sensible point is that it seems a shame to devote so much time and effort to maintaining control groups with constant conditions when it could be directed toward achieving a greater impact with more work groups and more people. At this stage in the development of Job Enrichment we don't really need to demonstrate effectiveness with controlled experiments. There is ample case evidence available to prove the effectiveness of making enriching changes in work content.

The other project model mentioned earlier, the full-scale program, appeals to many organizations. Their hope is to enrich either the whole organization or a multitude of work groups all at one time. Once they are convinced that the Job Enrichment approach is appropriate, they seem unwilling to concentrate the effort and investment in one work group to sort of get their feet wet. They want to plunge right in and cover the whole distance with one quick effort. Too often management comes to believe that job enrichment is really pretty simple, and that all the managers in the organization should be given enough education to perform their own enrichment at the outset of the program. Perhaps it would be worthwhile to take time out to examine this approach, for such dilution presents many problems. Job Enrichment is not likely to produce a real impact if its installation depends on an educational process for a large number of managers or the inclusion of Job Enrichment principles in various management development workshop seminars.

Let there be no doubt that in most cases successful Job Enrichment does require substantial changes in the style and behavior of management. Very few managers are accustomed to the guiding developmental role in which employees are given a great deal of individual responsibility and encouraged to use their talents and judgment. Most managers have been taught that managing consists of giving orders and maintaining extensive follow-up control. They have grown up in a somewhat threatening environment in which it is a dangerous risk to give true responsibility and accountability to subordinates. And organizational reward systems do not pay off for that kind of risk. And yet, it is just such willingness to experiment to find out the true capacities of subordinates that is at the heart of Job Enrichment. If jobs are to be enlarged enough to provide truly meaningful tasks for people, managers and supervisors must grow accustomed to putting a much higher level of trust in their subordinates; they must accept some degree of error as those subordinates grow, and accept the risks of allowing them to assume true responsibility. This kind of managerial approach does not come easily, and certainly is not likely to develop out of a classroom learning situation or a laboratory training experience.

A research study recently conducted by Professor Wallace Wohlking of Cornell University reviewed the results of hundreds of attempts to change management behavior in numerous organizations through the use of management development workshops and seminars. The basic assumption of these programs was that the attitudes of managers and supervisors must be changed first before any meaningful change in their behavior could be expected to occur. Wohlking found that extremely few, if any, of these programs resulted in any lasting change in the behavior of the participating managers and supervisors. His conclusion was that you cannot bring about sustained changes in management behavior by first attempting to change management attitudes. He linked this finding with his own hypothesis that lasting changes in management behavior come about not through a prior change in attitude but by *first* making some distinct structural change in the way managers are required to act towards subordinates. This allows the managers to become accustomed to the new behavior, and the change in attitudes follows.

Briefly, then, while an organization may try to initiate Job Enrichment by providing new learning experiences for managers and supervisors with the expectation that they will then install Job Enrichment themselves for their subordinates, it is almost always unwise. It is simply not likely that enough managers and supervisors will become actively committed to the newer style of managing to make Job Enrichment effective. A project founded on this model probably will fail; the effort is most likely to peter out and slide into oblivion, becoming "last year's big program." Or it may cause considerable disruption as some managers either force the process down reluctant throats or let their management practices become so lax while trying to give employees freedom that they lose complete control of their operation. Either eventuality is a prescription for failure. Most attempts to enrich most or all of an organization in this way will very likely amount to no more than a long series of educational sessions which generate very little change in jobs. Most organizations cannot muster a large enough force of Job Enrichment specialists to provide the required guidance and follow-up monitoring of the process which is required for real job change. If the program is undertaken with too many groups at the same time, the specialists' activities become spread too thin and cannot be effective.

For the process of redesigning jobs and installing the job changes, follow-up monitoring is the key. Successful redesign of jobs requires intensive concentration on the selected jobs, careful education of the management team, frequent follow-up by competent specialists to monitor the activity and pace of change, and a great deal of guidance for the supervisory team as they install job changes and cope with the problems inevitably generated. Failure to give that kind of guidance has been probably the largest cause of failure in Job Enrichment application.

The pilot project, carefully measured but without the taxing restrictions and dissipated energy of running experimental control groups, has been found to be the most successful model. We strongly recommend that an organization select carefully one good-sized work group in which an improvement in results will make an impression on others in the organization. Sound measures should be available for performance in the selected work group and capable people must be assigned for development as Job Enrichment specialists. That pilot project should be nurtured like a hothouse plant to ensure every chance for its success. This may seem like a very high initial investment for one work group, but the woods are full of people who are skeptical about behavioral applications like Job Enrichment—people who need convincing. It is not the traditional way of managing, and if the initial efforts fail or arouse too much skepticism the future of Job Enrichment for that organization will be very short. The pilot project gives the greatest assurance of establishing a strong foundation and is the best way to develop a sound group of internal practitioners. The guiding theme should be to proceed without a great deal of fanfare, work diligently using the best advice you can get, and produce a resounding success the first time out on the track. Then address top management and other managers in the organization with convincing proof of success. If you do not, the effort is likely to become just another fad—and wily managers have become expert at riding out passing fads.

Some additional emphasis may be warranted on the point of Begin Your Job Enrichment program with as little fanfare as possible; the effort is far more likely to succeed if it is begun with a low profile. You're likely to meet less opposition if your changes seem like natural steps in the evolution of the management process. The less said about last year's fantastic Job Enrichment program, the better; in fact, we recommend that the phrase "Job Enrichment program" not even be used. The process should appear to be as natural a part of the day-to-day process as possible. Success does not depend on whipping up a frenzy of excitement among the employees—it depends rather on the managers' and supervisors' quiet, day-by-day determination to redesign the jobs, install the job changes, and ensure that they work. Fanfare is likely to cause trouble.

A single group pilot project is also desirable from another point of view—it's easier to sell to top management. Gaining commitment for a widespread, full-scale treatment of an entire organization (or a large part of it) is very difficult. A much better case can be made for keeping the investment modest until it's known what the concept can do for the organization. The impact can be effectively and quickly expanded throughout the organization by training one group of specialists on the initial pilot project, then assigning each of them to expansion projects with their own set of specialists to train—and so on. When an external consultant is used it should be his or her responsibility to train the first set of specialists, gradually shifting the lead consulting role to the internal specialist and withdrawing. Further discussion of the expansion pattern will be covered in a later chapter.

This discussion of the type of project and selection of the work group raises questions about what level of the organization should be selected for the first application. Is it more effective to start with jobs at the top of the organization, at the bottom, or at the middle? Enrichment of jobs in many organizations is needed as much at the top and middle as at the grass-roots level. We have met countless executives and managers who, after exposure to Job Enrichment, asked "Why didn't you start with my job? I'm really doing nothing meaningful either, I'm just spinning my wheels." This is certainly a major factor in the increasingly common pattern of "second careers" among business men, as many of them find they must undergo the rigors of changing careers at mid-life in order to find work that will challenge them.

The fact is that Jobs Enrichment is needed and appropriate at all organizational levels, and there is no standard rule about where to begin. In general, however, it has been found best to start at the bottom with grass-roots jobs. The process then spreads upward naturally, since much of the technique of enriching jobs depends on enlarging them by loading on tasks and responsibilities from the jobs at levels above them. This naturally creates some vacuums in the higher-level jobs, which can then be enriched with tasks and responsibilities from jobs at still higher levels—and so on.

Acceptance of demonstration pilot projects is often better when they are proposed for grass-roots jobs. The organization then grows accustomed to enrichment principles and activity and there is less reluctance to make applications at higher levels. Also, for initial projects the measurements of results generally are more effective with lower-level jobs. The elements of time, volume, quality, and cost are more readily determined at lower levels. Results in professional or management jobs are more difficult to establish in the objective, verifiable figures which are so crucial to spreading of the program. However, if it is important enough to the ogranization to start with a set of jobs at higher levels, there is no reason not to do so.

QUALIFICATIONS FOR THE JOB ENRICHMENT SPECIALIST

Because the best set of ideas in the world can come to naught without the right people to use it, the organization must choose very carefully from within itself the specialists who are to implement the Job Enrichment program. For that reason we have developed the following description of the "ideal" person to serve as an internal organization specialist for Job Enrichment.

Foremost among the requirements is the ability to become an effective consultant. This is a very demanding role which requires an individual who can sell an idea persuasively without being dogmatic and who possesses more than an ordinary sensitivity to the needs and personal situations of the management people with whom he must work during the course of the program.

The ideal Job Enrichment specialist is above average in intelligence and is oriented more toward the pragmatic application of ideas than toward their theoretical ramifications. In addition, the ideal specialist has a high energy level which is manifested by a desire to work intensively and the ability to persevere through tense and difficult situations.

Since the specialist must be able to gain the respect of the people he or she will be working with, people with a history of successful experience as the supervisors or managers typically have the best chance of succeeding. Such individuals are likely to understand the operational problems of line personnel and share their concerns, particularly with respect to the pressures of delivering measured results.

Although successful line management experience is very important to a specialist, individuals with experience in systems work, work-flow analysis, or general operational troubleshooting are often successful in that capacity.

Regardless of work background, however, the successful candidate for the position of Job Enrichment specialist is open-minded and receptive to learning about the behavioral consequences of work situations.

STAFFING THE PROJECT

Now that criteria for the selection of Job Enrichment specialists have been established, some thought should be given to the deployment of the selected specialists for maximum effectiveness. When staffing an initial project, consideration should be given both to the needs of the selected pilot work group and enrichment for the organization as a whole. To that end, a good combination would include specialists from the line organization (either the pilot work group itself or a departmental staff group) and from some centrally located staff group. It has been found that the most preferable staffing pattern consists of one or two specialists from a central staff group (such as personnel, power planning, or training and development) or a systems and method group and one individual from the line department—either a line supervisory individual or a departmental staff person.

The specialist selected from the line organization should plan on devoting approximately one-third of his or her time to Job Enrichment for the duration of the pilot project.

The specialists assigned from the central staff group should plan on spending about half their time on the pilot project for the first six to eight months, increasing it to full time toward the end of the project as plans are made to expand the program to other groups. They should first concentrate on the strategies and techniques of Job Enrichment installation, then they must develop the training and guidance ability that will enable them to train other Job Enrichment specialists as the program expands. Since the eventual objective of the staff group specialists is to present Job Enrichment to the whole organization, they must have other skills besides the techniques required by the Job Enrichment program. Specifically, they must: (a) be able to deal with the outside consultants that may be employed, (b) be able to handle top and middle management tactfully and in such a way as to advance their programs, and (c) know how to measure impact, present results, and negotiate the inevitable obstacles.

It is also recommended that the department or work group to which the pilot project is being applied assign one of its own number to the program as a specialist. This individual should be on the scene at the work site daily, or at least frequently enough to observe, assist, and gather measurement data. Approximately one-third of the time of this individual would be required for project activities (possibly more at a later date). The frame of reference for the departmental specialists should be enrichment for their own department or, more specifically, the pilot work group alone. They may later be absorbed into the central staff when the program is expanded, but their initial purpose is to give close assistance to the pilot project group. The great advantage of assigning departmental specialists is to have them available on the scene after the pilot project is ended to keep the enrichment process going. They will be critical to the perpetuation of enrichment for the pilot group, for in the early stages of its introduction Job Enrichment does not normally sustain itself. It needs constant care and follow-up activity, which is only likely to occur if some individual is held responsible for it. The departmental specialist should be held clearly accountable for perpetuation and for seeking any necessary assistance from the central staff after the pilot project is concluded.

Both central staff and departmental specialists should attend all Job Enrichment meetings and most of the on-site planning and problem-solving sessions. Each of them must, as much as possible, observe and direct experience in the installation process. This recommended combination of specialists from the central staff and the line department is certainly not the only way to staff a Job Enrichment effort. The organization may not be able or willing to devote that much manpower to the initial effort. However, this arrangement has been found to be optimal for a good balance of attention to the pilot work group and for preparation to expand the effort.

A word of caution to the organization that is willing to provide more than two or three specialists for training at the start. The advantages of training more specialists at the outset, in order to have a larger core staff of specialists, should be weighed against some of the disadvantages of assigning too many. Too many specialists can sometimes overpower the supervisory teams participating in the pilot project. If you have more than three specialists on hand, it becomes difficult to give all of them enough direct experience with installation; that is, the coaching, of supervisors, and leading of training and problem-solving sessions. A good deal of care should also be exercised in teaming specialists from different departments for the Job Enrichment staff. There can be considerable strain on the team when all the members are from different departments of the organization. They all have different allegiances and the existing political and power realities among work groups are never suspended during a Job Enrichment project. Those opposing allegiances can cause frequent pulling and hauling and some counter-productive tensions on the job enrichment team as they try to work together.

SIX-PHASE PROJECT MODEL

Experience with numerous job enrichment applications has led to the development of a carefully structured model of the activities to be included in the pilot project. It is wise to use a long-range blueprint to establish order and control over the project activities. Figure 6.1 shows a Gantt chart representation of the main activities in a six-phase project model, the approximate duration of each phase in months, and the relationship of activities in each phase. This model has produced numerous successes with good control of all project activities.

The right-hand column shows the approximate number of man days required for an outside consultant, if one is engaged to guide the effort. The blocks in the bottom row show the approximate frequency of status reports to higher management as the project proceeds. More or fewer progress reports may be required.

Phase	Month / Month No.	0	1	2	3	4	5	6	7	8	9	10	11	12	Man Days
						Roy W. Walters Job Enrichment Programs Six-Phase Activity Model									
I															8
II															8
III															15
IV															15
V															5
VI															4
Reports															

Phase I: Data Gathering and Analysis
- Diagnostic study of conditions, problems, job attitudes, and work content
- Work flow diagramming
- Design of project measurements
- Design of implementing model

Phase II: Education Phase
- Orientation workshop for middle management
- Training the departmental management team in concepts of motivation and Job Enrichment implementation
- Development of initial lists of possible changes in job structure

Phase III: Primary Implementation
- Implementation programming
- Implementation problem-solving
- Implementation of first items with selected individuals

Phase IV: Expanded Implementation
- Involvement of entire work force and full-scale implementation
- Measurement of progress
- Refresher workshop if necessary
- Interviews to assess effectiveness of installation

Phase V: Building Autonomy
- Preparation of the staff and line teams for independence in their respective function to assure continuance of the program

Phase VI: Final Analysis
- Final review of project status and programming for longevity
- Interviews with employees to assess impact
- Job reaction survey retest

FIGURE 6.1

After meetings and presentations for top management have been completed, then commitment to a pilot project must be gained and the pilot project work group and the internal specialists must be selected. Once these steps are completed a general orientation session should be conducted with the managers and supervisors of the pilot group to acquaint them with the overall plan, the objectives of the program, Job Enrichment concepts, and the project activity model. When this has been completed, the six phases then proceed as shown in Fig. 6.1.

Phase I: Data Gathering and Analysis. This consists of essentially the same activities described in the section on Job Enrichment Feasibility Study; the process is the same. If the Feasibility Study has already been completed for the purposes of gaining initial commitment, then Phase I is complete.

Phase II: Education Phase. This phase consists of orientation workshops for middle management and training workshops for the managers, supervisors, and workers (if desired) of the pilot work group. It is especially important to hold the orientation workshop for middle managers before proceeding with further project activities. Attendees at the middle-management workshop should be managers or executives at levels directly above the pilot work group—or any others who may have a key interest in a job enrichment project or will later be in a position to oppose suggested job changes. In a later chapter more detail is offered on the orientation workshop for middle management and the supervisory/worker workshops in the education phase.

Phase III: Primary Implementation. These activities are implementation programming, implementation problem-solving, and implementation of the first items with selected individuals. Programming implementation refers to the establishment of an installation road map, or a graphic representation of the order in which items of job change will be considered, planned, and installed. Without such a detailed blueprint items of job change can easily be installed in conflict with each other or in the wrong order of priority for maximum effectiveness. Examples of the installation road map will be discussed in the section on Organizing for Action. Implementation problem-solving in the Primary Implementation Phase requires a series of weekly or twice-weekly meetings with teams of first-line supervisors, managers, and workers (if desired) for the purpose of subjecting proposed job changes to an intensive critical review called *problem-solving*. These sessions are intended to anticipate all the problems and consequences of proposed job changes, plan them out carefully, program the action, and work out the "bugs" prior to installation. This phase is entitled Primary Implementation since in all likelihood such items will at first be installed and tested for effectiveness only with selected members of the work group. Or it may be that at first only a few members of the work group are ready to receive such items of new tasks or responsibilities.

Phase IV: Expanded Implementation.   Just as the term suggests, this involves spreading the installation of job-change items to as many individuals in the work force as possible. By this stage measurement of progress should be well developed and in full swing. At some time during this period, possibly from the fourth to the ninth month of the project, a refresher workshop may be advisable for the same members of the enrichment group who participated in the initial training workshop. The purpose of this is to address any problems of installation, improve on installation techniques, and, if commitment to the project seems to be lagging, introduce new material to stimulate renewed activity. A fuller discription of the refresher workshop is offered in Chapter Seven, The Education Phase.

Phase V: Building Autonomy.   Beginning approximately with the ninth month of the project, this phase focuses on building autonomy on the part of both the internal Job Enrichment specialists and the teams of line supervisors in the project work group. From this point to the end of the initial project year a good deal of attention should be devoted to devising means of fostering independent activity on the part of both specialists and supervisory teams. This will prepare them for the time when they will be continuing the project very much on their own, with only minimum assistance from the outside consultant or central staff specialists.

Phase VI: Final Analysis.   This phase occurs during the final month of the pilot project year. Included in the analysis are interviews with members of the work group to assess the impact of the job changes and the gathering of data on all measures established for the project, including readministration of the Job Reaction Survey. All of this data should be worked up into a final report to be presented to appropriate members of the organization. The remaining steps are to establish a continuation plan for the pilot project work group and to make individual assignments of accountability for continued activity with the pilot project group.

A WORD ABOUT PROFESSIONAL CONSULTING FOR JOB ENRICHMENT

Within organizations considering Job Enrichment there is always controversy about hiring outside consulting assistance for the project. As consultants specializing in Job Enrichment we have often been asked to state the case for it. Aside from gaining the advantages of superior knowledge and expertise from an outside consultant, there are some other advantages to engaging a professional for assistance in the Job Enrichment project. The following are a few brief comments on the subject, offered with as much objectivity as we can bring to it.

1. Gaining initial commitment is difficult in most organizations. But an outside consultant is constantly marketing his services, and can apply many of the same approaches and strategies to help you gain that initial commitment from top management. The assistance of a professional can be invaluable for making top-level presentations, developing strategy for gaining commitment, and answering the many detailed questions which will surely be asked at this stage of the game.

2. An outside consultant is often better able to deal with reluctant managers and executives than are inside specialists. In many cases the outside consultant will be viewed as not having the usual internal political motivations which often make inside practitioners suspect.

3. In general, the outside consultant is in a position to be more objective in his approach to the project and the process of job redesign. He may often be able to find more opportunities for job changes than an insider may notice.

4. Job Enrichment seems deceptively simple to some people. There are, however, pitfalls and problems which can ruin a project. The experienced outside consultant who has handled numerous projects can be very useful in helping the organization to avoid mistakes that others

have made. Bear in mind that the initial project for an organization is a critical one. Learning by trial and error alone can bring the entire effort to an early and unnecessary end.

5. Finally, while a sense of urgency and high commitment to results may or may not exist within the organization, it is always one of a consultant's major concerns. A capable outside consultant can often provide just the amount of push needed to help overcome the inevitable inertia which must be conquered to get the project started and to sustain momentum once it is established.

SUMMARY

There are two difficult tasks facing a manager, line or staff, who wants to introduce a beneficial change program in his organization. The first is to obtain initial approval to introduce the change itself. The second is to pull it off successfully. To help meet those challenges, we have conveyed in this chapter much of what we have learned about the process of gaining initial commitment for a Job Enrichment program or project. In addition, we have described a process—the Job Enrichment Feasibility Study—which is designed to assess the viability of a work group for a Job Enrichment implementation program. A model for such an implementation program has been presented along with recommendations for staffing the project. Finally, while we believe it important for an organization to develop its own staff expertise in Job Enrichment if it contemplates widespread implementation, we recommend that it seek professional consulting advice at the outset.

REFERENCES

1. Raymond E. Miles, *The Affluent Organization,* Harvard Business Review, (May/June, 1966).

2. Frederick Herzberg, *One More Time: How Do You Motivate Employees?*, Harvard Business Review (Jan/Feb. 1968).

3. Exploratory research has just begun in conjunction with New York psychiatrist Dr. Robert A. Ravich to determine potential applications of the Ravich Interpersonal Game Test (RIGT) to business supervisor-subordinate relationships. See Robert A. Ravich, M.D., and Barbara Wyden, *Predictable Pairing* (New York, Wyden, 1974).

chapter
SEVEN
The Education Phase

INTRODUCTION

As indicated in Chapter Six, Phase II of the six-phase model includes certain educational activities required to provide members of the organization with a conceptual understanding of work motivation theory, the principles of motivational job design, and the beginning of the actual job redesign process. Education sessions also serve the critical purpose of overcoming existing biases about supervisory technique and gaining commitment to proceed with the hard work of redesigning jobs. In this Chapter the objectives, techniques, and mechanics are presented for a middle-management orientation session and the supervisors/workers workshop.

THE MIDDLE-MANAGEMENT ORIENTATION SESSION

Assume that top-level commitment has been gained, work groups selected, and specialists assigned for training; there is one more particularly helpful step to be taken prior to starting work with the project group. We refer to an orientation session for middle-managers. This orientation session is a two-day seminar for middle-level executives in positions generally one to three levels above the managers of the selected work groups. The organization chart should be carefully examined to identify all the middle-level executives who could become involved in decision-making or approval of job changes at any time during the project, and any others who may have a key interest or need to be informed as the project goes on. Attendees need not be limited to those directly above the selected work group. They may be from other work groups or departments whose staff may be effected in some way, or they may be from various staff positions. Particular care should be given to invite any key executives who may be involved in future decisions about expansion of the Job Enrichment effort and anyone who is likely to be following progress reports on the project. The guiding principle for selecting attendees for the orientation session should be: neglect no one who could have significant influence on decisions or approvals during the entire project, or on the decision to expand the effort to other work groups. It is helpful to have this orientation session introduced with supportive remarks from some influential individual near the top of the organization. Every evidence of support and commitment from the top-level executives will be a great help in gaining the support and commitment of the middle-level executives.

The purpose of the orientation session should be quite obvious. Those who will be asked to decide on and approve changes in jobs that involve new procedures, increased responsibility, and the attendant risks involved in this kind of change should have an appreciation of the purposes, techniques, and conceptual background of a program such as Job Enrichment. Never forget that some of the activities and job changes brought about by a Job Enrichment program can be shocking to traditionalist and conservative executives. Every attempt should be made to help them fully understand what will be involved in the project and what their own role in the process will be. There is sure to be opposition from such individuals if they do not understand the purpose of the changes or the potential value of the project. Once again, as with the process of gaining top-level commitment, every effort must be made to direct the attention of these middle executives to the potential effects of Job Enrichment on profitability and bottom-line results. In most cases, the careers of these individuals rise and fall with short-term, highly measurable results, and they are not likely to be interested in organizational matters which do not appear to be important to those careers.

Where this orientation step has been neglected, the most common result has been very stiff opposition from middle-level executives whose approval and support are needed. On the other hand, such a session can be the key to smooth advance of the project with minimal opposition. In addition, some of the attendees at the orientation session may well be the heads of work groups who will want to include Job Enrichment among their own objectives in the near future. When these individuals have a good understanding of the pilot project's objectives and plans, and receive periodic data on its progress, the task of convincing them to proceed in their own work groups can be made considerably easier.

The specific objectives of the orientation session for middle-management personnel are to:

1. Give them sufficient understanding of Job Enrichment principles and project plans to reduce opposition from those who may be in a position to influence the project in any way.

2. Help them understand potential results.

3. Establish understanding of techniques, controls, and measurements for the project.

4. Encourage their acceptance of a supportive role in the process, regardless of their level of involvement.

5. Give them some participative experience with the methods to be used by the local management of the project group. Such participative learning experience at the orientation session can often heighten the chances for commitment from those attending.

6. Allow for open controversy and questioning to bring doubts or fears into the open for discussion before the project begins.

Suggested Content for the Middle-Management Orientation Session

The topics and training designs used may vary a great deal, but the following guide should be helpful in designing an effective orientation session:

1. Provide appropriate pre-conference reading related to organization change, new styles of management based on findings in behavioral research, and new insights into superior/subordinate relationships.

2. Arrange for supportive introductory remarks from an individual near the top of the organization.

3. Give a briefing on factual information about the selected work group, staff for the project, and the object jobs. Add information on the purposes of the project, its duration, and plans for recording of results.

4. Conduct small group discussions on the pre-conference reading.

5. Conduct participative training designs based on recent findings in behavioral science related to personal growth in the work situation, achievement needs, the Motivation-Hygiene theory, and growth oriented superior/subordinate relationships.

6. Use some of the numerous films available on the Motivation-Hygiene theory or Job Enrichment case histories.

7. Conduct a briefing on the principles of motivational job design as described in Chapter Five.

8. Describe and discuss the six-phase model or whatever plan has been established for the project.

9. Describe the *greenlight* brainstorming process for gaining ideas for job changes from supervisory groups (the greenlight brainstorming process is described in detail in the section titled greenlighting, later in this chapter).

10. Conduct practice greenlight brainstorming on a sample job description, either an actual job in the organization or some practice case.

11. Give a description of problem-solving (which is also described in detail in the greenlighting section just mentioned).

12. Allow sufficient time for questions and discussion about the project and its implications.

It is strongly recommended that such an orientation session be held before a project begins. In many cases active support and enthusiasm can be gained from these middle-management groups if that session is well done. If not all the attendees have become converts at the orientation session, at least it is possible to identify, before it begins, those who will oppose the project. This can be an advantage in itself.

THE SUPERVISOR/WORKER WORKSHOP

The process of redesigning jobs is normally begun with the workshop session attended by the first-line supervisors, managers, and workers (if desired) of the selected work group. The main objectives of such a session are to give the supervisory team and workers a chance to learn about and understand new findings in the field of work motivation research and to have them list all the ways they can think of to change the contents of the work in the object jobs.

Many will ask why the workshop and the redesign process does not involve the personnel who hold the object jobs. After all, they have a detailed knowledge of those jobs and they should be kept fully aware of what's happening to the jobs as they change.

Well, in some cases it may be unwise to exclude them from the enrichment process. Certainly it would be in organizations where there exists a high degree of employee participation in all changes and decisions, or where the employees, either directly or through their union, have been voicing complaints about the nature of their work. In such instances, involving the workers in the change process could be the first step toward enrichment.

However, in many situations, the disadvantages of involving the job holders in redesigning their own jobs will outweigh the advantages. Some of the problems are as follows:

1. Although some employees may respond to an effort to improve the content of their work, it is unlikely that the majority can be completely objective about it. Employees dissatisfied with a job situation are often not entirely certain why they are dissatisfied. Commonly, all they know is that something seems wrong about the total experience. It is likely that much of their thinking about changes in the job will be related to hygiene problems with little insight about true changes in work content.

2. To many people, involvement in the process at the beginning may seem somewhat like being asked to conspire against themselves to squeeze out more work; response is not likely to be enthusiastic. For most individuals handling a larger job with greater responsibility, autonomy, and achievement opportunity is something that must be tried before the satisfaction becomes apparent.

3. Resistance to anything new should be expected from some people in the work force. This resistance is much easier to handle if changes are introduced gradually, without a great deal of fanfare. Resistance is likely to be less if the process is introduced casually, without any special announcement, as part of the normal course of supervisory activity.

4. If employees are told all about the process at the start, or involved in the redesign process, there is a danger of raising expectations too high and then not being able to deliver action fast enough to satisfy those expectations. There is a risk of making Job Enrichment appear to be just another unfulfilled management promise.

5. Involving members of the work force in the redesign process can require too much time off the job for planning sessions. Complete redesign of jobs often takes three to six months of regular meetings. This amount of time off the job could disrupt production.

6. Involving workers in the workshop and redesigning process could make the group too large for effectiveness in the planning sessions, resulting in very little action for the amount of effort and discussion expended.

7. During the planning process some sweeping moves and changes are often discussed, such as the drastic combination of tasks, changes in work flow or elimination of certain positions. Such proposals are not always adopted but discussion of them with members of the work force can generate great and unnecessary alarm among the people in those jobs. This can be destructive. Excluding the employees from the redesign of their jobs may sound like doing things deceitfully or behind their backs but experience shows that the process goes smoother with less trouble and awkwardness if changes are introduced gradually, discussed individually with people in the jobs, and carried off in as natural a manner as possible.

It has been shown that supervisors are generally close enough to the details of jobs to do an effective job of redesigning them without the problems associated with involving the work force in the redesign. Many of these supervisors may have been in the same jobs at some time in the past. After learning the principles of job design they frequently know exactly what to do with the jobs. In most situations the chances of success are improved if the redesign is done by the first-line supervisors and managers. This approach has been found to be best in situations with people in clerical, manufacturing, processing, or service jobs. It may be advisable to involve people in highly individual, professional, technical, or supervisory positions in redesigning their own jobs. In such situations, the people in supervisory positions above these jobs may not know enough of the detail to do an effective job of redesign and individuals in jobs such as these are more likely to demand involvement in the redesign process. Each situation warrants careful individual consideration, but as a general rule it is advisable to carry out the redesign process with supervisors just above the object jobs. The question of involving the workers—or some of the workers—is one that cannot be answered without careful analysis.

Who Should Attend the Supervisor/Worker Workshop?

Generally the best group for the supervisory/worker workshop is one made up of first-line supervisors and managers who will be directly involved in introducing the changes to the work force. Occasionally it is wise to include staff or technical people who have intimate familiarity with the content of the object jobs. Lead clerks or senior workers in a quasi-supervisory role between the first-line supervisors and the work force should be included in the workshop if they will be involved in the installation of job changes and discussions with the workers.

Arrangements should be made for a middle-level executive in an influential position to attend the first part of the workshop if only to give kick-off remarks. It is important to have a show of support from some high echelon person to ease the minds of the managers and supervisors about their involvement in the program and the commitment of the organization. When such a middle-level executive is invited he should be briefed in advance as to his role in the process and the importance of his show of support at the commencement of the workshop. If he has not been so prepared, he may inadvertently say things that cast doubt on his own conviction or the commitment of the organization to the project. Managers and any middle-level executives who will attend the whole workshop should be carefully briefed on their role in the workshop process and the tensions which can be created in the group by the simple fact of their presence. They should be warned not to dominate discussion in the subgroup sessions. It may even be advisable to keep them out of the subgroups to avoid restricting discussion.

With large supervisor/worker groups it may be necessary to split the group into two or more sections, running a workshop with each. In some situations this is required in order to allow adequate coverage of the work force during the period of the workshop. It is recommended that the workshop be conducted over a period of at least three, and preferably four, days.

Advantages of An Off-Site Location

It is strongly recommended that the supervisory workshop be conducted on a live-in basis for three or four days at an off-site location away from the place of work. Normally a convention center or a well equipped motel will be ideal for the purpose. Attendees should be encouraged to wear informal attire.

There are many compelling reasons for recommending an off-site workshop. Experience with both off-site workshops and those conducted at the work location indicates that the accomplishments of off-site workshops far exceed those held at the place of work. Perhaps the simplest reason for an off-site workshop is to avoid constant interruptions and telephone calls related to the day-to-day work. Then too, there will always be the temptation to go back to one's desk at lunch time or at the end of the day, which only serves to dilute the participants' concentration on the business at hand. At an off-site workshop, the entire state of mind changes. People are freer, less inhibited, less concerned about the day-to-day job strains. They are much more inclined to fully concentrate on new learning and to be creative. In a practical sense a great deal more can be accomplished at an off-site workshop. Evening sessions are possible, at which a great deal of progress can be made; a great deal more problem-solving and planning can be done on proposed items of job change. This means that fewer planning sessions will be required back at the work-site, where they are so difficult to conduct in the midst of the daily routine. In this sense the investment in an off-site workshop is a wise one in the long run.

Working together with superiors one or two levels above them may be a new experience for most first-line supervisors. If the work shop were conducted in business clothes and the traditional business meeting atmosphere, it is not likely that supervisors would be able to relax or be creative. It is more likely that they would be defensive and guarded in their contributions to discussion. The mere fact of seeing the bosses appear in Bermuda shorts and sport shirts can often be just what it takes to bring this group together.

There are bound to be many strains and stresses during the project, and the special feeling that can be generated at an informal off-site workshop can help set the project over all rough spots it might hit. If it can be arranged, a cocktail party or two among the workshop attendees can often go a long way toward building a new working relationship. These allow personnel from different organizational levels to get to know one another as people, rather than just as fellow employees. Also, the mere fact of being sent away to an off-site workshop can often be quite a mark of distinction for first-line supervisors. Normally this kind of affair is reserved only for managers and above, and the significance of being sent to an off-site learning experience is not lost on supervisors or workers. And, finally, the willingness on the part of the organization to spend the extra money for an off-site session is a visible commitment to the importance of the project.

Workshop Objectives

The following set of objectives will be helpful in planning an effective supervisors workshop:

1. To establish a basic understanding of new behavioral concepts about work motivation.

2. To begin breaking down biases about supervisory technique that would be detrimental to the approach required for effective enrichment of jobs.

3. To establish understanding and acceptance of the new supervisory role required in the Job Enrichment process.

4. To learn the principles of motivational job design.

5. To identify every possible change in job structure and content which may have motivational value.

6. To complete the analysis and action programming for at least one item of job change to be installed on return to the work group.

Workshop Activities

It is generally advisable to devote the first workshop day to discussions about the need for new styles of management, the need for organization change, and learning the Motivation-Hygiene theory. There is a great deal of material available which can be used to generate discussion that will indicate how aware the group members are of problems in the organization and just how willing or reluctant they may be to change their own supervisory behavior. It will be important for the workshop leader to determine where the group stands on these matters at the start. The leader can then spend more or less time as needed to gain commitments to the kind of change required for job enrichment. Rushing into the principles of motivational job design and the redesign process itself without reasonable commitment from those attending may be a great mistake. After discussions about organizational problems, supervisory behavior, employee behavior, and the need for new approaches to motivating people, it is appropriate to introduce the Motivation-Hygiene theory. There are many books, articles, and training designs available for that purpose.

It cannot be emphasized too heavily that participative training designs and exercises are best. Lecturing should be kept to a minimum. It is not our purpose here to discuss training methods, but suffice it to say that new concepts and a developing commitment to new ideas are far better achieved by doing than by listening. There is an old aphorism that has meaning in this connection: "I hear, and I forget; I see, and I remember; I do, and I understand."

GREENLIGHTING

Using the motivational principles we have been discussing, no doubt there are many ways to get a group to generate ideas for making changes in their jobs. However, a particular method of brainstorming called *greenlighting* has proven successful time and time again. This is followed by a conservative and critical process of analyzing the ideas generated, using a structured problem-solving process. Let us first consider the greenlighting form of brainstorming. It is always difficult to get a group of people to think about their jobs in new and different ways. Each is accustomed to doing his or her job in a particular way; they are afraid that they will be ridiculed or laughed at; they are reluctant to suggest what may seem to be weird ideas in front of superiors. But radical and drastic ideas are exactly what is needed for this kind of brainstorming, and they will be generated only when the group members are in the right frame of mind.

This frame of mind develops best in a creative environment in which people can feel free and easy, confident, and unselfconscious, in which freewheeling and spontaneous ideas are welcome. To help achieve the right conditions the workshop leader must emphasize that there is to be absolutely no ridicule or criticism of any idea advanced during a greenlighting session. The object is to change the jobs being considered to include more of the elements of Motivation-Hygiene theory, and even the most extreme ideas must be accepted and recorded without question or analysis. Evaluation of ideas comes later.

The workshop leader should outline the following rules for a greenlighting session:

1. The group should strive for innovative and imaginative ideas, no matter how drastic or radical they may seem.

2. One person will be designated to write down each of the ideas as fast as he or she can on a piece of easel paper, and these are to be posted on the walls as the group generates more and more ideas. The remaining members of the group are to shout ideas as fast as they can be written down.

3. No idea tossed out by a participant may be rejected.

4. The objective is the greatest quantity of ideas that can be generated.

5. Combining and improving ideas is encouraged as the process proceeds.

6. No criticism or questioning is allowed. That is a form of problem-solving which means stopping, and is not permitted during a greenlight session. The idea is to generate every imaginable creative idea, realizing that some will be useless, impractical, or impossible. There will be time later to separate the wheat from the chaff, but if the

restrictions and hesitations are not removed, many good ideas will not be advanced simply because people feel at first that they are too radical for consideration.

7. Those who insist on problem-solving during the greenlighting session must be ostracized by the other members of the group. This is usually done by hissing or booing or generally making the problem-solver feel uncomfortable. Not many problem-solvers insist on continuing their obstructions when faced with group ostracism. Remind such a person that there will be time for problem-solving when the current session is finished. Such ostracism may seem like a harsh suggestion, but actually it becomes a humorous matter. Most groups will join in the greenlighting spirit and delight in booing problem-solvers.

It is a good idea for the leader of a greenlighting session to devote some time to getting rid of the stiffness which always exists at first in these situations by telling those present about the usual behavior in business groups that try to generate creative ideas about any situation. What normally happens is that truly unusual innovative ideas are often squashed immediately by "killer phrases" offered by other members of the group. We've all heard these "killer phrases" devastatingly delivered —statements such as: "They'll never buy it top-side." "We tried that the year before last and it didn't work." "It costs far too much." "You can't be serious." Phrases like these have unquestionably killed off innumerable imaginative ideas. They pop up in almost every group unless defense mechanisms are set up to prevent them. A useful technique with your group would be to give a few examples of killer phrases, then have the group think up every other killer phrase they can imagine, write each of them down on a slip of paper, and go around the room having each person in turn deliver a killer phrase. This will be fun for the group and will generate some good laughs, but the point cannot be missed that such phrases will be distinctly unwelcome and not allowed during a greenlighting session.

Another useful and entertaining way to prepare for good greenlighting is to have the group practice greenlight brainstorming on some unrelated but commonplace subject that allows for some humor—for example, innovative uses of a paper clip, ball-point pen, or some other simple item. The group should be allowed five or six minutes to think up every possible radical and innovative use for the item, then the person doing the recording should take down the ideas one at a time to build up as long a list as possible. Often a couple of exercises such as these, to loosen up the group and prepare it with humor, will easily generate the readiness and free state of mind for effective greenlighting. After preparatory sessions such as those described, it is also effective to have the group practice more serious greenlighting on a hypothetical job other than the actual job they are scheduled to work on. This will give them the feel of dealing with work motivation concepts, work flow, and job structure, and will enable them to seek ways to change the jobs motivationally, using recently learned principles of job design. Effective training designs can easily be developed for practice greenlighting.

With these preparatory steps completed the group should be ready for the actual greenlighting session. Now an easel writer should be appointed to record the ideas offered. It is normally best to allow the group to begin with *free greenlighting;* That is, to toss out ideas on any subject or any aspect of the job that occurs to them. The chances are that each member of the group will have developed several ideas during previous discussions which he can contribute to the greenlighting. When the free greenlighting tends to slow down and the group appears to be having difficulty thinking of new ideas, it may be useful to use *focused greenlighting.* In focused greenlighting the group concentrates on job design principles (as described in Chapter Five) one at a time, to explore each particular concept for new ideas about the object job. Such sharpening of the brainstorming process can often produce more ideas than the free greenlighting by itself.

Work-Flow Diagrams as Aid to Greenlighting

To help make the greenlighting session productive, it is a good idea to prepare, prior to the workshop, large graphic displays of simplified work-flow patterns for the object jobs and post them on the walls of the workshop room. When greenlighting activity seems to be slowing down, or questions arise, the group's attention can be directed to certain portions of the work-flow diagram to help the members see possibilities for specific and detailed job changes. It will be important to establish simplified and straightforward work-flow diagrams without a great deal of footnoting or symbols. Each diagram should be easily understood and used only to focus the group's attention on a particular part of the job; those attending will be able to fill in the details from their own minds when directed to a certain part of the job process.

Subgroup Greenlighting

Another technique for structuring greenlighting sessions for effectiveness can be used with a large group or groups of supervisors and workers from related but separate work groups within a department or division. They can be assigned to greenlight in subgroups in separate sessions. The optimum size for effective greenlighting is somewhere between six and sixteen members. With less than six members the activity is often too slow to generate a feeling of excitement about creativity. With more than sixteen members people often must wait too long to get their ideas listed, and so the personal involvement is less. However, subgroups of five and six may be appropriate, especially when several different jobs are being considered and it is desirable to have the participants concentrate in small groups on jobs in their own sections. In some cases it can be useful to establish or encourage some degree of competition among greenlighting subgroups. It is also useful to have each group take a break to review the lists generated by the other groups, seek ideas for their own lists from them, and then reconvene for continued greenlighting. Normally, greenlighting is productive only for periods of less than one hour at a time. Some break in the process should be scheduled for lunch time, a rest period, or a review of other groups' lists. When such breaks are taken (such as lunchtime), each individual in the group can be assigned to do some more thinking about greenlight items on his or her own, and to return with at least one additional item for the list.

Some Words of Caution

To be of any use, greenlight items must be sharply stated and to the point, rather than broad generalizations. They must deal in detail with the nuts and bolts of the job. When it comes time to actually make a change the intent of the suggestion must be entirely clear. A good analogy for the difference between good and poor greenlight items is the difference between the spade and the steamshovel. When thinking of ways to change the job, use the detailed spade-like approach, not the generalized steamshovel approach. For example: A spade-type greenlight item, detailed and to the point, might be, "Make machine operators responsible for ordering their own supplies and arranging maintenance of machines themselves." A steamshovel type greenlight item (which is common in groups which have not been advised against it), might be, "Give machine operators more responsibility for doing the work."

Another aid to effective greenlighting is to have the team or Job Enrichment specialists meet before the workshop to review the details of the job and to anticipate where the most likely areas for effective greenlighting exist. In this way the specialists can anticipate the direction the greenlighting may take and give some guidance or direct the group to consider certain areas. If the team of specialists can develop a good outline of the optimum job design, they can often be helpful in sparking new greenlight items when the group has temporarily run dry. In short, in order to give effective guidance, the leaders of the workshop should have worked out in advance a reasonably complete idea of what the redesigned job should be.

It is unwise to attempt to greenlight too many different jobs in one workshop session. More than three or four related jobs in a work situation is probably too much. More greenlight sessions may be required in order to be able to handle additional jobs.

Conditioning the List of Greenlight Items

A lively, no-holds-barred greenlight session will normally result in a list of from 60 to 200 detailed items of possible change in a job. The total greenlight list will probably be a conglomeration of good ideas, poor ideas, and impossible ideas. Also, no matter how much emphasis is placed on seeking items that are related to Motivators, there will normally be a number of Hygiene items mixed in the list. Although emphasis should be placed on thinking up items related to Motivators, the Hygiene items that do appear should not necessarily be discouraged. Some of the Hygiene items may be very well chosen indeed and should not be ignored. In fact, at some point a separate list of the useful Hygiene items should be constructed for implementation along with the Motivator items.

The next task in the process is to go through all of the items to sort them into categories and to code them by type. This process, called *conditioning,* consists of separating the wheat from the chaff in a greenlight list, separating the really useful items from the useless or frivolous. Conditioning can be done by the entire greenlighting group together or by small teams. Each item in the greenlight list should be considered separately, with the group or team deciding first whether the item is obviously outlandish or impossible. However, do not allow them to be hasty about this decision; there will be those who will be tempted to take this opportunity to expel any risky or adventurous item, and the group may be tempted to discard excellent items that seem at first glance to be a little too difficult. However, items which are obviously useless or frivolous should be removed (e.g., such items as "Fire the Boss," which often appears humorously on greenlight lists). Even though that may be a sound suggestion it's not exactly a practical way to begin enriching jobs.

Retain any item which has been seriously presented that has any change of implementation, no matter how remote. Any item retained should be designated either a Motivator or Hygiene item. It should then be coded according to the job design principle it represents. Work through the entire list in this fashion, not hesitating to add items where possible or to improve items on the list. If the group has been split into smaller groups for subgroup greenlighting on different but related jobs, have each group review the other lists, since items on one list may spark ideas for another group. Put good Hygiene ideas on a separate list. When conditioning is complete have the Motivator and Hygiene lists with the assigned conditioning codes typed up for easy reference in later sessions. Conditioning of the list should be approached with these four purposes in mind:

1. Separate the useful ideas from those that are useless.

2. Separate Motivator ideas from Hygiene ideas so there will be no doubt about what kind of change is being made.

3. Identify the job design principle involved with each greenlight item

in order to determine whether any job design principle has been neglected in the greenlighting. This may require additional greenlighting if a weak area is found.

4. Conditioning can provide valuable reinforcement for the training previously given on the Motivation-Hygiene theory and job design principles. The questioning and discussion, which often becomes lively in the group as they condition the items, provides a valuable backup training experience.

PROBLEM-SOLVING

Problem-solving (once known as "redlighting") is a cautious approach used to prepare greenlight items for installation. As the term suggests, problem-solving is the opposite of the radical "all systems go" process of greenlight brainstorming, in which no stopping, questioning, criticism, or analysis is allowed. Problem-solving requires a very hardheaded and objective analysis of what might be wrong with an item, since no such analysis has been allowed during the greenlighting process. Problem-solving forces the management team to return to the real world after the euphoria of greenlight brainstorming. The objectives of problem-solving are:

1. To gain a clear understanding of exactly what the suggested item means, since it is often unclear on the greenlight list.

2. To anticipate all possible negative aspects of installing the item.

3. To decide whether or not to install the item.

4. To program all the steps required for installation.

It is a sound idea to describe both the greenlighting and problem-solving processes to reluctant and conservative executives before the project begins. We would recommend that greenlighting, which sounds rather wild and radical, be described first, and that the description of problem-solving follow. This reassures your listeners that however extreme the notions generated by the one may be, they will receive the cold and objective evaluation of the other. Structure and discipline become important at this point in the process, and problem-solving provides both of those elements. Many proposals for changes in jobs look deceptively simple and easy to install at the start, but unless some mechanism is employed to ensure that all the problems and consequences of a change are anticipated and planned for, the results can be surprising and disruptive. Problem-solving is no mystery, nor is it applicable only in Job Enrichment applications. Once it has been tested and used, many have found it to be helpful in all kinds of situations.

The 10 Problem-Solving Steps

Problem-solving analysis of a proposed job change is a 10-step analysis that covers all the essentials required to meet the four objectives in preparing an item for implementation. Not all items will require intensive problem-solving, of course; some are simple and straightforward, involving little or no risk. The 10-step method is really intended for those job-change suggestions that are complex and carry high risk. It is wise, however, to give brief problem-solving consideration even to simple items to ensure that there is no unforeseen problem involved before implementation. For the more complex or risky items proposed, the following 10-step process will give a complete problem-solving method for anticipating and planning for all eventualities before installation of a proposed change.

1. *Define the item.*   Clearly define the item in exact detail. All team members must have the same understanding of the item. The quick statement of the item during the greenlighting session often is not nearly exact enough to be useful. Often what begins as one item becomes several items which should be worked on in series.. Give the item a number, name, or label for easy reference later.

2. *List advantages.*   An effective way to do this is to have the group greenlight freely all the advantages they can think of that would result from installation of this item. Then go back and discard any listed advantages that may be invalid and compose a final list.

3. *List disadvantages.*   Here, again, it's effective to use the same greenlight process. Think of every possible disadvantage which may be involved with installation of this item. Think of disadvantages as things

that would result after the item is implemented. It may be helpful to think of disadvantages in three categories:

a) Risks
b) Impracticalities
c) Other negative consequences

4. *Plan to minimize disadvantages.* Take each disadvantage and think of every possible way that it may be reduced or eliminated. It will be found that many, if not all, the disadvantages of a proposed item can be dealt with, lived with, or removed entirely.

5. *Weigh advantages against disadvantages.* This is a judgment process in which the group as a whole considers whether the advantages of installing the item outweigh the disadvantages. Obviously, the *number* of advantages or disadvantages does not greatly matter; it is their *importance* that will enable the group to decide whether to: continue planning the item, drop it, or defer it for later consideration.

6. *List roadblocks.* Once the item to be installed has been decided on, use a quick greenlighting process again with the group to think of every possible roadblock or obstacle that must be cleared before the item can be implemented. Examples of roadblocks are: approvals required, changes in rules, training required, changes in job descriptions. As can be seen from these examples, roadblocks are different from negative consequences of installing the item. They are things that must be gotten around or compensated for before the item can be installed. Once a valid list of roadblocks has been established, consider quickly, again, whether the item should be planned for installation, dropped for good, or deferred for later consideration.

7. *Plan to clear roadblocks.* This is simply a process of listing the specific action steps that must be taken to clear any roadblocks standing in the way of implementation.

8. *Program the item for action.* The method of implementation should be decided on. In what is called "broadside implementation," some items are installed with all of the work force at the same time. Other items either involve more risk or are appropriate only for the more

competent or more experienced employees. Installation then is selective, at first involving only certain of the employees. List each step that must be taken to implement the item, then establish a target date for each of those steps. Where appropriate, assign individual responsibility for the action steps required for implementation, and plan for any required approvals.

9. *Anticipate individual response.* This is a critical step which is frequently overlooked with disastrous results. Once the item has been decided on and planned, some time should be spent in anticipating the response of the individuals who will be involved—individual by individual, if possible. Bear in mind that not everybody will respond in the same way, and certainly not all of them will welcome every item. Plan the optimum method for introducing the item: whether it should be separately to each individual involved, or to the whole group at once. In any case, it is generally advisable to use the customary means of communicating new procedures, whether to the individual or to the group. Keep your procedures as natural as possible.

10. *Design item control and feedback.* Where appropriate, devise methods of gaining data on the effects of the installed change, and provide feedback to the individuals involved on how they are doing it.

At first glance, this 10-step method of item analysis seems formidable and laborious to many people. It need not be. With a little practice those installing the process can guide it along without undue delay. Not all items require an intensive analysis. Some are simple and the problem-solving solution is readily arrived at. There is no need to be laborious with such items. A fast run-through in such cases will ensure that nothing major has been overlooked. The full process is very important, however, in the case of complex items that involve high risk or sweeping changes in work-flow. A good job of problem-solving before rushing into implementation can avoid many headaches.

Write Down the Main Points

For several reasons, many groups have found it helpful to write out the essential points in the problem-solving process as it goes on. A written record is important, for example, when more than one session is

needed to complete an item. Also, a written record of the essentials of
the problem-solving reasoning can be very convincing to the problem-
solving team itself. Often, the supervisors on the team are reluctant or
fearful to install a particular item. When they see the problem-solving
process written out clearly on easel pages, their response often becomes
less visceral and more cerebral, and they can see not only the advantages of the item, but also how they can handle the disadvantages. The
written record of the problem-solving solution may also be helpful when
other parties wish to review a proposed item. Problem-solving may be
done with the entire supervisory team together or, if the group is large,
it can be done by smaller subgroups. With written records each group
can review the work of every other group and attempt to add to it or
improve it, as well as having the benefit of every other group's review.
The pace of problem-solving an entire greenlight list of items can be
quickened in this way. In cases where supervisors and workers from
different but related work groups are at the same workshop, they can
be divided up by function to problem-solving the list of greenlight items
that pertains to their area of work.

Problem-Solving Beyond the Workshop

For any job that is at all complex there will be a vast number of items
to be problem-solved. Only a beginning can be made at problem-solving
the list during the workshop session. After the workshop, problem-solving should be continued at full group or subgroup sessions once or twice
a week until all proposed items have been analyzed and prepared for
action—which may take anywhere from two to six months. Items that
have been problem-solved, however, can be installed while the remaining items are being problem-solved.

It is of great importance to complete problem-solving of at least one
or two items of real substance while at the workshop. If the group can
accomplish this they normally gain a great sense of achievement which
establishes a momentum that carries over into their activity back at the
work site; then they know that they can master the discipline of the
problem-solving process. The object should be to have, at the very least,
one item completely ready to install the day they return to their work
group.

Choosing Items for Quick Implementation

The last step in the workshop should be selection of a list of items
for quick implementation. It will be important to get action going immediately to convince the supervisors and workers that things are truly
going to happen; that they have not been to another of those talkfests
that are followed by nothing. Items that can be installed soon after the
workshop are items that:

1. Do not involve sweeping changes in workflow or equipment.
2. Involve no great risk.
3. Can be approved at a relatively low level of authority.
4. Do not require lengthy problem-solving.
5. Effect a fairly large number of people in the work group.
6. Require no lengthy training period for installation.

SUPERVISORS' WORKSHOP PLAN

So far we have dealt with two major *action* phases of the workshop,
greenlighting and problem-solving. To show how these crucial activities
can be effectively integrated with the learning phases of the workshop,
we offer below an outline of workshop activities. This is certainly not
the only way to structure the workshop and there is great latitude for selection of training material and designs. To be sure, selection of training material on the conceptual background of Job Enrichment will
vary a great deal with the sophistication of the group. Some workshop
groups may already have had considerable exposure to behavioral theorists and the Motivation-Hygiene theory prior to their attendance. With
such a group only a brief review may be required before launching
into a description of job design principles, greenlighting, and problem-
solving. Other groups may require a fairly intensive review of recent
findings in behavioral research, starting at the beginning and building
up gradually. However, the following basic format has been used in
numerous projects with proven success.

Preworkshop Reading and Preparation

One week before the workshop is scheduled to meet, send the participants articles about: (1) the relationship of behavioral science to man-

agement, (2) new insights into management and supervisory style, (3) the growing need for organization change and renewal, and (4) the Motivation-Hygiene theory (or available programmed instruction on motivation theory). Also effective are various training designs intended to cause participants to examine their personal supervisory assumptions or their organization's values and goals. All of these materials should be carefully chosen to form the basis for guided discussions to make specific points at the workshop. Some of the reading should impart new learning and some should stimulate controversy. The discussions based on these materials will be helpful in assessing the group's state of readiness to explore new approaches to motivation.

Day-to-Day Schedule

First day: morning

1. Develop group and subgroup discussion or training designs based on preworkshop reading. Generate as much discussion and controversy as possible to assess readiness of the group for new concepts. Identify members of the group who may need special attention before undertaking job redesign activities.

First day: afternoon

1. Provide theory inputs on Motivation-Hygiene theory using lecturette, exercises, and film.

2. Hold discussion and use testing devices to assess grasp of new concepts and ability to distinguish Motivators from Hygiene factors in work situations.

First day: evening

1. Arrange for additional reading and discussion groups.

Second day: morning

1. Reinforce understanding of Motivation-Hygiene theory.

2. Hold additional discussion as needed.

3. Show films and/or presentations on case histories of Job Enrichment applications in other organizations with discussion of the kinds of job changes that were found to be motivational.

Second day: afternoon

1. Given conceptual input on job design principles (as presented in Chapter Five).
2. Introduce greenlighting.
3. For warmup, practice greenlighting on some topic unrelated to job design.
4. Practice greenlighting on a sample job other than the object job to be redesigned.

Second day: evening

1. Prepare simple work-flow diagrams for each job to be redesigned for reference during greenlighting and to heighten awareness of job details.

Third day: morning

1. Introduce the process of conditioning the greenlight list.
2. Hold a brief practice at list-conditioning with a critique of participants' work.
3. Discuss the practice greenlighting and critique to sharpen awareness of the need for motivator items.
4. Greenlight the actual jobs to be redesigned.

Third day: afternoon

1. Condition the lists.
2. Conduct additional greenlighting if required.
3. Introduce problem-solving.
4. Introduce team effectiveness criteria (a means of improving the effectiveness of team action using group critique of its own process. This is discussed in detail in Chapter Nine).
5. Problem-solve a selected item from the greenlight list.
6. Critique the team's effectiveness at the problem-solving process.

Fourth day

1. Select a list of quick and easy items for installation on return to work group.

2. Problem-solve the quick items if necessary.

3. Problem-solve as many items as possible; prepare and schedule them for implementation.

4. Brief the group on how to communicate about the project on return to the work group, and on plans for the remainder of the project

HOW TO COMMUNICATE ON RETURN TO THE WORK GROUP

Supervisors who have returned from the workshop and made unwise communications to their work group have gotten many projects off to a difficult and unfortunate start. Such a situation can be avoided, as we have already emphasized, by keeping the project at a low profile and making no special communications about it at all. Supervisors should not attempt to give their workgroups an offhand, extemporaneous description of Motivation-Hygiene theory or any other aspects of Job Enrichment, no matter how close their relationship may be or how badly they want to impress the work group. In the first place, it simply is not necessary. In the second, it is all too easy to give incomplete and/or incorrect information even when one has the very best intentions, and such information can easily make the rest of the project an uphill fight. In fact, it may even be unnecessary and unwise to make any announcement about a special project at any point of its existence. And in cases in which some mention of the project's purpose and techniques *must* be made, the first day back is not the best time for it.

Even when there must be some announcement about the project, there should be no special mention of Job Enrichment; it is even better not to use the term "Job Enrichment" at all. Further, supervisors should particularly avoid discussing items on the greenlight lists. By their nature these lists are probably still very rough and contain some hair-raising ideas that could greatly upset some members of the work force (who have no background for proper evaluation of those ideas), or at least give them unreasonable expectations of the project. The workers' reactions to the greenlight lists is completely unpredictable at this point, and no risks should be taken.

To be sure, the people in the work group will wonder what the supervisors have been doing away from the job for the past three or four days, but it should be enough to tell them that the supervisors have been at a training session to learn improved supervisory techniques—which is in fact fairly close to the truth. If this suggestion causes some supervisors to have misgivings about misleading the work force, we can only emphasize that our recommendations are based on practices that have been found to be effective in the projects that have been most successful. We should also emphasize that some projects have encountered serious difficulties as a direct result of *not* following these recommendations.

If supervisors are questioned further about what kind of supervisory training they received, it should be sufficient to indicate that the purpose of the session was to examine the content of the jobs in order to find ways to make the work more human and meaningful and to make boredom less likely. It may also be helpful to point out that the company has involved the supervisory team in this examination of the work because it is convinced that both the organization and the employees in it will benefit if something can be done to allow them to get more enjoyment from what they are doing. If some workers were involved in the workshop these concerns are minimized.

SUMMARY

In this chapter we have described two sessions designed to educate managers in the concepts and process of Job Enrichment, including the Motivation-Hygiene theory, the principles of good job design, and the process of making job changes. One program is an orientation session that is conducted for middle management. The other is a workshop for lower management, first-line supervision and workers (if desired). In addition to their educational function, both programs are intended to gain commitment to the Job Enrichment project. To that end they are focused not only on giving their participants an understanding of the concepts involved, but also on developing a list of actual job change items, selected for their motivational potential, and a program for their implementation. The design and content of these educational sessions have been distilled from a great deal of experience in the conduct of Job Enrichment training and implementation projects and offer, we believe, the best opportunity for successfully beginning and carrying out such a venture.

chapter
EIGHT
Organizing for Action

INTRODUCTION

Some Job Enrichment efforts have failed to get off the ground or have stalled somewhere during the project period for either or both of the following reasons:

1. The process is mistakenly regarded as principally a reeducation effort, with heavy emphasis on the workshop learning experience and little organization, guidance, or follow-up during the actual on-site job change period. Often the project supervisory team is left too much on its own without having been prepared to act effectively, and the result is apt to be the quiet, rapid demise of the project. It must be remembered that by the time the workshop is completed, little or nothing has actually been done to make the job changes. The workshop is primarily preparation for what comes after.

2. Middle-management people often are not given active roles in the job change process. Commitment tends to be contingent on involvement. If middle-management people are not kept involved, they tend to lose touch with the activity, become distant, and lose their sense of responsibility for the project's completion.

To avoid these two pitfalls, action on the job site must be carefully organized. This requires establishment of a new organizational entity for the job enrichment activity. As noted earlier, management people are not likely to change their attitudes towards subordinates and begin to fully use available talent until they are required to. This chapter will describe a method of organizing the workers who will spearhead the job change process. The point is to so structure their efforts that they can generate effective action while maintaining close contact with key middle-management individuals.

A number of organizing strategies have proven to be extremely useful: establishing a Job Enrichment steering committee, setting up implementation teams, detailing a "road map" for implementation, establishing means of measuring project success, and making plans for progress reporting.

Let us first consider the organizational steps of setting up a Job Enrichment steering committee and implementation teams. Figure 8.1 shows the organizational setup for the steering committee and implementation teams as used in many successful projects.

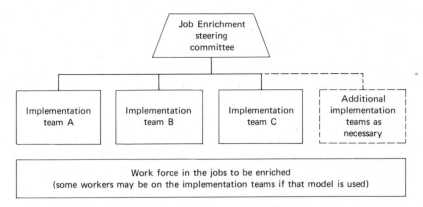

Note: The implementation teams are made up of first-line supervisors, with attendance by higher levels as appropriate. The number of implementation teams will vary with each situation; in some cases only one will be required.

FIG. 8.1 Organizing for implementation

THE JOB ENRICHMENT STEERING COMMITTEE

Just after the workshop a steering committee for the project should be established to provide an overview of all the project activities and to function as a planning body which can devote its attention to long-range concerns. Normally, the Job Enrichment steering committee should consist of the Job Enrichment specialists, the outside consultant (if one has been engaged), the management person just above the first line of supervision in the work group, and in some cases the next level of management (which is usually middle management). Other members may be added from appropriate staff positions or from those possessing particular technical knowledge of the jobs which can be helpful in long-range planning of job changes. The makeup of the Job Enrichment steering committee may vary greatly from organization to organization and need not follow any strict pattern. However, two concerns should be borne in mind. When deciding on membership for the steering committee, one must keep in mind that: (1) It should include those people above the supervisory team necessary to effectively analyze all of the activities going on in the project, make long-range plans, and evaluate progress as the project goes along. (2) It should provide a continuing structure which includes the key middle-management individuals who are likely to be faced with frequent decisions about critical job changes. These individuals must have some form of active role in the process even if it is only to review and analyze what is going on. It is normally sufficient for the Job Enrichment steering committee to meet monthly for planning and review of progress.

Specific functions of the steering committee are as follows:

1. *Long-range Planning.*
    a) Establish models for the optimum job designs in each job that is to be redesigned.
    b) Establish "road maps" for implementation to guide the implementation process. These are simply graphic displays of the sequences in which items chosen from the greenlight list should be put through the problem-solving process and installed for maximum effectiveness and minimum conflict. More detailed discussion of the road map for implementation is given later in this chapter.
    c) Set long-term goals for the job changes to be installed.
    d) Anticipate positive and negative consequences of the job changes to be installed and plan accordingly.
    e) Coordinate job change efforts among the implementation teams to avoid conflict, where more than one team is established.
2. *Management of the Implementation Process.*
    a) Set short-term goals for implementation team activity.
    b) Review problem-solving and installation progress.

  c) Clear roadblocks standing in the way of implementing items of job change.
  d) Seek solutions to various problems generated by the job changes.
  e) Select items for problem-solving.
  f) Gather, analyze, and report data on results.
  g) Maintain records of key activities in the project. To accomplish this record-keeping function, some individual on the steering committee should be assigned to maintain a project chronicle or journal which describes all of the key activities undertaken, the problems encountered, how they were handled, the job changes installed and the results gained. Such a chronicle will provide invaluable guidance during the course of future projects. The keeping of a project chronicle will also ensure that details are not overlooked and that matters discussed at previous meetings can be picked up and continued at succeeding meetings.

3. *Communications.*
  a) Make appropriate communications and reports upward to higher levels in the organization.
  b) Initiate appropriate communications about the project to members of the work group involved.
  c) Make communications to other work groups in departments as necessary.

The steering-committee concept has another key purpose in addition to these specific functions outlined above. That is to establish a structure which assures the continuous involvement of middle-management individuals who are likely to become defensive or obstructive if they are not included in the planning and installation of the job changes. If they are left out, such people often withdraw to a position somewhat like that of a high tribunal which sits in judgment on all of the job changes worked out by implementation teams. They can become overly cautious and unnecessarily critical of job changes planned below them with which they have had little to do. The solution is to maintain their involvement and identity with the job change process by including them in an organizational structure such as a steering committee. Involvement means ownership, and that is a large part of the key to handling middle-management resistance. However, the Job Enrichment specialist and the outside consultant must not allow the steering committee to take over the implementation program to the extent that the first line supervisors and workers, who are actually charged with the implementation process, feel that they are losing responsibility for the project.

A steering committee established for the purpose of long-range planning and review of activities during the project can naturally become a Job Enrichment management committee after the project period is completed and specialists and consultants have withdrawn from the work group. Such a management committee will be required if activity is to be sustained over the long term. The steering committee structure provides just such a management body to keep the process alive after the project period.

IMPLEMENTATION TEAMS

Right after the workshop, the first-line supervisors (and workers, if they are involved) who have participated in the workshop and who will be installing the job changes with their subordinates should be organized into one or more teams. The teams' purpose will be to perform the problem-solving process as previously described for each item of job change to be installed and to plan the necessary installation steps. These implementation teams should meet for a period of about two hours on an average of once or twice a week.

The number of problem-solving/planning teams established will vary from project to project, being determined by the number of separate and distinct functional groups to be supervised. Supervisors whose work groups have something in common should be grouped together. In some cases the work being done throughout the work group is similar enough that the concerns of all the supervisors will be very much alike. In such cases, and provided the group is not too large, only one problem-solving/planning team may be necessary.

It has been found that implementation teams of from four to six members are ideal for effective team action. Planning teams with from seven to ten members will probably encounter some difficulty simply because there are too many people on the team to interact effectively and too much time will be lost while each person has his say. Teams of

over ten are inadvisable and should be avoided. The specific functions
of the implementation teams are as follows.

1. Complete the 10-step problem-solving process for items of job
   change to be installed.

2. Members of the problem-solving/planning teams are the principal
   implementers of job changes, each with his own group of subordinates.

3. Members of the problem-solving/planning teams discuss among
   themselves the details and problems of implementation, giving assistance to each other where possible.

The implementation team structure, with its regular meetings, gives
the specialist frequent opportunities to work on installation problems and
progress and to give close assistance and coaching to first-line supervisors
(and workers, if involved) as they install the job changes decided on.
A principal objective for implementation teams should be to achieve a
high degree of autonomy and develop the ability to conduct their planning and problem-solving sessions without the assistance of the Job Enrichment specialist. As the project progresses the specialist should seek
to foster such autonomy so that toward the end of a project period the
implementation teams should be able to function on their own and continue the process with fewer meetings.

A method of generating autonomy among these teams is to have
members of the team chair the sessions. They can be trained to prepare
and conduct the problem-solving sessions, assuming the role of the Job
Enrichment specialist. It is sometimes a good idea to rotate the chairmanship; that is, give each member of the problem-solving/planning
team the opportunity to chair sessions himself. This can be especially
useful for team-building where managers are attending problem-solving/
planning sessions with first-line supervisors. Rotating the chairmanship
changes working relationships and builds up the independence and confidence of the supervisors reporting to the manager. In some cases,
however, the manager may need considerable conditioning before he will
accept a subordinate role at such sessions.

(*A Caution:* It is desirable to develop teams to the point where they can run their own sessions. But this capability develops at different rates with different groups, depending on their commitment, workload, and other factors, and forcing them into autonomy could have strongly negative results. Encourage them to be independent but make sure they're ready to be.)

To avoid any possibility of confusion, we'd like to summarize the difference between the Job Enrichment steering committee and the implementation teams. The steering committee is set up to look at the broad view and coordinate all the activities in the project. The implementation team is intended to deal with the minutiae of installing job changes on a day-to-day basis. Because of its concentration on detail, the implementation team may sometimes be unable to see the forest for the trees— and this is when the value of the steering committee, with its broader view, is obvious.

THE IMPLEMENTATION ROAD MAP

Just after the workshop, one of the first tasks for the Job Enrichment specialist should be to construct an implementation "road map" to serve as a guide, first through the process of problem-solving, and then through the installation of job change items from the greenlight list. In some cases the implementation road map may be designed by the Job Enrichment steering committee with assistance from the members of the supervisory team.

The implementation road map is a graphic plan showing the order in which to do problem-solving and install items of job change. It charts the future of the project, shows what has been installed, and gives an overview of the relationships of the items being worked on. A graphic display is recommended because it allows more effective analysis of the plan of action and shows the optimum priority of items in both problem-solving and installation. It also shows where some items may conflict with one another, or where one item may actually prevent the installation of a later item.

The first step in establishing a road map for implementation is to review the greenlight list to ensure that all useless items have been purged and that Hygiene items have been separated from the Motivator items. The next step is to group these items that have something in common as one of the keys to planning the installation activity. Some items on the greenlight list may have in common only the job design principle they represent. Since the items on the greenlight list were coded by job design principle during the conditioning process at the workshop, it should be a simple matter to group them accordingly; that is, to group them under the headings described in Chapter 5. You will recall that these were the:

Implementing Concepts	and the	Core Dimensions
Natural Units of Work		Task Variety
Client Relationships		Autonomy
Task Combination		Task Identity
Vertical Loading		Feedback
Feedback		

In some cases one job design principle may include several types of items, and in each of these instances it may be advisable to group the items under headings that are more specific and more directly related to the particular job. To illustrate, in many service jobs the Natural Units of Work may include some items related to background clerical duties and other items involving direct customer contact. When this happens it may be appropriate to set up separate Natural Units of Work not for the whole job but for each function and for each individual. Thus the items concerned with background clerical duties can be considered apart from those related to direct customer contact. Careful scrutiny of the greenlight list for any job may very well turn up many other headings under which related items may be grouped. For example:

1. Sales related items.

2. Service related items.

3. Repair related items.

4. New signing authorities.

5. New write-off authorities.

6. Internal feedback items.

7. External feedback items.

8. Good Hygiene items.

9. Reduction of controls.

10. Direct contacts with other groups.

11. In-office duties.

12. Outside duties.

Normally, from two to four main groupings are sufficient for a given job. The point of this grouping, of course, is to gather together items that are likely to be problem-solved in a sequence and installed in the same way. Often the priorities of the groups themselves become obvious as their lists of items are completed. Then, when the items within each group are given to their own priorities, both the groups and their items can be entered on the graphic display road map for review and reference.

When deciding on the priority of items as they are selected from the greenlight list, keep the following four considerations in mind:

1. *The problem-solving time required.* The priority of an item can be affected not only by *how much* time is available for problem-solving but also *when* the time is available. In the first case, if the most convenient time selected is not enough to problem-solve the item properly, it might better be postponed—or moved ahead. In the second case, if an important item is scheduled for problem-solving in the middle of the vacation schedule, it might be better to install simpler items first and delay the more complex problem-solving items until all members of the team can be presented.

2. *The pace of installation.* Too many complex items one after the other could prove discouraging to the members of the implementation team. Such items might also make the rate of change too rapid for the job holders to absorb. Thus it might be wise to schedule simple items between the more difficult ones.

3. *Changes and reorganizations required.* Physical changes, equipment changes, or rigid rule changes may, be involved in some items. The

group may wish to delay installation of some less complicated items and start on preparatory action for those items that require it.

4. The priority for items which are not affected by the preceding three paragraphs should be governed by plain logic and common sense (which, by the way, are important tools for all stages of Job Enrichment). Review of the greenlight list may show that some items cannot be installed until certain others have been done. These, of course, should be scheduled later as appropriate.

The scheduling and execution of required training steps will also be highly important. We cannot expect people to become excited about items of job change if we do a poor job of preparing them to handle those items. The wise Job Enrichment specialist will pay close attention to the completion of training steps decided on by the implementation teams. These steps must be carefully planned with thorough follow-up to assure readiness.

TWO BASIC PATTERNS OF JOB CHANGE

The redesign for most jobs normally assumes one of the following two basic patterns, depending on the main job design principles:

1. Mainly a series of vertical loading items involving added responsibility and autonomy.
2. Mainly task combination, natural units of work, and client relationship.

The principal difference between these two patterns is the presence or absence of task combination and the need to set up Natural Units of Work. The redesign of most jobs will include some vertical loading of new responsibilities and the addition of appropriate feedback mechanisms. However, not all job redesigns will involve combination of tasks, Natural Units of Work and client relationships. Certain deductions can be made before installation begins by determining which of the two basic patterns are to be used. Since pattern one involves only vertical loading of new responsibility, with no great changes in work flow or procedures, the process can move quickly and impact is comparatively prompt. On the other hand, when task combination and Natural Units of Work are to be involved, as in pattern two, the problem-solving and installation process is longer and more complex, which means that the impact on working behavior is likely to be delayed. Such foreknowledge can be useful in predicting how soon to look for signs of the impact of job changes being installed.

Figures 8.2 and 8.3 show how such a road map for implementation might appear.

It may be necessary to construct separate implementing road maps for each implementation team to follow. Each problem-solving/planning team should review the implementing road map constructed for its use. First, (from a technical standpoint) the supervisors on each team should review the selected items, the priorities assigned to them, and the overall plan they are about to follow. Since they are very close to the jobs being considered, they may be able to see changes or improvements that should be made before implementation begins. Second, if each implementation team is assigned a task of reviewing and approving the road map devised for it, the chances of their accepting it as their own and becoming committed to its use will be enhanced.

The foregoing point raises the question of which is the most appropriate group to construct implementing road maps. In some situations, if time permits and the necessary expertise exists within the implementation teams, it will greatly increase the involvement of the problem-solving/planning team if its members devise their own road map for implementation. There is a strong case to be made for involving members of these teams in every possible aspect of project activity, for that will heighten their identity with the project and their sense of ownership over everything that happens.

MEASURES FOR THE PROJECT

We have made the point that every project should be established with a high regard for the line manager's need to demonstrate results and for the importance of demonstrating the quantitative effectiveness of any activity such as job redesign. This, of course, means that effective methods of measurement are of major importance. A great deal of care should be devoted to establishing sound measures of the impact of

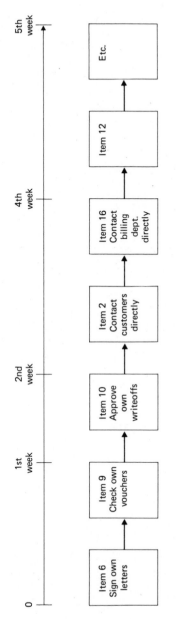

FIG. 8.2 Series of vertical loading items (pattern one)

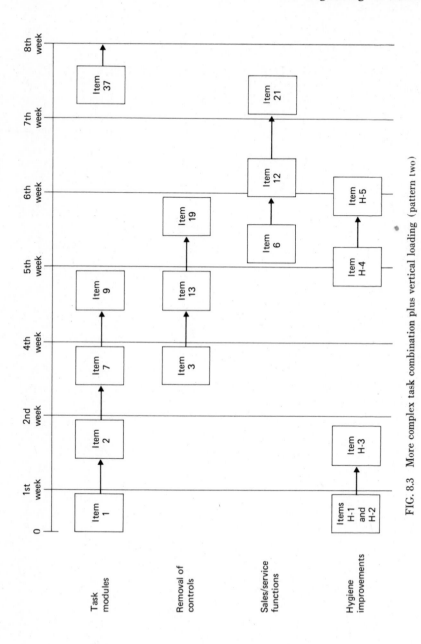

FIG. 8.3   More complex task combination plus vertical loading (pattern two)

changes introduced over the course of the project. It is the data gathered from the project, validly measured and properly presented to top management and other members of the organization at the conclusion of the project, which is the most effective means of expanding the process of job enrichment throughout the organization. Failure to measure impact has been the weakness of many other applications of behavioral science to management. Conversely, a concern for impact measurement has characterized most successful Job Enrichment applications, and has made all the difference in its rapid acceptance among managers in recent years. When the measurements have been collected and historical data assembled, it is best to assign one individual to be responsible for continued updating and analysis of the measurement data. It must not be forgotten that the purpose of a pilot project is to intensify effort in one work group to demonstrate in every possible way the effectiveness of Job Enrichment and to establish credibility within the organization. A challenging sales job lies ahead at the conclusion of the pilot project, and concern for measurement throughout the project will provide the basis for an effective selling approach for expansion.

Hard and Soft Measures

"Hard" and "soft" measures are both available for measuring the impact of Job Enrichment changes. Wherever possible, emphasis should be placed on obtaining hard or clearly quantitative measures. Generally stated, hard measures deal with improvement in strictly measurable items, such as rate of output, error rates, reduction of costs per finished item, and other such quantitative items. Soft measures include such things as improvement in job reaction survey scores, interview data drawing on quotes from job holders, and other less quantifiable but valuable organization changes. Emphasis should be placed on hard measures, since these are the only ones which are truly convincing to line-management people.

For some specialists accustomed to personnel staff work and other behavioral science applications, the process of obtaining hard measurement may be new and somewhat uncomfortable, but adroitness at gaining hard measures must be developed in order to relate to the line-management state of mind effectively. Beyond that, line people are usually favorably impressed to find staff individuals who can relate to the realities and pressures faced in a line-management position. If it can be shown to be truly effective in solving cost-of-operation problems and problems with operating measures, Job Enrichment will have a bright future in the organization. It is a very unusual line manager who is willing to participate in something like Job Enrichment solely to improve the quality of life for his employees. The day may come when more and more managers will be willing to devote their energies to such noble objectives, but at the time of this writing that day has not quite arrived. The only way to effectively mobilize their support, given today's realities is to show that Job Enrichment impact can be measured and that it can assist them significantly in dealing with the pressures and problems facing them in discharging their line responsibilities.

There are some standard measures of Job Enrichment impact which have frequently been used in projects. These include:

1. Rates of output (productivity)
2. Error rates (quality or accuracy)
3. Turnover (rates of force loss)
4. Overtime reduction
5. Reduction in cost per unit
6. Customer service surveys
7. Absenteeism

Many other measures are likely to be appropriate in a given situation. The key is to meet early in the game with the managers of the project work group or the middle-level managers above them—or both of these groups—to discuss which measures of impact will be most meaningful to them. The needs and expectations of these individuals can be determined by questioning them about current operating problems. What are they having trouble improving? What things are causing pressure on them? What things do their bosses most want improved? Have specific objectives been set for the project work groups for the coming months? If such objectives have been set, try to relate the project measurements to them. Any manager is likely to respond if Job Enrichment can be shown to have helped him achieve his objectives.

These individuals will have a key role in convincing others of the value of Job Enrichment at the conclusion of the pilot project, and once their needs and expectations have been identified, measures can be designed which will be both valid and impressive.

Before going on to the types of hard and soft measures, let us offer a word of caution about discussing with managers what should be measured. Most managers will be cautious and somewhat defensive about talking over the problems and weaknesses of their work group. Many of them may even deny at first that any significant problems exist. The specialist must start early to build a close relationship of trust between himself and the managers of the work group. He must seek ways to generate an open dialogue about problems. He must use every possible strategy to avoid identifying himself as an interloper from the staff at head office and to gain acceptance as an on-site counselor who is to help solve local operating problems. The managers must feel that they can speak safely with the specialist about operating problems. If the managers get the impression that information is being spread around the organization about themselves and their work groups, the project can be severely jeopardized.

Types of Hard Measures

1. *Productivity.* Almost any work group will benefit from the mere fact of having established a measurement system of its output, and most work groups do have one. Where no such system exists, however, it may be necessary to devise one for purposes of the project.

Bear in mind that there will be a need for historical data on whatever measures are selected. Assign someone early in the process to start assembling such data for comparison with the data generated during the test period. Even when new measures have been constructed it may be possible to go back and reconstruct historical data along the same lines. In stating measures of improvement and productivity, look for ways to translate those improvements in rates of output into dollar figures. Try to express production rates in terms of dollar cost per item generated. In fact, the dollar savings principle should be used with every possible measure. It can also be applied to quality improvement, improvements in cost per error, waste material reduction, turnover reduction, absence, and overtime reduction.

2. *Throughput Rates.* In many kinds of clerical work the key measure of productivity is expressed as a "throughput rate," the total processing time required to complete the handling of a given item of work. Throughput rates apply to insurance claims handling, applications of all kinds of complaint processing, and bank teller work. Reduced throughput rates in these kinds of work result in reduced costs and improved customer service.

3. *Quality Measures.* Measures of quality may take precedent over measures of productivity in service oriented jobs. Once again, try to express improvements in quality in terms of dollar savings wherever you can. It may be possible to establish a measure of improvement by calculating the costs of having to correct errors or duplicate work when errors occur.

4. *Force Reduction.* A Job Enrichment project presumably is not intended to reduce force but rather to humanize and personalize the work for the members of the existing work force. However, there may be times when it's advisable to reduce the cost of doing business by reducing the staff. In such cases, Job Enrichment may indicate either (or both) of two reasons:

a) *The work force may be overstaffed to begin with.* Many operations are found to be overstaffed with people in poorly designed jobs that do not require them to do their best. Also, many organizations have become so complicated, departmentalized, and specialized that managers and supervisors lose sight of the effect of their operations on the overall cost of running the business when they are not held accountable for those costs. They often are conditioned to pursue numerical objectives which are not related to the managing costs of the business, and this can discourage concern for the true cost of an operation. In such situations many management people become adept at forms of organization gamesmanship. They are regularly promoted while actually becoming rather poor managers—at least to the extent that they do not get the highest return on investment by controlling costs, among other variables.

Many managers will refuse to consider the possibility of being overstaffed because any force reduction may make it more difficult to achieve some other objectives for which they are held directly accountable. In such cases, Job Enrichment may bring about productivity increases which demonstrate that the force can be reduced, and force reduction may then become an explicit measure of the impact of job changes. However, the manager may still be very reluctant to match his work force to the actual work load.

b) *Some jobs may be essentially unnecessary and may actually diminish the motivational content of other jobs.* This situation is being found in more and more organizations. Over the years certain jobs have come into existence solely to control or check or verify the output of people in other jobs. In many such cases there would be no need (or less need) for such checking and verification if the production job had been designed well enough to encourage involvement and good performance from those holding it. The Job Enrichment specialist should take immediate interest in any job that is based on checking the work of others. Often these jobs take the meaning and accountability right out of other jobs. While there are some exceptions, such jobs are often found to be unnecessary. When they are, the best way to enrich the basic job may be to dismantle and remove the verification function or at least reduce the amount of verification.

Care should be taken to avoid giving the impression that force reduction is the object of Job Enrichment in all situations. Force reduction is not always possible, nor is it always appropriate. It should be emphasized also that when and if certain jobs disappear as a result of Job Enrichment, the workers who held those jobs should be placed elsewhere in the organization.

Whenever possible, it is better to allow force reductions to occur naturally by attrition. If management insists on abrupt and arbitrary force reductions as a result of Job Enrichment, this can doom the whole project.

5. *Turnover.* Oftentimes the prime reason for starting Job Enrichment is to reduce job turnover. Loss of personnel due to job dissatisfaction, especially among young people in urban labor markets, has become so common that many companies are being forced to begin redesigning jobs. Problems with turnover provided the principle reason for serious trials to test the validity of Job Enrichment theory in the early 1960's at AT&T. Results were so impressive with urban labor groups that the Job Enrichment approach to job redesign has become firmly established in

recent years. Reduction of turnover can be a most impressive measure of the impact of a project, but where turnover is seasonable it will be necessary to compare like months or periods in successive years.

It should also be mentioned that where turnover reduction is concerned, establishing the validity of results can be difficult. Many things besides job content can effect turnover, and care should be taken to separate preventable termination from unpreventable termination. Such reasons for termination as leaving the city, medical discharge, and maternity should be excluded from the evaluation, leaving only those terminations that appear to be related to job dissatisfaction.

Ascertaining true reasons for termination can also be difficult. In order to avoid discomfort and unpleasant confrontations, people leaving a job often give other than their true reasons for going. They may say they are leaving for more money, but the pertinent question is: What led them to look for another job in the first place—which then enabled them to discover that they could get more money? In order to gain valid data from post-termination contacts it may be wise to use some form of survey which is likely to give objective data on reasons for termination. The beginning of the project also is a good time to institute an exit interviewing procedure. Each individual leaving the job after the start of the project should be carefully interviewed to determine as much as possible about his or her reasons for termination. The specific values of an exit interviewing program are that it gathers data on: (a) reasons for termination, (b) job content problems, and (c) the success of the project at making meaningful changes in the job.

6. *Overtime Reduction.* Reducing overtime can also provide a measure of impact which will capture the interest of many a manager. If overtime is a problem at the start, this can be an important measure. In service and clerical work data on overtime reduction must be compared with changes in incoming work volume which can effect the need for overtime as well as worker motivation. The reduction may not have been due to improved motivation.

7. *Absence.* Measuring absence can be a useful measure of impact but its validity is usually in question because so many other factors can effect it. Here again it is necessary to compare like months from year to year to get useful measures of change in absence rates.

Types of Soft Measures

Although the hard quantitative measures are more impressive to line-management people, do not ignore the numerous sources of data for soft measures of impact such as:

1. Job reaction surveys.
2. Quotes from taped interviews of employee response to job changes.
3. Anecdotes about changes in both workers and supervisory behavior.
4. Measures of customer complaint levels where appropriate.
5. Surveys of customer opinion about product or service.
6. Changes in the use of time by supervisors—using a simple survey instrument. Data on changes in the way supervisors use their time and what they devote their attention to can be very useful—particularly where there is concern that the first line of supervision is not really supervising and may not be developing talent among subordinates. This is a very common weakness in most organizations.

Another point to consider in establishing measures for the project is that they can often provide the basis for individual feedback on performance, which is a powerful motivation missing in most jobs. This involves converting measures of group performance into measures of individual performance, then using the data as positive reinforcement of behavior and as the basis for individual goal setting and performance appraisal.

PROGRESS REPORTING

At the beginning of on-site activity the specialist should discuss with middle management the preferred media for reports and the intervals at which they should be submitted. There is no set pattern for reporting on all projects. Some higher-level executives want to be kept informed of each move in the project; others wish to hear nothing until the end of the project when the results are in; there may be a need for informal memorandums to several departments or individuals as the project goes on. Problems can be avoided by analyzing the organization's needs for communication about the project. Once those needs for communication have been determined, it is important for the project team to make definite commitments for reporting and to see that the steering committee keeps those commitments. The format and media for reports may vary. Some situations will require written communications in all cases; other situations may require oral presentations matched with a written report; in still other situations round-table discussions of project activities and results will be useful.

It is important to involve the management team of the project work group in report preparations in every way possible. Such involvement gives them a periodic detailed review of their own progress as well as the opportunity to identify with results. It is important to avoid the appearance that the project belongs to the staff people or the specialists—it must not be labeled "their project," or "the head office project," or "What are they doing for us?" Success in job enrichment depends in part on making the project the property of the work group itself in every way. If the project is to be sustained after the project period, the work group must feel that they own it. Give the management team, including first-line supervision (and workers, if involved), a role in the oral presentations if at all possible. Taking part in oral presentations and round-table discussions will heighten their involvement and sense of ownership.

If no requirements are set by upper management for reporting, we suggest the following pattern:

1. Full written and oral reports of feasibility study before the workshop.

2. Written reports of workshop results showing the greenlight lists after they are Conditioned.

3. Brief progress report memos at least monthly to key individuals.

4. Detailed reports of changes installed and progress midway through the project. Round-table discussions to allow questioning and review of progress are also advisable at this time.

5. A full final report at the conclusion of the project period with a clear description of the changes made, giving heavy emphasis to results obtained. This report should become an effective device for getting others in the organization involved in their own areas. The final report

should include an oral presentation as a springboard for discussions about the future of Job Enrichment in the organization. One suggestion for oral presentations and discussion with middle management is to use excerpts from taped interviews of employee comments on job reaction before and after job changes. It makes a strong impression when people are heard describing in their own words the impact of changes in the content of their work.

6. When results are evident at the time of the mid-project report or the final report, do not hesitate to seek high-level exposure in the organization. Meet with the top man if at all possible. If Job Enrichment is to have a significant and lasting impact on the organization and serve as a catalyst for organization change and growth, the effort needs the support of the man at the top. Make it an objective to see the man who heads the organization not only to present results but also to persuade him to give the project exposure and encourage participation by others when he meets with top-level department heads.

A final note about report procedures. Beware of preparing reports and giving presentations outside the structure of the steering committee without its full participation. There is a definite risk of losing the support of members of the work group management team if you include certain things in the report which they may disagree with or wish to state differently. When reports are prepared without their participation there may be inaccuracies that unwittingly expose the committee to criticism which can destroy the trust that exists between the specialist and the management team. Their participation in the report preparation, review of report drafts, and involvement in presentations prevents such misfortunes—which could cost you their support. Reports should never be taken lightly or considered as routine matters—improperly handled they can be dynamite. Reports should be scrutinized with great care for possible negative reactions.

SUMMARY

At the completion of a job enrichment training workshop the participants frequently experience a state of euphoric excitement about a new discovery. But this should not deceive the unwary specialist into thinking that such a state of mind can be relied on to continue and sustain the supervisory team over a long period of time. The participants are returning to the same work site, and to the same set of problems, stresses, and strains which they left before the workshop. As the group starts the hard grind of installing the job changes they have creatively brainstormed, they will begin to lose that initial hope and excitement. In order to preserve the momentum of the workshop and to transform energy into action we have presented in this chapter a program for organizing the Job Enrichment effort. The plan includes establishing organizational entities that are responsible for carrying out the project and for measuring and reporting on its success. Details and recommendations for effective measurement and reporting have been reviewed to present those techniques which have proven successful many times.

chapter NINE

Problem-Solving and Installation of Motivational Job Changes

This chapter presents guidance and strategy for successful implementation of new job designs. Details of the installation process will be covered, including problem-solving and the introduction of job changes to the work force. Attention is also devoted to the multitude of obstacles and problems often faced at this stage of a project.

EFFECTIVE PROBLEM-SOLVING SESSIONS

Since the process of problem-solving (as described in Chapter 7) may go on for many weeks, it will be important to organize these sessions with care to avoid losing direction and momentum. Problem-solving will be hard work and there may be times of fatigue and discouragement. Good organization and structure for these sessions can make all the difference between problem-solving sessions that are highly productive and those that are a waste of time.

At the start some thought should be given to subgrouping the supervisors and managers if they are not to work together as a whole group at every session. As previously mentioned, in some cases the entire management group may be too large to work together effectively or the work groups may so differ in function that it may be necessary to problem-solve in small groups whose concerns are somewhat homogeneous. Even in cases in which the various sections or units are doing a very similar job, it may be useful to divide the supervisors into small problem-solving groups each working on a different item of job change. Where they might waste time in a large and ineffective group, these small groups of supervisors may be able to work separately on items and significantly increase the pace of problem-solving.

The role of the manager in problem-solving sessions should also be given careful consideration. In some cases it may be useful to have him in attendance at most—if not all—of the sessions. If it is judged that his contributions are necessary for thorough analysis of proposed job changes, he should, no doubt, be asked to attend. In other cases it may be found that the manager tends to dominate all discussions and force all decisions. In such cases it may be advisable to conduct problem-solving at the supervisors' level, meeting with the manager periodically for review and decisions. In any event, a balance should be sought between periods when the manager is present at or absent from problem-solving sessions. He must not be allowed to become too distant from the process, but he should not be allowed to dominate all activity in the sessions, as this will discourage his subordinates from participation and many of their ideas will be lost.

The schedule for problem-solving sessions must fit the situation comfortably. In many instances it may be unwise to schedule problem-solving sessions during a main portion of the working day; it may be difficult to have supervisory groups away from the work process so frequently during the height of the work period. In such cases it may be possible to meet in the early morning or late afternoon, or even after hours if that is absolutely necessary. Obviously early morning sessions are likely to be far more productive than late afternoon or after-hours sessions when people are fatigued from the work day. Normally, problem-solving sessions should not extend beyond two hours. The work in these sessions requires a kind of concentration which is exhausting, and if they are extended beyond two hours the result will often be fatigue and restlessness which will make it difficult to accomplish anything.

For obvious reasons, every attempt should be made to locate a bright, airy space in which to hold problem-solving sessions. Such a space should be in close proximity to the work area if possible, but wherever it is located it must be conducive to extended periods of concentration and discussion. An agenda should be established for the sessions in order to give the meeting some basic structure. Establishing too firm an agenda for the group, however, can have the effect of reducing the participants' sense of ownership of the session. It has been found effective for the specialist to establish a tentative agenda or a rec-ommended agenda which is sent to each supervisory group in advance of the meeting for their review and comment. At the beginning of the session the recommended agenda can be reviewed, additions or changes can be made according to the suggestions of the members, and the meet-ing can be gotten underway. Every attempt should be made to make the agendas and the activity in problem-solving sessions belong to the groups of supervisors who participate.

At the beginning of each problem-solving session a recording secre-tary should be appointed, either one of the Job Enrichment specialists or one of the supervisors in the group. It will be essential to have a record of discussions, problems, and decisions that occur in the course of each session. This record need not be an exhaustive word-for-word replay of every point discussed at the session, but it must be inclusive enough to allow a review of all the main points in preparation for the following session. Such a record becomes extremely important when it is found that more than one problem-solving session is required for completion of an item. Without such a record much of the critical detail of problem-solving and planning can be lost and must be reconstructed before any further progress can be made at a later session. The need for someone to record minutes of these sessions may seem minor. Ex-perience has shown, however, that such records are vital to effective problem-solving. Minutes also can be used for short-interval communica-tion to higher management or to other problem-solving teams who should be kept informed of progress.

Make a habit of having the problem-solving group start and finish their sessions on time. A great deal of productive time can be lost if various members of the group hold up the others by failing to observe the established starting times. A fair amount of discipline and structure will be required to make these sessions fully productive; punctuality and adhering to a schedule can add a good deal to the effectiveness of that structure.

Many problem-solving groups have discovered that a visual record of the points discussed in the problem-solving process has often helped them avoid confusion and find a breakthrough where no solution was thought possible. Flip-chart easel paper is best for this purpose and should be available at every problem-solving session. Once again, it is not necessary to record *every* comment made but simply to keep a prominent visual record of the point being discussed, the various options that may be available for the solution of a problem, a list of the advantages or disadvantages of each option, and a record of the decisions made as discussion goes along. It may seem like duplication of effort to have a secretary recording the session and keeping a visual record on the easel paper as well, but the two processes serve different purposes. The visual record on easel sheets is principally used as an aid in visualizing solutions to problems. Experience with numerous problem-solving groups has shown that when discussion of an item becomes complex, or when a number of options are considered as possible solutions to a problem, very few people can keep a clear mental picture of all the possible options and their relative strengths and weaknesses as discussion moves along. In many cases when solution was thought impossible it was just this simple device of prominent visual recording that led to a solution.

Effective problem-solving sessions normally consist of four main components:

1. Review of key events related to the project which have occurred since previous meeting.
2. The problem-solving process for the item selected.
3. Guidance, coaching, or role-playing in preparation for the introduction of job changes to the work force.
4. Setting objectives for installing job changes and future problem-solving sessions.

Within this structure of activities it is important to get the problem-solving group accustomed to using the 10-step problem-solving process on all but the very simplest of job change items. Most such groups will be unaccustomed to group problem-solving. Early sessions are likely to be very disorganized with a great deal of miscellaneous conversation and meaningless contributions. Few groups will be fully effective right at the start without previous group problem-solving experience. The specialist should expect to encounter lack of discipline in discussion, a good deal of meaningless talk, wandering from the subject, and generally ineffective group action. Either at the workshop or early in the series of problem-solving sessions the specialist will have to assess the level of team effectiveness of each of the teams with which he is working.

Some teams may easily develop the ability to work together without additional training; others may have a great deal of difficulty working together and waste much time in the sessions. A decision should be made as to the need for training to develop greater team effectiveness. There are, of course, many methods and training techniques available for this purpose—from a very simple set of criteria which the team can use to evaluate its own effectiveness to much more elaborate team-building designs which may be required in groups in which conflict and dissension have halted progress. When some form of team effectiveness training is necessary, we recommend a simple process, one in which the team evaluates itself by a set of criteria provided by the specialist. Deeper involvement in team-building exercises can often get the group so wrapped up in their own trust levels, confrontation processes, and encounters that they become diverted from the business at hand and make little or no progress on the examination of greenlight items for job changes. This is not intended to derogate the more complex forms of team-building; they may be entirely necessary with some groups. It is suggested, however, that simpler techniques be explored first, as the more complicated methods can often raise more problems than specialists are prepared to resolve. The following five items form a set of simple criteria for evaluating team effectiveness which can be introduced with little effort. Introducing the group to this means of evaluating their own effectiveness has often proven successful in raising their consciousness of —and willingness to fill—the need for greater team effectiveness.

I TIME

Premeeting preparation Someone review status as of last meeting and plan a short summary. Prepare the room and materials needed.
Starting—start on time Set time goals and agree to time discipline.
Finishing Either finish on time or review what you are working on and decide whether it must be finished now.

II DIRECTION

Set goals
Redirect when course is lost.
How is direction maintained? Does one or a few lead and dominate? Does a "chairman," formal or informal, keep things organized?

III DECISION-MAKING
>   *Bandwagon*
>   *Compromise*
>   *Bulldozing*
>   *Thorough consensus*
>   How well are all the personal resources used?

IV COMMUNICATION
>   *Perfunctory*
>   *Polite*
>   *Probing*, seeking understanding
>   *Creative listening*
>   *Hostility*

V CRITIQUE
>   *Scheduled or concurrent*
>   *Unconstructive criticism*

These five criteria provide for most groups all the structure necessary to enable them to carry out a thorough evaluation of their effectiveness in each session. The training process is a simple one. At the beginning of the problem-solving sessions each member of the team is
given a handout containing the five criteria with an explanation of how
they will be used for self-evaluation at the conclusion of each session.
The following discussion of these criteria should be helpful in introducing the suggested self-evaluation process to the implementation teams:

I Time

Time will surely be of the essence during these implementation sessions.
The teams will most likely consist of line supervisors and managers (and
workers, if involved) for whom time taken away from their daily jobs
will be of great value. Every attempt must be made to structure the time
available for these sessions and to make every minute productive. Three
things are suggested for making effective use of time:

>   Premeeting preparation
>   Starting
>   Finishing

Some individual should be given responsibility before each session to review the status of the last session and to prepare the room and materials needed so that everything is in readiness at the appointed starting time. That individual should plan a short summary for the others to bring them up to date on the last session and the objectives and agenda of the current session. If time is to be used properly in the session, quite obviously discussion must start on schedule. Every individual team member must accept the responsibility for getting himself free of other responsibilities to join the team at the appointed time ready to begin. Meetings should start exactly on time, goals for various parts of the discussion should be established, and team members should agree to adhere to time discipline during the session. Finishing on time can be as important as starting on time. A characteristic of ineffective teams is that they often let meetings run open-ended. This is almost a guarantee that some time will be wasted and some unproductive activity will occur. Establishing an outside limit for finishing the meeting will establish the boundaries for time discipline. When the appointed time for finishing arrives, the group should then decide whether or not it is necessary that discussion be completed before the next session. If not, discussion should be dropped and the meeting terminated at the appointed hour. Encouraging this pattern usually develops time consciousness and an increased willingness to adhere to time discipline.

II Direction

It is not uncommon for a discussion to wander away from the direction it is supposed to take. Members of an ineffectual team may not even notice the digression—or if they do, may for some reason (lack of confidence, timidity, disinterest, etc.) not say anything about it. The result, of course, is a waste of time, money, and manpower.

All of the team's members should clearly understand that keeping the meeting on course is not just the discussion leader's responsibility; any of the team members who think that the discussion is getting off the track should feel it both their privilege and their duty to state their concern. The group should not arbitrarily reject the question but should examine the direction of the discussion and redirect it if necessary. The ability to objectively monitor their own direction-keeping is one of the most useful tools a team can have for developing its effectiveness.

III Decision-making

Each team should examine its own pattern of decision-making with the object of drawing on all of the personal resources available to forge truly sound decisions. It may be helpful for them to examine several different common forms of group decision-making and to identify which method they are using. For example:

Bandwagon. Most members jump on the bandwagon when a member (usually a prominent one) of the team assumes a position. This makes decisions easy, but does not ensure that they are sound.

Bulldozing. One or more dominant personalities force their decisions on the team, even over what might be legitimate objections from other members. This gets a decision made, but it stifles the creative efforts of other members of the team. And again, it does not guarantee that the decision will be a good one.

Compromise. When two (or more) positions are taken on a question that conflict in various ways, it may be fairly simple for everyone to give a little and settle on a compromise position. Usually this does not involve a careful examination of the original positions, so the result may be a poor decision.

Consensus. This requires imaginative questioning and probing of all positions, with full participation by all team members. Using the full resources of the team, it gives by far the greatest probability for sound, workable decisions.

IV Communication

It can be valuable also for the group to evaluate the characteristics of the different communication patterns among them. Exchanges among team members may be perfunctory or formal, in which case there may be little active involvement in problem-solving. Team members may not be digging for solutions to the extent necessary. Hostilities may be developing within the team. Often just having to step back and examine patterns of communication may show group members that hostilities are reducing their effectiveness. The group *should* be striving for probing and imaginative patterns of communication, with all members actively seeking to understand divergent positions and to evaluate them toward the best possible solution. Often when the going gets difficult it is obvious that the team members are not really listening to each other at all; rather they are developing their own arguments and waiting the chance to break in on the speaker. It should be pointed out to them that creative listening to divergent positions is essential when disagreements develop about proposed solutions.

V Critique

In many ways this evaluating criterion may be the most crucial, since its object is to encourage team members to be conscious of the need for constant evaluation of team effectiveness. The team members should be striving to develop their critiquing ability concurrently with the discussion. No doubt they will be unaccustomed to the process of constantly evaluating the discussion and problem-solving in which they are involved, and so it is suggested that critiques of team effectiveness be scheduled for the end of each session. However, as the team members become more comfortable with self-critique, they become more likely to express concern about their effectiveness during the course of the meeting itself. There should be less and less need to schedule a critique at the end of the session. Wherever time discipline is lost or poor decisions are made, comments should be forthcoming from team members as they realize these failures. The truly effective team develops a special consciousness of team process in the midst of discussion.

Once again, this is surely not the only set of criteria for judging team effectiveness. However, we suggest that a simple process of developing team effectiveness will be sufficient with most groups. The fact that such a process is introduced will make team members aware of the importance of working together effectively.

A final bit of advice to the specialist: Every effort must be made to make these team sessions action-oriented. The teams must be pressed to take action on ideas, which means that they must establish target dates and individual accountability for the steps decided on. Many outstanding ideas die a sudden death when someone exclaims, "That sounds like a good idea," and the subject is dropped with no specific action steps, individual assignments, or target dates having been worked out. Once an implementation team has established an action spirit, their pride in their own achievements will sustain them from one achievement to the next.

THE MOMENT OF TRUTH: INSTALLING JOB CHANGES

Let us turn our attention now to what might be called the moment of truth, the critical business of executing the plans developed for changes in job design. Up to this point our concerns have been devoted to theory, creativity, brainstorming, planning, and problem-solving, but all of these efforts, exciting as they may have been, will have gone for naught without effective methods of execution.

Bear in mind that many supervisors will never have introduced this kind of change before. It may be necessary to give them a good deal of guidance and coaching before they have their first discussions with employees about new responsibilities and job changes. To ensure that they are not taken by surprise and thrown off balance by unusual responses from the job holders, make certain that the team pays attention to the problem-solving step of anticipating responses of the work force before introducing job changes. Responses from the job holders are not always as expected, nor are they always positive. However, a little time spent in anticipating the most likely responses can be of great help in preparing the supervisors to successfully implement the changes.

Types of Installation

One of the steps in preparing to implement job changes is the selection of an installation method. There are two basic methods of installation: *broadside* and *selective*.

In the broadside approach to implementation all members of the work force are involved in a given job change at the same time. This is appropriate when the necessary job changes involve widespread rearrangements in work flow and task combination which must be applied to the entire work force at once. The broadside method is also commonly used for installation of job changes which are of lesser complexity or lesser significance, in which no great risk to the organization is involved. However, the problem with the broadside approach is that not all workers are at the same level of experience or competence, and so it often happens that not all of them are ready for their job changes at the same time. Because of this, broadside installation has sometimes proven disruptive, causing a downturn in rates of production, accuracy, or other measures of performance.

On the other hand, the selective approach allows the installation of job change among the more experienced and competent workers first, while the less proficient workers have their job changes installed at times when they are better able to handle them. This is particularly important when the changes involve complex and/or important jobs whose disruption could be very costly to the company.

As a rule of thumb, then, job changes that make a significant impact on job content probably should be installed with the selective approach.

Telling Subordinates About the Job Changes

The very best items of job change cannot succeed without the acceptance and commitment of the work force. It is therefore very important that the supervisor communicate the information about the changes to his subordinates in a manner which will elicit their acceptance and commitment.

Choosing the Communication Method

How supervisors tell their subordinates about the job changes to come can have a great deal to do with how those changes are received. Certainly the quickest and easiest way is for the supervisor to meet with his or her subordinates as a group and discuss the scheduled changes with them. While this technique may very well be appropriate in some cases, it contains too many potential hazards to be the best approach for our purposes. For one thing, though many people find it easy to voice approval of a program in a group situation (or at least withhold disapproval) this does not necessarily mean that they are committed to it— or even that they fully accept it. For another thing, people in a group are less likely to raise all the questions they would in private, feeling that some of their questions are too personal or that they might make themselves look foolish to other group members. Then there is the possibility that one or two dissidents may dominate the discussion and cause other employees to react negatively to the program.

The preferred method of communication for our purposes is for the supervisor to sit down individually with each subordinate and discuss the nature of the job change, explain how it will affect the subordinate, and solicit the subordinate's questions and comments. This preference applies even when the broadside approach is being used to install job changes across the entire work force at once. The advantages of this technique over that of the group meeting are important ones. First, any approval of or commitment to the program that the worker makes is made as an individual, not as a member of a group; it is personal, and the worker cannot easily ignore it thereafter. Second, the subordinate is free to raise any question he or she would like to (particularly if the supervisor/subordinate relationship is a good one) without fear of criticism or ridicule from coworkers. And third, the individual in this situation is not swayed by any dissidents in the work force, as might have been the case in a group meeting. In fact, when the supervisor meets with such dissidents in a one-to-one meeting such as we are recommending here, he or she can handle their objections or resistance without giving them a platform from which to influence other members of the work force, which they would have had in a group meeting. Furthermore, the dissident is likely to be a less difficult person without an audience to play to.

A fringe benefit of the individual meeting is the fact that the supervisor can use it as a supportive performance-evaluation interview, reviewing the worker's previous job performance and emphasizing his or her competence and readiness to handle the proposed job change. This is particularly helpful when the job change involves new areas of responsibility and independence. Recognition of the subordinate's achievements should help to build his or her self-confidence and encourage the acceptance of new responsibility.

This type of interview, evaluating the individual's performance, should be standard periodic procedure in most companies. If this is the case in your organization, fine. If it's not, this could be a good beginning.

Helping Supervisors Prepare

Job Enrichment specialists will sometimes find that some supervisors are very hesitant to communicate job change information to their subordinates. They are used to communicating daily with the workers about the job at hand, but this is something new and different—and it's not at all uncommon for people to communicate very poorly on matters that are outside of their previous experience. Also, it's becoming more common to find supervisors who never have actually supervised—who achieved their position just by outlasting everybody else in the department or by some other nonqualifying means such as politics or good bluffing. (Unfortunate, but it happens.)

The specialist can help supervisors over this problem by having them take the time to make brief notes of what they must say to their subordinates to introduce the job changes. This act often helps them organize their thoughts and identify parts of the change about which they are uncertain. For very complex items of job change it may even be necessary for the specialist to go a step further and prepare a set of guiding notes for supervisors to refer to as they prepare themselves for discussions with their subordinates.

Many supervisors have found it very helpful to practice role-playing before they have their first discussions of job changes with employees. This is not a difficult technique to set up; simply have one supervisor prepare notes of what has to be said and have another supervisor play the role of a subordinate. The two then act out the interchange between supervisor and subordinate. Such a real-life role-play can often identify in advance some of the questions that subordinates will have and will give reluctant supervisors an added measure of confidence prior to introducing the first job changes.

What To Cover

When preparing to introduce an item of job change—whether by individual meetings or by one group meeting—the supervisor should keep the following four points in mind:

1. Each individual will want to know the details of the proposed job change.

2. Each individual will want to know why the supervisor feels that he or she is ready to accept this change in task and responsibility. This means that the supervisor should review and discuss the individual's strength and capability on the basis of past performance.

3. The supervisor should review any preparatory steps or training that may be required.

4. The supervisor should emphasize that reactions, comments, and suggestions from the employee are very much desired. It will be important for the supervisor to keep communication channels open with each subordinate as items of job change are introduced.

When items of job change are being introduced, the reasons for them will inevitably be questioned by the job holders. It is generally best to make the explanations in everyday language, avoiding the use of theoretical jargon. The supervisor should not attempt to explain theories of work motivation as may be understood from the workshop. The supervisor probably will not have the time, and may very well not have the skill, to do the subject justice. And as we said much earlier, it simply is not necessary.

How To Say It

It is very important that the supervisor avoid words and terms that give a negative meaning to the program. To illustrate: In one project a particularly important item of job change was nearly ruined by a supervisor who introduced each item of job change to subordinates with the statement, "I want to talk to you about a new duty." Now, it's very easy to interpret "new" as "additional," because it's often used that way, so the supervisor's constant use of the phrase "new duty" gave subordinates the impression that the supervisor was trying to load more and more work onto them. After several repetitions of the phrase their reaction became extremely negative.

It is generally far more effective to advise employees that the proposed job changes are part of a plan to give them more control of the work process, to treat them more as adults, to free them of restrictions and make work more personally satisfying. The supervisor should keep the answers to the subordinates' questions on a personal level, avoiding descriptions of great schemes for improving motivation which are much more likely to arouse suspicion than interest. The supervisor can legitimately use such statements as: "We'd like to make you more of your own boss, to let you use your own judgment more." "We'd like to make work here less like being in a kindergarten." or "You've proven that you can do this work without constant follow-up, and it's time we let you do it that way." This type of statement is both honest and reasonable, and does not concern itself with the abstract area of job motivation.

Acknowledging Unofficial Leaders

In almost every work group there is at least one person who, because of seniority, competence, special skill, personality, or a combination of these, has achieved higher status than the other workers—even though that status may be completely unofficial. Intentionally or unintentionally, such a person often sets the mood of the work group toward anything that affects its members. Because of this, the supervisor might be very wise to discuss the proposed job change with these people before introducing the subject to the rest of the group. Commitment or resistance from them can set the mood for the whole introductory phase of the program.

If the supervisor has chosen the individual meeting as the way to introduce job changes to the work group, seeing these "bellwether" people first presents no problem; the supervisor simply schedules meetings with them before meetings with anyone else. However, if the supervisor has chosen to introduce the job changes at a single group meeting, seeing these unofficial leaders first could cause difficulties. If the group does not recognize its unofficial leaders as the supervisor does, or if it recognizes and resents them, any private advance meetings could conceivably prejudice other workers against the program. This is a case where the supervisor can be guided only by his or her own judgment.

These bellwether people usually represent a great deal of knowledge and experience. Their advance comments and suggestions could help the supervisor discover pitfalls and make improvements in the proposed job change.

Informing the Absentees

This point may seem too minor to rate its own subsection, but it's not. Some personnel may be absent when the first communication about the job change is made. The good supervisor will see to it that these people are brought up to date on the proposed job changes immediately on their return to work. Not next week, not tomorrow, but today, before they can be filled in with second-hand (and possibly incorrect) information and before they can feel resentful about not being informed officially. Keep in mind, too, that the uninformed person cannot play his or her part in the scheduled job change as effectively as one who is informed.

TOOLS FOR PROJECT MANAGEMENT

As a program of job redesign progresses, key activities, problems, details of implementation, and needs for follow up proliferate on many levels and in many directions. The act of redesigning jobs affects many other aspects of organization activity. For example, supervisory and management roles change, training needs are generated, data must be gathered, manpower planning is affected, and presentations and training events are required if Job Enrichment is to become a concerted effort for organization change and renewal. Several tools have been developed for control and management of the details of implementation, for charting of results, and for coordinated programming of all activities and details. They are:

Implementation Chart
Item Control Chart
Supervisory feedback records
Job Enrichment calendars for supervisors
Project Follow-up Log
Project Chronicle

The Implementation Chart. Each supervisor who will be involved in implementing job changes with his or her subordinates should be equipped with a simple matrix device such as the one shown in Fig. 9.1. On the matrix, each item of job change to be installed is entered in the diagonal spaces across the top. The names of the individuals in the work group are listed in the column at the left. As each job change is selected and readied for installation, the supervisor reviews each member of the work group to decide which of them are ready for the item

Items of Job Redesign

Names	1	2	3	4	5	6	7	8	9	10	11	12	13	14	15	16
Art	X	X	X	X	X	X	X	X		X	X	X	X		X	X
Betty	X	X	X	X	X	X		X			X		X			
Carl	X	X	X		X	X		X								
Dave	X	X	X		X											
Edie	X	X	X													
Frank	X	X														
Gloria	X	X														

FIG. 9.1 Implementation chart

at that time and for which of them the item should be delayed until a later date. As each item of job change is implemented for a given individual, the appropriate box should be checked off. When implementation is to be delayed—and it can be determined when the individual will be ready for implementation—a target date is entered in the appropriate box. Observation, training, and development will work gradually toward full implementation, which will be shown on the implementation chart when each item has been checked off for each person.

If the names of subordinates are listed in order of decreasing experience and competence, the pattern of implementation marks in the matrix normally forms a triangle, as shown in Fig. 9.1. Those with the most experience and competence will normally receive the greater number of items at first. Implementation marks for those individuals will no doubt extend far across the matrix. Newer or less capable individuals will probably have fewer implementation marks at first. The triangle pattern shows graphically how supervisory activities must vary with different employees. The immediate task will be to implement more of the basic items with the newer, less experienced people. This will be a time-consuming supervisory process, evaluating needs for development and providing training and encouragement to make those individuals ready for the expanded job.

An even more challenging task, however, is that of providing greater autonomy, responsibility, and growth opportunities for the more competent and experienced people at the top of the list. Enrichment of a job is certainly not a one-time, static situation in which work experience can be expected to remain rich forever, and the supervisor will need to identify new activities, responsibilities, or projects for these people. He or she will have to keep the job ever-expanding, providing opportunities for creativity and new learning (see Fig. 9.2).

When carefully kept by the supervisor, the Implementation Chart shows several things:

1. Relative status of job redesign for each individual, which is especially useful where the job changes consist mainly of giving added responsibility and autonomy on an individual basis.

2. Target dates for development of each employee.

3. A graphic view of increasing competence of each employee. This

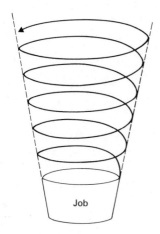

Job

FIG. 9.2   The supervisor keeps the job expanding with added responsibility

becomes a useful source of specific data for the appraisal process which is traditionally based on very unspecific and subjective judgments.

Entry on the Implementation Chart should be made during the implementation planning sessions and reviewed frequently with supervisors by the Job Enrichment specialist.

The Item Control Chart.   Once implementation is in full swing, with several items of job change implemented, the implementation of each item of job redesign throughout the work force must be controlled. Implementation can become very disorganized and incomplete unless all the pertinent information about each item of change is charted as it is installed. Whereas the Implementation Chart just discussed is used by the supervisor to show the status of *individual workers* and their progress with job changes, the Item Control Chart is used by the Job Enrichment specialist to keep up to date on the status of *each item* implemented in the course of the project. (See Fig. 9.3.) Time and again this device will prove useful for ensuring thorough implementation, reviewing items installed, and following up those items which have been

Description	Type of Item	Installations Schedule and Status Notes	Follow-up Steps	Supervisory Controls	Measures of Impact	Remarks
(A serial number or brief description of the item)	(Job design principle used)	(Dates of installation and notes on number of workers involved)	(Action required to make installation complete)	(Various sampling, spot-check, or other devices as required during transition period)	(Data on the impact of particular items where appropriate)	

FIG. 9.3   Item Control Chart for job redesign

implemented with only part of the work force. Without a clear view of the status of each item, the specialist cannot determine the extent of implementation, especially when implementation has been selective.

The Item Control Chart also will be indispensable to the specialist in preparing for status reviews with supervisors, as he or she attempts to stimulate their activity toward complete implementation of items with as many of their people as possible. Reviews of job changes that have generated less than the expected impact often reveal that the specialist used no means of item control, and items assumed to be fully implemented were actually tried with only a few individuals. Effective use of an Item Control Chart shows clearly when, and by how much, an item is not completely implemented.

Supervisory Feedback Records.   Among the most common flaws found in the implementation of new job designs is that supervisors often pay too little attention to the need of their subordinates for feedback on their performance with a new task or responsibility. This is probably the most universal weakness among supervisors, and their sudden involvement in Job Enrichment is not an automatic remedy. As previously discussed, not all employees are likely to respond enthusiastically at first to every job change, and others will be hesitant and need encouragement. When changes in job design are made the need for effective supervisory feedback is intensified. The supervisor must make frequent observations of the workers' performance, gather data on how well each is doing, and give them frequent reviews—either formal or informal— of their progress. This process is at the heart of establishing a new value system among people on the job. The object, of course, is to get people oriented toward task achievement and striving for excellence. To do this, the supervisor must do three basic things:

1. Provide the worker with a job structure that allows maximum opportunity for individual achievement.

2. Arrange that feedback from the task itself will make the worker aware of his or her own contributions and accomplishments.

3. Reinforce the worker's desire to continue achieving by frequent supervisory recognition of his or her accomplishments.

To do an effective job of providing recognition through feedback, each supervisor should set up a feedback record of some kind in which notes may be kept on the performance of each individual in the newly designed task. This can be simply done in a loose leaf binder with a tab for each individual. Every week or so the supervisor should attempt to jot down a few notes on the performance of each person for use in informal reviews of progress and day-to-day words of encouragement.

Job Enrichment Calendars For Supervisors.   Every supervisor who will be involved in implementing job changes with subordinates should be equipped with a planning calendar of some kind to be used for Job Enrichment planning only. This seems almost too elementary to be worth mentioning; anyone whose supervisory job requires any degree of planning for future activity would naturally use such a device to keep track of due dates for training steps, installation of new tasks and responsibilities, evaluations of performance, and various assignments that may be necessary in the course of the job redesign. But the fact of the matter is that many first-line supervisors in all kinds of organizations do not handle planning activity at all well. For this reason Job Enrichment specialists will often find it useful to provide each supervisor with some simple planning tool such as a calendar book and encourage them to use it to keep all their Job Enrichment planning separate from other activities. The pace at which new job designs are installed and the period required to demonstrate results in a pilot project can be greatly affected by the ability of each supervisor to execute all the details of implementation. Tools for planning can increase effectiveness in this area.

The Project Follow-up Log.   If planning and control of details are important for the supervisor who implements the job changes, they are doubly important for the internal Job Enrichment specialist. The specialist will also have a myriad of things to follow up to ensure that key steps are not overlooked, that efforts are made to involve the entire work force in the job changes, that data are gathered for measurement, and that the many other implementation details that make the difference between success and failure are taken care of. Some form of follow-up log should be established in which all future follow-up steps are recorded. The specialist's visits with the project management team can then be thoroughly planned by use of the Item Control Charts, reviews of the Implementing Charts, and the Project Follow-up Log.

The Project Chronicle. It is very helpful, particularly on initial projects, for the Job Enrichment specialist to arrange for the establishment of a Project Chronicle, or narrative of key events—including such things as the main activities in the project, key steps taken for job redesign, problems encountered, the solutions chosen, reactions of the supervisory group and the work force to job changes, and the impact of the project on other work groups. Such a narrative can be of great value as a reference for other specialists as they are introduced to the program on later projects, or for anyone who has a need to review all the details of the project.

PROBLEMS OF SUPERVISORY STRUCTURE AND DEPARTMENTAL ORGANIZATION

As the process of redesigning jobs gets underway, the structure of supervision and supervisory roles should be closely examined. The deployment of people in supervisory positions and their relationship to managers and subordinates can be a crucial factor in several ways. Less than optimum arrangements can create problems such as those discussed below.

Overlap

A problem very common to the vertical hierarchy is the high degree of overlap among jobs. Often the concerns and responsibilities of the worker, supervisor, and one or two levels of management overlap to such an extent that it becomes difficult to distinguish the accountability of one from the accountability of the other. Final outcomes are difficult to link with individuals and achievements have little personal meaning. Overlapping job content and accountability often assume the pattern shown in Fig. 9.4.

Worker, supervisor, and manager are often found to be involved in the same concerns, sometimes even performing the same functions. Periods of stress, frequent breakdowns, high error rates, or a combina-

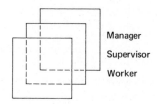

FIG. 9.4   Overlapping job content

tion of these often cause management to apply controls, and these controls frequently result in job overlap. Also, over a period of time, job overlap can result from the unwillingness of supervisory people to relinquish authority. In addition to its wasteful duplication of effort, the involvement of supervisory personnel in a high-overlap situation has negative effects in two ways: (1) It denies workers the satisfaction of knowing that their work assignments and responsibility are truly their own, and (2) it means that supervisory people are not free to perform the more challenging and innovative parts of their management role. In examining supervisory structure and job content, therefore, one principal objective will be to load responsibility downward and to lessen the overlap among jobs. The result will be a healthier set of job relationships (Fig. 9.5).

When serious efforts are made to give workers the freedom to perform their jobs on their own, make decisions, and be responsible for outcomes, a foundation is established for truly effective use of human

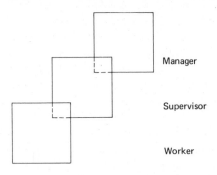

FIG. 9.5   A healthier relationship

resources. Job overlap becomes minimal, and the focus is on the results of activity rather than on control of it.

Inadequate First-line Supervision

The existing supervisory structure may be inadequate for the kind of supervision required for redesigning jobs and developing talent among subordinates. Some organizations simply fail to set up adequate supervisory positions, especially during periods of rapid increase in work volume, opting instead for a group of people to perform checks, quality controls, or troubleshooting to control errors and breakdowns (Fig. 9.6).

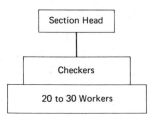

FIGURE 9.6

A work group structured in this way has two principal problems. First: the checkers have been set up as a stopgap measure to catch errors, and this means that the workers will inevitably feel less of a commitment to error-free work. Second: no effective first-line supervision occurs, since the section head cannot effectively evaluate performance or give developmental help and feedback to so large a work force. The result of these two factors is often a decline in productivity and work quality as people feel less and less responsible for their own performance. This usually leads to more controls, more checking, less autonomy for the job holders, and a descending spiral of effectiveness.

In many of these instances the work force may include several individuals with the skills and attributes that would qualify them for supervisory responsibility. In fact they often rise to the top as senior technicians or lead people to whom the others turn almost as though they were supervisors. A very good way to handle such situations (good both for the organization and for the personnel involved) is to make full use of the talent of such lead people by giving them true supervisory roles and titles. Keeping the responsibility where it belongs will avoid the build-up of layers of people whose only role is to check and catch errors—which, in turn, will avoid the steady erosion of job content.

Unnecessary Assistants

Another common problem in growing organizations (though it is also found in long-established organizations) is the tendency to create positions for assistants in various parts of the organization chart. We are not saying that assistant positions are always useless or unnecessary; in conditions of rapid growth the technical requirements of system changes can create a pressing need for assistance to people in line management capacities. However, such positions often become permanent features of the organization chart, creating several one-over-one reporting relationships that have undesirable consequences for both boss and subordinate.

At the lower supervisory levels assistants are often appointed when volume increases or breakdowns in work-flow are frequent—or even as a reward for past performance. Such appointments often reflect both a desire to give someone a measure of recognition and a reluctance to entrust that someone with true supervisory responsibility. Supervisory structure in these situations may resemble that shown in Fig. 9.7. In this pattern the assistant department head, or whatever the title may be, often finds there are real limits to the authority one can exercise on his or her own. It is often difficult for this individual to find opportunities for achievement, growth, or measurement of his or her own contributions. The assistant's job is often constrained and limited by that of the boss, because they are essentially sharing a function. (While this refers primarily to an assistant in a line capacity rather than an assistant performing a staff function, job emasculation can occur in either case.) On the other hand, it is possible for the boss to delegate so much responsibility to the assistant that the former finds himself or herself left with just the shell of a job; one in which there is little need or chance for continued involvement and growth.

The appearance of assistant supervisory positions in the organiza-

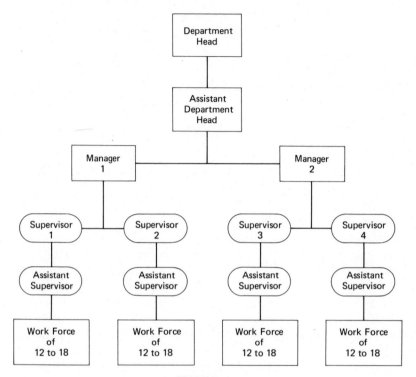

FIGURE 9.7

tion structure is often symptomatic of management unwillingness to entrust additional people with supervisory responsibility when volumes increase. It may also signify a reluctance to face the task of developing new first-line supervision, a common malady in many organizations. In either case the establishment of assistant's positions at these low levels can, and often does, result in several problems of job design. For example:

1. Responsibility shared at the lower levels often becomes a greater problem than at higher levels. Supervisory roles at these levels are frequently ill-defined at the start and often become obscured. Achievements and accountability become shared, which means a

distinct loss of motivation. Also, subordinates become confused as to who actually has the authority—the supervisor or the assistant.

2. Feedback to subordinates is often conflicting, when not simply neglected.

3. Many assistant supervisors become frustrated in their assignments as they begin to gather the confidence to supervise on their own. Without an official or meaningful capacity in which to act as supervisors they often become the most disgruntled individuals encountered in a work group.

4. If control over work assignments and employee development is retained by the supervisor, this often means that he or she has too many subordinates to be able to effectively implement and follow-up on job design changes during a job redesign project.

There is surely no all-purpose formula to follow in making decisions about supervisory structure. In the situation shown in Fig. 9.6, consideration should be given to keeping the jobs whole by eliminating or reducing the layer of checkers and establishing first-line supervisors for technical supervision and employee development. In the example shown in Fig. 9.7, the assistant's positions raise serious questions about the motivational content of jobs throughout the work group. The tasks and responsibilities in each assistant's position should be carefully reviewed to determine where one position may seriously impair another and to identify situations in which shared accountability may breed uncertainty and lack of fulfillment. From the standpoint of good job design the guiding principle for supervisory structure should be to set up separate and individual accountability for supervisory people wherever possible, using assistants only when forced to do so.

A review of supervisory structure should be a standard part of the analysis early in any Job Enrichment application. Waste of human resources is by no means confined to the nonsupervisory ranks and implementing new job designs can be a nightmare when obscure and overlapping supervisory relationships exist.

Organizing Work Groups by Function

Among the hundreds of organizations we have come in contact with, this is the most common error in organization structure that we found. The key problem is this: As volume or complexity increases in a business, the need arises for dividing up the work force into subunits, each with their own leadership. The most common tendency is to break up the work into areas of specialty, or functional units (if that has not already been done to reduce the span of tasks one employee must perform). Work-group organization then assumes a strictly *functional* orientation. The major consequence of this is that no single group, and certainly no single individual, can turn out a completed product or a whole service. As a result the key concept of "closure" in the work process is lost for both individuals and subunits. Since no group completes a whole job, there is invariably a lessening of commitment to the customer or client who receives the finished product or service. Feedback on task performance is less relevant, and significance of the task is reduced.

A variety of other ills stem from this approach to organization structure, not the least of which is intergroup bitterness among groups who depend on each other for completion of the work process. Figure 9.8 shows the structure of an organization with a functional orientation.

There is another crucial aspect to this question of the concept of work organization. A careful examination of supervisory structure and work-group organization should be made at the outset of any change effort. Also, if the organization of subunits in the work process is based on a fragmentation of the whole job, that will often mean that no meaningful Job Enrichment can occur without some significant combination of tasks across the subunits. This will later require reorganization of the structure of all work groups in the manner discussed in the next paragraph. To concentrate on only one or two sections for enrichment without including the others in a broader approach may well be a waste of time.

Our experience with such organization problems indicates that there are great advantages in having a customer or client orientation, the structure of which is shown in Fig. 9.9. In the client-oriented organization, work groups are so arranged that each one is responsible for a complete product, process, service, or assembly operation to the greatest extent possible. We have described here a concept which might be referred to as cross-functional organization of work groups. The rationale for it, of course, is to "nest" or gather all the various functions into a work group that is "whole," or responsible for a complete operation.

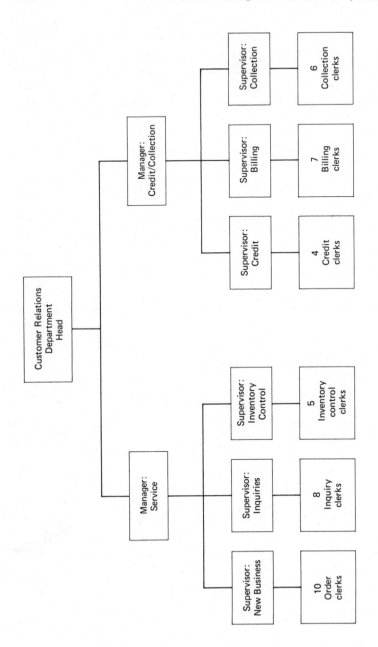

FIG. 9.8   Before redesign: Functional organization

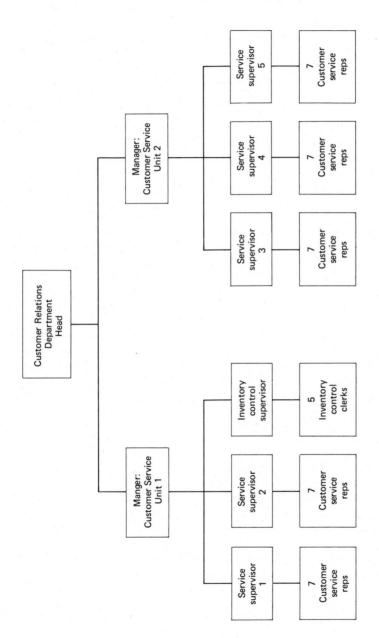

FIG. 9.9   After redesign: Customer- or client-oriented organization

The same concepts about whole jobs and task combination provide an excellent approach to work group organization as well. This is the concept that has generated the growing popularity of decentralized "profit centers," which so many companies are now using. The same concept can be seen in the organization structure of the mammoth General Motors Corporation. Alfred P. Sloan's genius for organization enabled him to see a long time ago the good sense of establishing separate whole product lines within a very large company. The various brand-name divisions of GMC operate much like separate companies in a sort of federal system. The sense of accountability and commitment to a particular whole product or service tends to provide a far greater motivational stimulus than would otherwise be the case and reduces the internal strain and dysfunction that often occurs with functional organization. The same principles apply on a smaller scale with sections, units, departments, and groups. In some cases it is even possible for a whole job to be done by one person—which has a terrific impact on that individual's motivation. Indeed, this job-nesting process has been the solution to many recent job-design problems.

Needless to say, it is highly important to examine the organization structure carefully as part of the total Job Enrichment process. Changing job content at low levels in a work group often stimulates redesign of organization structure, and is part of a very positive spreading of influence by the Job Enrichment activity. This can become a continuing stimulus for a total process of organization development on a broad scale. More is offered on this subject in a later chapter, under the heading "A Pebble in the Pond."

WHAT'S LEFT FOR THE SUPERVISOR TO DO?

This question is frequently raised in discussions when Job Enrichment is being considered. In fact, it is often asked by the supervisors themselves once they are included in the process of redesigning jobs for their subordinates. The answer is that there is plenty for the supervisor to do when enrichment gets under way—but the changes that occur both in perspective and in the supervisory role require the acceptance of responsibilities which may be new to most supervisors. The principle of vertical loading frequently causes certain tasks and responsibilities from the supervisory job to be loaded into the lower-level jobs which are the object of Job Enrichment. When this is done thoroughly, many supervisors find the content of their jobs substantially altered. This is especially true for any supervisors who have been heavily involved in the production work itself.

While these changes often come as a (sometimes unsettling) surprise to many supervisors at first, they do clear the way for each supervisor to step into a new role that can be vastly more satisfying than what he or she has been used to. As responsibility for the work is turned over more and more to those doing it, the role of the supervisor should become one of setting directions and goals, providing the work materials and training, and ensuring that conditions for his or her people are conducive to the fullest exercise of their abilities. The new role for the supervisor should include the following activities (which are sadly lacking at first-line supervision levels in many organizations):

1. Data gathering for trends and forecasts.

2. Work volume projections and work-force scheduling.

3. Training, both initial and remedial.

4. Goalsetting with subordinates.

5. Evaluation of performance and making performance reviews.

6. Continuous management of the enrichment process with each subordinate.

7. Counseling on both job and personal problems.

8. Innovative thinking about methods and procedures.

9. Effective communication about changes in company policy, objectives, and procedures.

10. Working on Hygiene problems that may be causing dissatisfaction or inefficiency.

In short, there is plenty left for the supervisor to do when enrichment gets under way. Effective enrichment of the jobs below them should enable supervisors to perform more truly the role of management. The corollary of that development is that managers at levels above the first-line supervisors should also become more free to pursue concerns of greater import and value to the organization than they have previously been able to do. This suggests an important point about the enrichment process: Far from being confined solely to people in jobs at the lowest levels in an organization, the influence of the enrichment process is often pervasive. As tasks and responsibilities are loaded from the supervisor's job to the jobs of subordinates, supervisors should be encouraged to examine with managers the relationships of their respective jobs. The result should be that supervisors reach up through the vertical loading process to take on some of the managing tasks and responsibilities formerly handled at levels above them. The enrichment process frequently results in a far-reaching reordering of roles in the management hierarchy, permitting a far wider use of talent at each level in the organization.

Supervisors commonly find the new role thrust on them to be a significant enrichment of their own work experience, and their responses are frequently enthusiastic. One supervisor in a recent project gave expression to a feeling shared by many others. She said of her job enrichment experience, "I had felt for a long time that something was wrong. I ran around putting out fires and trying unsuccessfully to control everything. Now my people are doing their own thing. I feel like a manager. Now I think I'm doing something more valuable."

Managers often complain that supervisors are not supervising and that the first-line of supervision is weak. The result, they say, is that they themselves become bogged down in the morass of day-to-day administration and concentration on short-term concerns. Among the most valuable by-products of a program of job redesign is a structured approach for getting lower-level supervisors to extricate themselves from production work and start administering their groups. Far from being left idle, supervisors will find that they have their hands full meeting the challenge of supervising in the truest sense of the word.

"BUT THEY'LL WANT MORE MONEY"

This is a fear commonly expressed by managers during early considerations of Job Enrichment. However, the best available evidence, from numerous companies, shows that few problems have arisen over pay in Job Enrichment applications. This is an indirect corroboration of the contention that workers do have things other than money on their minds, and it should be noted by those who view motivation solely in economic terms. In our experience, enrichment of work content has rarely led to demands for higher pay. Nor have we encountered refusals to accept added responsibility without increases of pay. Except where a great dissatisfaction over pay already exists, changes in job content to allow for greater use of skills and autonomy to make work more meaningful have not led to demands for matching pay increases.

This is not to say that matters of compensation should be ignored as Job Enrichment proceeds. Wise management reassesses job content as enrichment occurs and will be willing to share gains in productivity by reevaluating jobs and upgrading them where appropriate. This is especially important where savings have been realized through reduction of layers of supervision, checking, or quality control.

The relationship of Job Enrichment and compensation has become a positive factor in some projects in another way. A number of companies have had success with putting production workers on salary in order to put less emphasis on time as a determinant of pay and more emphasis on performance. The need to address compensation issues related to Job Enrichment should be recognized early in an application. Appropriate contact should be made with those who control compensation and salary administration in order to have them prepare for later reviews of job content and reevaluation of pay grades. Enrichment is normally done by identifying specific blocks of added responsibility or combination of tasks. When this is done selectively, by involving employees in job changes individually according to their readiness to accept them, the Job Enrichment changes can be grouped into blocks which can provide a useful framework for the establishment of new pay grades within an existing compensation structure. It should be obvious that matching newly established performance levels within a job with corresponding pay incentives yields a most potent combination for inducing improved performance.

Improving job designs for enrichment of work experience should not be viewed as a solution to employee dissatisfaction over pay. A problem of that nature is likely to persist even after improvements in job design; it may even become more acute. We must be aware that Job Enrichment is by no means a panacea for all forms of employee discontent; Hygiene problems call for Hygiene solutions. Furthermore,

Job Enrichment should never be used as a diversionary tactic in the hope that employees can be persuaded to accept more meaningful work and forget existing dissatisfactions about pay. (Recall our discussion in Chapter 4 of the basic dichotomy between Hygiene and Motivation problems in work behavior.) Long-term results are far more likely to be satisfactory if these sets of factors are considered separately and appropriate solutions developed for each.

WHAT ABOUT THE UNION?

Our long-range view is that union leadership will ultimately become a positive force pressing for increased attention to the quality of work life in industrial nations. After all, unions in the United States have led the fight for improved working conditions and laws that correct conditions that are detrimental to workers. This will include pressure for improvements in job design to allow more meaningful tasks and greater worker autonomy in the management of day-to-day work. Survey upon survey and study after study are driving home the significance of work as a key determinant of mental and physical health and avoidance of worker alienation. Although broadening of the base of union concern to include negotiation with management for more meaningful work will probably be a slow process, there are even now some definite signs of interest beginning to appear. Union leadership in several industries is beginning to recognize the growing unrest among rank and file workers in jobs that dull the spirit and deny any sense of personal significance. Indeed, the call for improved work content through job redesign is already appearing on bargaining tables in the U. S. auto industry and several others.

In today's environment, however, union interest in Job Enrichment is generally not keen enough to ensure a receptive attitude toward Job Enrichment initiated by management. In some companies the long established win/lose relationship between union and management may assure opposition to Job Enrichment simply because it is a management initiative. In one recently publicized case an innovative executive in the auto industry began serious, wide-spread efforts with all his subordinate managers to redesign jobs and improve the quality of work.

The undertaking was made solely on the initiative of management without union involvement in decisions or development of the program. Though significant successes have been scored with the redesign of a number of jobs, and reactions of workers have been favorable, official union response in this situation has ranged from tolerant skepticism to some vocal opposition. The key factor seems to have been the decision to deny union officials any direct involvement in the program. Opposition seems to stem from suspicion that management cannot really be so altruistic and a feeling that the effort is no more than a smoke screen for attempts to increase productivity or reduce staff. Perhaps an additional measure of opposition is generated by a "not invented here" attitude as well. Not many companies have yet tried major applications of Job Enrichment in a union environment and no definite procedures have been developed for that purpose. The bulk of experience and the most notable successes have been with white collar clerical or service work populations. But one characteristic is common to all the successful applications with unionized jobs: The legitimacy of union interest in matters of work content has been acknowledged and the union has been given a significant role in the initiation and development of the program. Some companies have begun by having union and management together explore the issues of employee and company goals and work satisfaction to identify areas of common interest. Others have been successful by starting with a management development seminar, attended by both managers and union representatives to explore together new approaches to management, behavioral science findings, and the importance of meaningful work. That shared experience then serves as a touchstone for establishment of a joint union/management effort to tackle the process of job redesign.

Whatever method of initiation is employed, the object must be to give union leadership a sound understanding of the fact that redesign of work using behavioral principles can serve employee and company interests simultaneously. It is certain that Job Enrichment has a far greater chance of success in a unionized organization when the union is given a continuing participative role in the development of job design changes to be implemented.

We feel it is not unduly optimistic to anticipate the time when joint efforts in the redesign of work will be recognized as a useful bridge between unions and management. It should become clear that this is one area in which employee and company needs coincide.

SUMMARY

This chapter has dealt with various problems and questions which commonly arise during the period of installing changes in job design. A number of techniques, strategies, and suggestions have been offered which have been found useful in clearing the numerous hurdles to be faced during this part of the process. Suggestions and techniques have been recommended for improved effectiveness in problem-solving, handling the first installation interviews with employees, overcoming resistance, and dealing with individual differences among employees. A number of tools for control of the project have been described for use by the Job Enrichment specialist and some questions related to the significance of supervisory structure have been explored. Other issues related to the impact of job enrichment on the supervisory role, matters of compensation, and union relations have also been addressed.

chapter TEN

Halfway Home

Several months of education, problem-solving, and installation of changes in job content are bound to raise a number of issues and problems that require attention, and the mid-project period is a good time to attend to them. This chapter describes a number of problems which can jeopardize a project at this stage and offers techniques for conducting different types of employee interviews, making an overall assessment of the project, dealing with factors that retard the impact, handling changes in the management team, and maintaining enthusiasm for continued hard work among the supervisors.

MID-PROJECT INTERVIEWING

A fatal mistake sometimes made by project specialists and managers is to measure the success of implementation at this stage by the items of job change installed and the number of people involved. Normally, it is premature to look for measurable signs of the impact of enrichment after only four to six months of activity. It is certainly too soon to expect reduction of such things as force loss and absenteeism. It is also too soon to look for definite improvements in attitudes about work. A longer period of time is required before new chances to excel and receive recognition in new areas of responsibility can produce attitude changes. Since the first hard assessments of impact may be months away, the tendency may be to assume that great progress is being made just because records show that a large number of items have been implemented and many people have been involved. That assumption *may* be well founded. Then again, it may not. The reactions of the employees affected should be sought periodically to be certain that the changes made are producing meaningful new experience in the work.

Sampling employee reactions at this stage will also indicate whether implementation has actually gone as far as records indicate.

Reactions from the work force can be gained through job reaction interviews, through exit interviews with those who are leaving, or through the establishment of group meetings using a sounding-board process described later in this chapter. As with the initial job-reaction interviews done during a feasibility study, interviews for assessment of job reaction should be done by the project specialist or someone who is not a member of the direct supervisor hierarchy in the work group. The interviews should be conducted in private, somewhere away from the immediate work site, with individual workers—or pairs of workers if some indicate a preference for that. It is also useful to tape-record these interviews for retention of data and for compilation of anonymous excerpts for reporting.

There are several objectives for mid-project job reaction interviewing. Among them are the following:

1. To determine how much positive or negative impact on work content has been achieved by the changes made.
2. To measure the actual extent of implementation.
3. To gain valuable insights into employee perceptions about the reasons for change.
4. To determine whether some items are working poorly or disrupting the work flow.
5. To evaluate the effectiveness of supervisor-implementing techniques.
6. To discover new items of job change through employee comments.
7. To determine whether there is need for additional communication or direct involvement of the job holders in planning future changes.
8. To determine whether there are factors involved that are retarding the impact or effectiveness of the changes in job content, such as significant Hygiene problems.

Before each interviewing session the interviewer should prepare a list of all the items of job-change that have been scheduled for implementation with each person to be interviewed. Checking this list against the information gained during the interview will enable the interviewer to evaluate the actual extent of implementation. The interviewer will also find it helpful to obtain some background data on each interviewee's past performance, absence, tardiness, and attitudes. Such information is useful in determining the significance of comments made during interviews.

Interviewing should begin with nondirective questioning similar to that used in the preliminary study. These nondirective questions are designed to elicit comments from the employee about critical incidents on the job. For example:

1. "What things do you recall from the last few months that have made you feel especially good on the job?"
2. "How could more of these things be made possible?"
3. "What things do you recall from the past few months that have made you feel especially bad on the job?"
4. "How could these things be reduced or eliminated?"
5. "How does your job as it is now compare with your job, as it was _____ months ago?"

The interviewer should encourage the interviewee to comment as much as he or she is willing to on these nondirective questions. Since the questions have not directed attention to any one item, the comments will show what job changes the interviewee considers to be the most significant. Next, the interviewer should ask for comment on specific job-change items that he or she wishes to know about. Finally, the interviewer should ask about those items of job change that the interviewee has not commented on: Have they in fact been installed? What is the interviewee's reaction to them? Can the interviewee suggest any improvements in these or other items?

Here are some additional questions that have been found useful:

1. "Have you considered quitting this job in the last _____ months? If so, what was it specifically that caused you to consider quitting?"
   (Or, as an alternative question: "Is it any more or less likely now that you would quit this job than it was _____ months ago?")

2. "Do you now feel any more or less likely to recommend this job to a good friend of yours than you did previously?"

3. "What do you feel still needs to be done to make this job better for anyone holding it?"

4. "Is there anything else at all you would like to comment on?"

These mid-project interviews often provide a wealth of information that is useful in assessing progress, identifying needs for coaching supervisors for improved implementation, and uncovering problems that impede progress. In many cases these interviews yield ideas for additional job improvements after employees have had some experience with new levels of authority, new tasks, and improved feedback. Much of this interview information will be very useful for feedback to the management team. Positive comments from the employees about improvements in job design will provide highly effective reinforcement and encouragement for the supervisors who have worked so hard.

EXIT INTERVIEWING

Exit interviewing can also be a prime source of valuable data about reactions to job experience, flaws in implementation, and possible new avenues for job improvement. To exploit this source of information, Job Enrichment specialists should attempt to interview every member of the work group who leaves or is terminated during the project. Further, the interviewer should use specific questions designed to probe for reactions to job content. Data from most standard exit interviews do not normally yield material that is of much use on this subject. Reasons given for leaving are usually evasive or innocuous in order to avoid unpleasantness, and rarely is very much learned about actual work experiences. However, when interviews are focused directly on experiences in the work, most people are willing to comment, and a great deal can be learned about job content as a factor in their termination. Often the honesty of people on the way out can uncover numerous weaknesses in the job design and indicate where redesign efforts should be intensified.

Numerous Job Enrichment specialists have found the following pattern of questions to be highly effective in exit interviewing:

1. "Why don't you begin by telling me how you happened to come to (name of company) to look for a job?"

2. "What was the deciding factor in your job choice?"

3. "How did you view your future here in the company when you first began?"
   (Note: Use this *particularly* with individuals who leave with less than one year of service.)

4. "Tell me *briefly* about your job assignments here up to your present job."
   (Note: Use this only if the interviewee has held several jobs in the company before the present one.)

5. "What did you expect of *this* job when you first began it?"

6. "Thinking over the past six months in your present job, tell me about some experiences or situations that made you feel exceptionally good."

   • "How long ago did this happen?"

   • "How did you happen to get the assignment?"

   • "What part did you play in it? What did you do?"

   • "Why did this make you feel exceptionally good?"

   (a) "Were there any other experiences or situations that made you feel exceptionally good that you can tell me about?
   (Note: this question is *optional*. If, in answer to question 6 the interviewee responds immediately by mentioning a good experience, the interviewer may want to ask about others, primarily because this program rests on and benefits from good experiences in a work situation.)

7. "Conversely, tell me of an experience or situation during the past six months that made you feel particularly bad."
   (Note: If the individual has been on the job less than six months, say "on your present job," instead of "during the past six months.")

   • "What would your feelings be about having an opportunity to discuss this with your boss?"

   • "Why do you feel that way?"

- "How would you have handled this situation?" (Regarding situation about which interviewer felt particularly bad?)

*8. "Let your mind turn back over your period of service here. Tell me when you first started to think about leaving the company."

  - "What happened to start you thinking along that line?"
  - "What else might have started you off?"
  - "Were there any other factors involved?"
  - "Why did this make you want to quit?"

9. "What finally made you decide to leave?"

10. "What are some of the things you'll be looking forward to in a new job?"
    (Note: Use this question with every separation category except retirement. If the individual is not going immediately to another job (e.g., if he or she is taking a leave of absence), acknowledge this fact with an appropriate preliminary statement and alter the question accordingly (for example, "If you should decide not to come back here after your leave of absence, what would you look for in your next position?").

11. "Pretend with me for a few minutes that you have the *complete freedom* to make *any changes whatsoever* in your job. What are some of the changes you would make?"
    (Note: If interviewee asks: "In connection with the work? Or other than the work?" the best response is, "Either or both. Whatever you feel should be changed.")

12. "If a friend of yours were looking for a job, what advice would you give him or her about coming here?"
    Optional probe: If answers are of a general nature, such as the

---

* *If the interviewee is being dismissed,* and has not mentioned that fact up to this point, use alternate questions 8 and 9 as set forth here. On completion of question 7, make some comment to the effect that "I understand that you've been dismissed." Then follow this immediately with: (8) "Tell me, what were the events that led up to your dismissal?" When this has been answered, ask: (9) "How do you feel these events could have been prevented?" When this question has been answered, proceed to question 10.

benefits are good, the people are friendly," the interviewer could ask: "What if your friend were interested in a job like the one you now have?"

13. "Are there any other comments you'd like to make about *anything* whatsoever that we haven't covered in the interview?"

CHECKING THINGS OUT WITH THE SUPERVISORS

Interviewing the job holders for reactions to job changes is only part of the process in "taking the pulse of the project," so to speak. The reactions of supervisors to their experience and their evaluation of the project's progress are equally valuable as feedback to higher management. Every supervisor who has been involved with implementation should be interviewed sometime in the mid-project period. Not only is it important to have their evaluation of their subordinates' job changes, it is also important to obtain their reactions to any changes in their own jobs. The supervisor's role and job content frequently change radically in the process of Job Enrichment, and their reactions to those changes can vary greatly. Many supervisors take to the vertical loading process readily and thrive on the newly found time to supervise—for which many have long felt the need without knowing how to obtain it. On the other hand, some supervisors may not see the importance of their new supervisory functions in developing the capacity and autonomy of their subordinates. They may feel uncomfortable with those new responsibilities. Some may feel out of their element when they become less involved in production work; they may think that they are losing control, and that their position or reason for being has been eroded and they may fear the risks involved in allowing greater autonomy for subordinates. It will be important for the Job Enrichment specialist to be alert for the development of such fears and, when necessary, to coach supervisors in accepting their new role.

The existence of such fears may become apparent as implementation proceeds, but individual interviews will usually bring them to the surface if they exist at all. In supervisory interviews it has been found quite useful to ask the following questions of supervisors:

1. "Please begin by describing what you feel has happened through

Job Enrichment over the last few months. What changes do you feel have been brought about?"

2. "How would you describe the impact of Job Enrichment thus far?"

3. "What would you say to supervisors elsewhere in your company if they were to ask you for an evaluation of Job Enrichment so far?"

4. "What things do you expect to see happening in the future with Job Enrichment?"

5. "What things do you feel have been especially good so far? And conversely, what things—if any—do you feel have been especially bad?"

6. "Are there things that you would have done differently?"

7. "How has your own job been affected? How do you feel about those changes in your job?"

8. "Are you concentrating your time on different things than you formerly did? If so, in what way?"

9. "How do you feel your role as a supervisor has changed?"

10. "Has your relationship with your boss changed with regard to your own independence and responsibility?

INVOLVEMENT OF JOB HOLDERS IN JOB REDESIGN

The need of workers to be involved in a job redesign program varies from group to group. In many cases the process can proceed smoothly and naturally with supervisors performing the entire redesign. In other cases the work group affected may show minimal or even negative response until its members are directly involved. The specialist and the management team must take care to sense the existing conditions and adopt a new model for implementation where necessary.

We counseled earlier that in many cases the members of the work force should not be directly involved in the redesign of their own jobs, and for organizations that have never included any of the work force in the planning of a change program it may be well to continue this policy. The reasons are pragmatic: Management is often very reluctant to allow workers time away from production to participate in planning; the increased numbers of those attending the planning sessions slows the progress of those sessions; and the participating workers, not knowing the responsibilities and limitations of management, may come to expect more and greater changes than are reasonable.

However, it must be recognized that when supervisors do all the planning of job redesign certain risks are involved. Employees may resent the fact that although this major change program will affect them, they cannot contribute to it—and this resentment could severely retard the progress of the project. Also, supervisors may not know the details of job content intimately enough to do a thorough job of design, and a number of potential ideas for job improvement may never be uncovered. And the workers' lack of direct involvement in the job improvement process may exclude them from a valuable job experience— one which could have been used as an effective selling point by management. The Job Enrichment specialist must therefore be on the alert for any signs that the workers should become directly involved in the enrichment process, or that they should at least be briefed or included in discussions about the program. The mid-project interviews provide a good opportunity to evaluate the extent to which the workers should be involved, for changes in implementation strategy can be made at this stage with less effect on progress than at other times.

Consider now an instance in which the workers show no signs of actual discontent over not being involved in the process but do raise frequent questions about what is going on. The case for the job changes being installed can be effectively presented at a briefing or meeting at which a Job Enrichment specialist discusses with the workers those features of the jobs which have made them monotonous or restricted in autonomy and feedback, the principles of humanizing job redesign, and the reasons why it is felt that both employee and company can benefit by improvement of the work content. As we have said before, there is no need at all to go into the background of behavioral science or the theoretical basis of Job Enrichment. Such information is completely unnecessary for the purpose at hand, and the workers understand and respond better when attention is focused on what is actually being done to improve their jobs.

When signs of trouble indicate that workers should be involved in job redesign there are at least three different methods of creating involvement. In some situations, the setting up of Natural Units of Work and task combinations may have led to the grouping of people into small teams. Where such groups have been formed it may be possible to have each individual group participate in brainstorming its own job improvement and implementation planning with supervisors. The groups' involvement should begin with a modified version of the supervisors' workshop described earlier. Once again, the focus is best placed on the practical aspects of job design principles rather than motivation theory.

Where such natural work teams do not exist, or where it is impractical to involve all the workers, certain workers can be selected, through whatever means may be appropriate, to join the supervisors' planning sessions after some orientation training. Another alternative is to form ad hoc groups of workers periodically to study certain aspects of a particular job change or to take full charge of planning for certain items.

To summarize this issue, our position is that organizations should try to involve people in working on the redesign of their own jobs wherever possible.

PERFORMING A PROJECT AUDIT

During the mid-project period (anywhere from the sixth to the twelfth month of implementation) it is prudent to step back from the daily activity of planning action and installation of job changes to take an objective, critical view of all that has transpired. A thorough evaluation should be done to look for weaknesses, areas of incomplete installation, missed opportunities, communication needs, and a host of other things which can effect ultimate success. Such a review is called a *project audit* or *project evaluation*. If performed carefully at a point in the project that leaves sufficient time to make changes and improvements, such an audit can make a very significant difference in the results obtained. The project audit is most effective when performed by an outside consultant or by a Job Enrichment specialist with extensive experience who may be guiding the efforts of subordinate specialists who in turn are directing their own projects.

The project specialist can make use of the guide as a self check to make a review of his or her own project. This method can be useful but the assessment is likely to be more valuable if it is done by someone other than the project specialist, someone who knows Job Enrichment but has not been closely involved in the day-to-day implementation. Observations by such an individual are likely to be far more objective. A complete project audit can normally be done in two to three days of interviewing and discussion with key people involved in the project.

Clearly there are a multitude of variables that can have an effect on the outcome of a project, and so it is sometimes difficult to know where to begin an audit. The subsection which follows presents a guide to how a project audit should be performed.

Guide for Job Enrichment Project Audit

The numerous variables that should be reviewed have been grouped into the 10 components listed below. The 10 numbered sections that follow offer suggestions for evaluating project effectiveness in each of the listed areas.

1. Work group selection and project model
2. Education
3. Staffing
4. Three P's of implementation: planning, problem-solving and pace
5. Implementation: real or imagined
6. Implementation management
7. Job design evaluation
8. Communications and dealing with the management hierarchy
9. Results and measurement
10. Management team autonomy and preparation for expansion

1. Work Group Selection and Project Model

1. Evaluate the choice of work group for the project.
   - Is it a "core job"? Will results from such a group be convincing?
   - Is it too large for the number of specialists assigned to it?
   - Are there too many in the supervisory team to work with at one time?
   - Is the project group so small that results may be jeopardized or considered not significant?

- Are there any obvious and unalterable limitations on the amount of job change that can be made?

- Has the project been limited to one part of a work group by prior choice when simultaneous involvement of other groups would have opened up far more potential for meaningful job change?

2. Evaluate the appropriateness of the project model for the particular situation faced. "Project model" refers to the series of activities and methods of implementation used. Specific things to consider here are:

- The timing of education sessions and implementation

- What parts of the total system of jobs are being addressed simultaneously

- How much attention is paid to follow-up and assistance during implementation by specialists

- Whether job incumbents are involved in the redesign of their own jobs

- The roles and responsibilities of project specialists and the management team

Setting up the project model requires care, for it is an area in which a number of debilitating mistakes can be made. For example: In some cases the project is overloaded with education sessions while there is very little implementation going on. This is often a holdover from earlier methods of management/supervisory development, in which the focus is usually on educating management to change attitudes in the hope that behavior will then change.

Some other projects have been weakened by the use of what may be called a "chain link" approach as opposed to an "integrated" approach. In the "chain link" approach a number of subgroups in a department or division are identified for involvement in the job enrichment project. There are two ways to involve them; in one a series of workshops may be held to achieve basic education of all the supervisory groups before any implementation takes place. The weakness here is too long a delay between the workshop phase and the implementation phase. The training for job redesign skills goes stale and commitment dissipates.

The other means of involvement is to complete a workshop with one group, then conduct implementation with that group, and then follow the same pattern with other groups. The problem here is that although a whole department or division may become involved over the course of a year or so, the process is piecemeal. Such an approach usually makes it impossible to see the whole operation as a job system in which all the functions are interrelated. The amount of improvement achieved may be only a fraction of what is actually possible through task combination, client relationships and feedback among the various groups.

The "chain link" approach also presents more risk of emasculating one job for the enrichment of another, because it focuses on only one job at a time. It also offers a greater likelihood of retaining fragmented jobs in the total work operation, since it may overlook many opportunities to combine tasks.

The integrated approach, on the other hand, avoids these pitfalls entirely. Conducting workshops among family groups of supervisors cuts across the spectrum of functions in a department or division. Having these different points of view brought to bear on related jobs will make the workshops more lively and much more productive. It will also make fewer of them necessary, which means a substantial saving in man-hours and money. This approach also makes it easier to identify supervisory or work leader jobs which may be unnecessary and which may, in fact, be having a detrimental effect on the work content of jobs below them. It will show up other problems as well, such as a plan that calls for fairly intensive early efforts to get action initiated but leaves the follow-up on implementation to local management. Follow-up and implementation assistance should be done by Job Enrichment resource people.

By all means use a systems approach and integrate the teams of supervisors to maximize the possibility of identifying task combinations, client relationships and feedback among work groups. Examine the job system as a whole before deciding on redesign steps and have the teams implement simultaneously. All factors bearing on the decision about involving incumbents in the redesign of their own jobs should be discussed with specialists and the management team. Later, interviews with people in the jobs will usually indicate whether the decision was sound and whether there is any need for change or for improved communications.

The roles and responsibilities of project specialists and the work group management team should be examined to determine whether a healthy balance is developing between assistance from specialists and autonomy for local management in the conduct of the project.

2. Education

The entire education phase should be reviewed to evaluate such issues as whether enough time was devoted to it, what training methods were used, and whether it was conducted in an environment that would maximize impact and learning. It may be useful to review all the training designs and materials used to identify weaknesses and suggest improvements. Interviews with supervision will usually indicate their grasp of theory and job design principles.

Examine also the need for education sessions with other groups, such as middle-level managers, managers of related work groups, systems and procedures specialists, and top management.

3. Staffing

Review of the number of projects underway and their magnitude should indicate whether the specialists are spread too thin to be fully effective or whether they could take on more than they are presently handling to expand the impact. Normally, three or four separate projects constitute a full load for a specialist. The principal consequence of having project specialists try to run too many projects at once is that they find too little time to dig for the data required for effective presentations on project results.

4. Three P's of Implementation: Planning, Problem-Solving, and Pace

There are several questions to be explored in evaluating these three aspects of project activity:

- Do initial brainstorm lists include effective methods for sorting out motivators from hygiene items?
- Are the selected items established in a sequence that both observes priorities and avoids conflict of one item with another?
- Was the objective of an overall optimum job design established and planned for early in the project?
- Is there an effective procedure in use for analyzing proposed job

changes before implementation? (This is to prevent later discovery of problems that result in withdrawal of an item because of failure to anticipate troubles.) If possible the audit should include evaluation of an actual implementation planning session for a critique of methods and team effectiveness to ensure that these sessions are maximally productive.

- With regard to the pace of change, is every effort made to capitalize on the workshop momentum of excitement and commitment in order to get things happening fast? For example, immediately after the workshop some simple items of job change should be installed to give the supervisory team some quick satisfaction at implementing change and to whet the appetite for more. A long period of delay with no actual implementation after the workshop will often result in a loss of enthusiasm which must be rekindled all over again later.

5. Implementation: Real or Imagined

Records of implementation kept by management should be reviewed to determine what items of job change should have been implemented, and with whom, prior to the date of the audit. During interviews with employees these items can be checked to ascertain the extent of actual implementation. There is often a great deal more on paper than has actually been implemented. It is pertinent to ask whether specialists have conducted their own mid-project interviews with employees to assess the extent of actual implementation.

6. Implementation Management

The audit should include evaluation of methods for controlling the multitude of details over which the Job Enrichment specialist must maintain surveillance in order to ensure effective follow through, analysis of overall project development, and analysis of the progress of individual employees. At the very least, there should be some way to see, at any point in the project, the status of each item of job change throughout the work group, records of the status of implementation with each individual employee, and a system for supervisors to use in gathering data for feedback on the performance of subordinates.

7. Job Design Evaluation

A crucial part of such an audit is a critical evaluation of the job design changes selected for implementation. All the items installed and intended for installation should be reviewed for effectiveness to determine whether the most meaningful new job design has been developed. It may be found that many Hygiene items have been mistakenly regarded as Motivators. Some specific areas for job design evaluation are:

- *Natural Units of Work.* If work is being distributed according to some system of individual units for employee accountability, are they the most meaningful that can be found in the type of work under study?

- Have opportunities for client relationships been overlooked?

- Has the redesign been focused too narrowly on one or two jobs, leaving too many others still fragmented?

- Could vertical loading of responsibility for increased autonomy and decision-making have been carried further? What is being done to encourage acceptance of added responsibility on the part of newer or less experienced employees?

- How effective are feedback systems? Are there sources of feedback data which have been overlooked? Do the feedback systems selected place too much of a record-keeping burden on the employees themselves to the point that the feedback value is destroyed? Is feedback established on an individual basis, and can each person see in some way the trend of his or her performance over a period of time?

8. Communications and Dealing with the Management Hierarchy

These two concerns are of special importance in evaluating initial projects, as the future of job design efforts and the commitment of top management depend on how well these things are handled.

- Are regular reports of progress made to higher management?

- Are other work groups kept informed of events in the project as appropriate to avoid conflicting activities?

- Even more important than formal communication is the relationship established with members of middle management who have a direct interest in the project. This should be thoroughly explored with the project team to determine what steps have been taken to go beyond mere communication and get middle managers involved in some way with project planning and surveillance. The steering-committee concept is an effective way to involve middle managers with this kind of planning and surveillance. Interviews with these managers will normally indicate whether they have been allowed to remain too distant from project activities with the attendant risk of their becoming obstructive at times when difficult decisions are to be made.

9. Results and Measurement

Once again, this is a matter which is especially important with initial projects. The following should be reviewed:

- Is someone specifically responsible for gathering data on the impact of the project and preparing it for recording?

- Evaluate the measures of impact selected. Are they the most effective available? Very often assiduous digging will reveal areas of impact which have been completely overlooked. The successes may be more impressive than specialists realize, especially if they are trying to deal with many work groups at once.

- Evaluate the process of surveying job reactions. How was the survey introduced? Is it likely that the person who administered the survey may have had any negative effects on trust and truthfulness due to his position in the organization or previous contacts with that work group?

- Are there any ways in which data on project impact can be translated into dollar savings or other terms which will be especially meaningful to line managers making an evaluation of the project?

10. Management Team Autonomy and Preparation for Expansion

As the project period nears an end and specialists prepare to move on to other work groups, attention must be given to the readiness of the management team to carry on with minimal assistance. Review the steps taken or planned for continuation of the effort. Once again, interviews with the managers and supervisors will give indications of their readiness to sustain activity by themselves. Has a continuation plan been worked out with the management team? If there are more items to be problem-solved and planned for implementation; have the managers and supervisors gained some experience in running their own sessions?

Or have other arrangements been made? What plans have been made for providing feedback on the project to the work force as needed? Have appropriate contacts been made with middle levels of management to ensure that continued interest is shown in keeping job design activity alive and that steps in the continuation plan are followed?

Plans for expansion of the effort beyond the pilot project should be reviewed. Are presentations to top management needed? Have contacts with new prospective client work groups been cultivated? Are there objectives set for additional projects in the coming months, and have advance preparations been made for adequate staffing?

THE MID-PROJECT REFRESHER WORKSHOP

After several months of implementation it is not uncommon to find that some doubts and uncertainty have developed on the part of the supervisory team. They have been working with concepts and activities that are new and unfamiliar. There are likely to be strains and tensions resulting from adding enrichment activities to their regular supervisory duties. Some will no doubt have difficulty handling the new role, which requires far more evaluation, feedback, and decision-making about the competence and development of subordinates than they are accustomed to. There may have been some periods of stress and confusion as a result of sweeping changes in work flow and task combination. In all likelihood the supervisory team has found that the transition from theory and conceptual mastery of Job Enrichment to actual implementation is a very taxing and difficult process. Their experiences with the day-to-day rigors of making Job Enrichment work may well have produced some wondering about outcomes and possibly some self-doubt about their ability to handle the new supervisory role. There may be indications of dissipating commitment as the going gets tough. For these reasons it is wise to consider a mid-project refresher workshop for the supervisory team. Purposes of such a workshop are to:

- Review the pattern of job changes to date and the purpose of each
- Review the extent of implementation
- Set goals for implementation in the coming months

- Share experiences with implementation and compare solutions to common problems
- Reinforce understanding of the principles of motivation job design
- Review results and anecdotes that indicate the effectiveness of job changes made. Every possible effort should be made to show this group the extent of their achievements and encouraging continued commitment. One day is usually sufficient time to accomplish the foregoing objectives. If at all possible it is best to conduct the session somewhere away from the worksite. This will permit complete concentration without intrusion by any of the daily work problems and will give the participants more of a feeling of stepping back from the details of implementation to take an objective view of what has transpired.

It is helpful to have a senior member of management attend the seminar, or at least deliver introductory remarks. He or she should emphasize the successes of those present, the signs of impact and the importance of their effort to the organization. This individual should strive to demonstrate in every way possible the continued support and enthusiasm from top management.

It is likely that a number of articles and case histories about Job Enrichment will have been published in the period since the beginning of the project. Some of this material may be used as the basis for discussion and comment for the purpose of adding new insights from up-to-date research and new findings about implementation techniques. Reviews of case histories and news articles about Job Enrichment activities in other organizations can help to stimulate an awareness of participating in an effort which has very broad significance and impact. There are also a number of films and videotapes available which can be used to review and reinforce understanding of motivation concepts and to provide a basis for discussion about implementation techniques.

Such a workshop can also include a fresh round of brainstorming for new items of job improvement or to tackle a job which has not yet been subjected to redesign.

Another useful activity, appropriate in some situations, is to have the supervisory team begin the process of redesigning their own jobs, using joint brainstorming by groups of supervisors and managers. This will be especially appropriate in cases in which a great deal has been accomplished toward loading functions and responsibilities from supervisory jobs into subordinate jobs. When this vertical loading process has been very effective, supervisors often begin to wonder about their own role, and the time is opportune for examining the content of jobs at higher management levels to identify those functions and responsibilities which would provide significant enrichment for the lower-level supervisory jobs.

chapter
ELEVEN
Finishing the Pilot Project

INTRODUCTION

Like a good story, most Job Enrichment projects can be viewed as having a beginning, a middle, and an end. In neither case does the ending come automatically or accidentally. It must be planned, and it must be integrated into the overall structure. Otherwise, no matter how interesting the story or project may be along the way, it simply comes to a halt without a payoff.

The previous chapters have described the activities that take place in the beginning and the middle of the pilot project. Now we turn to those that provide the final thrust toward completion.

Exactly what must be done in the completion phase differs from project to project. However, three basic objectives can be identified:

1. Finish implementing any job changes not already installed.
2. Develop autonomy for the internal management team.
3. Report the results as appropriate.
4. Planning for continuation.

If the project has followed a typical course, the roles and relationship of the work group's management team and its consultants—internal or external—will have changed along the way. In the completion phase the pace of change should be quickening considerably as the management team assumes more responsibility for Job Enrichment. In this chapter, therefore, we shall distinguish particularly between the roles of the management team and the consultants in each major area of activity.

WINDING UP IMPLEMENTATION

A given Job Enrichment project typically follows one of two basic patterns, and the dominant pattern determines how many loose ends of implementation remain to be tied up. In the first pattern, usually involving clerical or production workers, the principal problem is fragmentation of tasks. Thus the basic method of attack is to combine tasks where possible, set up natural units of work, and develop client relationships. In this pattern, the changes are usually so interrelated that they have to be made all at once, or in no more than a few clusters. The changes are done in neat packages, and the completion phase usually has little concern for further implementation.

The second basic pattern occurs frequently in the jobs of technicians, professionals, and managers. The problem is generally not fragmentation, but a lack of autonomy and feedback. So the emphasis in enriching the job falls on vertical loading. Since task combination is less important, implementation can be more selective. Thus, as the completion phase arrives, project personnel generally find that some proposed job changes have been introduced fully to some employees, partially to some others, and not at all to a few.

The first concern in the completion phase is to finish implementing the planned changes. Chapter 9 described the Item Control Chart as an aid to implementation. On this chart the project director writes down every item of job change, how it was implemented, with which workers it was first implemented, the dates, a description of any development or training required, and other appropriate comments.

The chart can prove very useful in the completion phase. The project director, and particularly the supervisors, can go back to the chart for a picture of the overall state of implementation. Then, working from the chart, they can take the following actions:

1. Install all job change items that have not been introduced so far.
2. Check the items already introduced to see if they can be extended. It is usually possible to extend the changes in one or two ways. They can be introduced in additional jobs, or jobs that have already been changed can be changed further. Vertical loading is usually full of possibilities at this point. Task combination is typically far advanced, but further enrichment is possible by adding to the new job module more autonomy by granting higher levels of authority, approval, or decision-making.

3. In all cases where there seems to be room for more enrichment, supervisors should prepare for each individual a plan that tells: (a) how the job has been enriched so far, (b) how the individual has responded, (c) what other possibilities there are, and (d) what kind of training or development is necessary for those who haven't been started yet.

In this process it is important to check for people who might not have been in the work group when Job Enrichment began, or who for some other reason were left out. Each supervisor should set up schedules for implementation and for any training that may be needed. Target dates should be firmly fixed.

Feedback

As a concept of job design, feedback should rank high, whether the dominant mode of enrichment is task combination or vertical loading. But precisely because one or the other of these concepts tends to dominate every Job Enrichment project, feedback is often unduly neglected. Of the major factors in job redesign, it is probably the most easily overlooked.

The completion phase is the time to check out the possibility of such oversight and correct it. The project team should ask such questions as: Are employees correcting their own errors in every possible case? Does the client relationship, if any, provide for the actual user of the employees' services to indicate how well the services meet client needs?

Two possible sources of feedback are especially likely to be overlooked. The first is the operating measures provided to top management. Chances are there is information in these measures that could be made available to the work group as a basis for comparing performance trends.

A second source is the technology or equipment being used. It may have features or possibilities that could provide feedback if someone took a Job-Enrichment perspective on it. For example, it might be possible to change a computer program slightly so that operators or other employees would get feedback in a printout or through a terminal.

Most work situations contain more feedback situations than are apparent. It may be useful in many cases to hold a special planning workshop in the completion phase, dealing exclusively with ways to improve feedback.

STRENGTHENING THE REWARD SYSTEM

An enriched job does not exist in isolation, but is a nodal point in many systems that make up the whole company. If Job Enrichment is to achieve maximum results, changes in the individual job and work group must be supported and reinforced by those systems as much as possible. Two systems are particularly important: the reporting system and the reward system. The first has been discussed in connection with feedback, which is the aspect most important to Job Enrichment. The second, the reward system, should now be examined in two aspects of its own.

Aspect 1. Job Enrichment almost necessarily implies new definitions of jobs. If task combination is the dominant mode of enrichment, tasks formerly split among several different job classifications are likely to be telescoped to make "whole" job modules for several people. If vertical loading dominates, employees will be given new and higher levels of responsibility.

The act of enriching jobs sends a message to employees. It tells them they are valuable to the company, and the company is taking steps to make sure that they have a chance to use their talents. Job Enrichment produces higher levels of value for the company. The reward system should be adjusted to reflect the changing job definitions and the increased productivity. If the reward system is not changed, employees are really subject to two conflicting kinds of messages: The job itself says "You're more valuable," and the pay structure says "Nothing has changed." Some employees are bound to think that Job Enrichment is just management's fancy name for getting more work at the same pay. This is a risk particularly in those cases in which job restructuring permits work-force reductions.

Aspect 2. Even when the supervisory job is not the target of Job Enrichment, it usually changes. As authority is passed down to the workers themselves, supervisors find themselves with more time for the responsibilities of planning and development.

For some supervisors the change in the content and focus of their jobs will create a challenge. They will respond by taking on new responsibilities, and by actively helping their workers adapt to Job Enrichment.

For other supervisors the loss of tasks and responsibilities will only create a void, not a new degree of freedom. They may see their jobs as being diminished, and perhaps because they feel insecure about this, they will be passive and shy away from unfamiliar challenges.

The reward system should be overhauled both to reflect the new responsibilities and tasks of all workers and to reinforce the behavior of those supervisors who respond well to the new challenges of their own jobs. The overhaul may mean raises, reclassification of some jobs, or perhaps creation of whole new classifications. The goal is to make the reward system confirm the constructive change made by enriching jobs, not to undercut it.

BUILDING AUTONOMY

As a Job Enrichment project gets underway, its leadership is quite naturally in the hands of the people who know the most about Job Enrichment. These may be staff specialists, outside consultants, or, very often, both working in cooperation. If Job Enrichment is to become integrated into the organization, its leadership has to be transferred into the hands of line managers. The trend should become increasingly evident as the project goes along. By the completion phase the transfer should be all but finished.

Just as the need for additional implementation in the completion phase is influenced by whichever mode of enrichment has dominated the project, so the building of autonomy is influenced by another characteristic of the project model: the degree to which employees themselves have participated in the process.

Direct involvement of employees in redesigning their own jobs is a possible source of problems, although it may be necessary in technical jobs where the worker himself knows the opportunities and limitations better than anyone else. This is, of course, the kind of job most likely to be enriched through vertical loading.

Where task combination and the building of work modules have dominated the enrichment process, direct worker involvement has probably been slight. However, the emphasis on team task modules provides a natural springboard for building up a large degree of autonomy in worker teams. After tasks have been combined to make natural units of work and/or team task modules, the completion phase is the time to round out the enrichment process with autonomy. The internal specialist or consultant can get this process under way by individual conferences with each supervisor to discuss ways and means. Another possibility is to run another round of greenlighting sessions focused on ways to increase work-group autonomy.

Two levels of autonomy. In the context of the completion phase, autonomy actually operates on two levels. First, it applies to the self-regulating aspects that are built into a job in the process of enriching it. Second, it applies to the capacity of line managers and supervisors to take on responsibility for continued management of the Job Enrichment function, which at the start of the project was almost entirely in the hands of internal specialists and consultants.

A key concern for consultants. At this point the consultant should be putting special emphasis on his or her own gradual withdrawal from a central role. The burden of implementation should have shifted to the management team.

The consultant should continue to be available as a resource person, but this is not likely to happen unless it is planned for and structured properly. At this point the management team needs coaching in the techniques of implementation, general help in problem solving, and perhaps some special help in overcoming resistance to change. In a few organizations—very few, in our experience—it may be enough to make clear to the management team that these forms of assistance are available on an open-door basis as needed.

A more satisfactory policy, for most organizations, is to offer such help in some sort of structure. One suggestion is to schedule sessions with individual supervisors, in which the consultant helps them with problems summarized beforehand in a resume.

If the problems come up frequently, with more than one or a few supervisors, the consultant may decide they can best be handled by a group session adapted to the particular problem. For example, if many supervisors are encountering resistance to Job Enrichment changes among their workers, the consultant may schedule a role-playing session in which supervisors can develop some insight into the sources of resistance.

THE FINAL PHASE OF MEASUREMENT

At various points we have laid special emphasis on the need for comprehensive measurement of the project. In the completion phase there are two principal sources from which measurement data can be gathered:

1. The performance data that have been monitored throughout the project should be scrutinized to see what facts will be most significant in management's evaluation of the project.

2. The Job Diagnosis Survey[1] given at the start of the project should be repeated—for several reasons:

    a) Comparison of the "before" and "after" results of the survey will indicate just how successful the job design changes have been in changing employee attitudes.

    b) The Job Diagnosis Survey will indicate the need strengths of the employees in the project, and will possibly indicate that the new job designs may require some revision of hiring criteria or other aspects of manpower planning.

    c) Such a survey may indicate some continuing weaknesses in job design. Even when the formal project test period is drawing to a close, it is usually not too late to hold further greenlighting sessions aimed at strengthening the job. Depending on the timing, the additional changes suggested can be implemented immediately or scheduled for a second phase.

PRESENTING THE RESULTS

There are two basic criteria by which a Job Enrichment project usually has to be judged successful. First, it should produce the measurable changes in attitudes and performance it set out to achieve. Second, it should persuade management that Job Enrichment is a valid intervention technique, worthy of wider use in the organization.

A Job Enrichment project can be expected to meet the first of these criteria if it is correctly diagnosed, carefully planned and controlled, and thoroughly implemented. But even this success is not sure to convince management unless the presentation of results is carefully planned.

In most cases the results are presented in two ways—in a basically oral presentation to a meeting of selected managers, and in a printed final report. These two formats of presentation are different but complementary, and each demands special planning.

The Oral Presentation

A Job Enrichment project that has gotten results usually provides mountains of statistics and other material that could be reported to management. Since consultants and managers who have achieved the results are proud of their success, they may be tempted to try to put all the facts into the oral presentation to management. This is a pitfall to be avoided.

The oral presentation is an opportunity to sell with facts. As usually set up, it includes not only selected members of top management, but also other middle managers, outside the original project, who might be considering Job Enrichment projects of their own. The presentation is thus a bridge to expansion of the Job Enrichment effort. Although based on facts, it should leave the heavy detail to the printed report, and concentrate on techniques of persuasion that are characteristic of any good sales effort.

The following general rules can generally lead to a convincing presentation:

- Since the basic material of the oral presentation will come from the printed report, plan to finish it in ample time for use of its materials in the presentation.
- The printed report is often distributed at the oral presentation. If you plan to do this, keep the copies out of sight—perhaps in another office—until you are ready to hand them out, so that your audience will not be distracted or tempted to take up specific questions out of the order you plan.
- Avoid surroundings that would make the atmosphere too heavy—for example, very formally furnished boardrooms. We have seen

some of these that, aside from their formality, are just too big to encourage face-to-face communication.

- Make it clear at the start that questions are welcome during the presentation—that you want to talk *with* your audience, not *at* them.

- Since you are structuring the meeting to handle questions, try to anticipate them and have answers ready.

- Be ready to distinguish between discussion on central points and digressions into detail. Use discretion in limiting discussion as necessary.

- State at the beginning how long you expect the presentation to take. Aim for an hour or less.

- Include lower-level supervisors and employees in the presentation whenever possible. Few things are as impressive to the president of a company as seeing lower-level employees swallow their nervousness and make a presentation at the highest level.

- Decide who will take part in the presentation. Assign responsibility for various aspects to various people. This adds variety to the presentation, and also takes the pressure off one or two people.

- Practice, practice, practice. Hold a dry run—or several. Objectives should be to coordinate various versions of what will be said; make sure no one will be surprised by what someone else should have told him but didn't (it happens); and get people more or less free of their notes, if they plan to use any.

- Avoid heavy detail, especially strings of statistics.

- Use graphics. They can make the cold statistics more dramatic and colorful and give participants a memory device that can be used less stiffly than notes.

- Don't shun humorous relief if it is natural and unforced in terms of the audience and the situation. It's probably a good idea to avoid the setup "First I'm going to tell a funny story" approach. If a key person in your audience has a reputation for humorlessness or strictly no nonsense, you may do well to avoid comic relief altogether. But in most cases a spontaneous one-liner, or a visual gag among the charts or slides, is welcome.

The Final Report

The audience for the printed project report includes the audience for
the oral presentation, but is broader and, in some respects, deeper. Thus
the printed report has to serve more purposes. Here are some uses we
have identified in our experience with varied companies:

- It gives members of the original audience a memory aide, a written
  record, and greater detail about what has been summarized in the
  oral presentation.

- It influences executives in other departments or divisions beyond
  the original audience to consider Job Enrichment efforts of their
  own.

- If these other efforts are accepted, the report gives other specialists
  a chronicle of the project.

- It fills a formal commitment to top management, either one made
  specifically in connection with the project, or one demanded by
  organization policy or tradition.

- It provides a source for general information about the project which
  may be disseminated beyond the organization. For example, an
  account of the project, its aims, and its results, without operating
  figures, might make good public relations material for shareholders
  or the general public. Or it might be a useful contribution to a
  management or behavioral science journal or conference. (All these
  last uses, of course, should be cleared with public relations staff in
  most companies.)

Contents of the Report

Any dozen reports on Job Enrichment projects might differ in many
ways yet all still be excellent. The differences arise from such factors
as who writes the report, who the audience is, and what kinds of pub-
lication resources the organization commands. There are probably no
unbreakable rules about format or order of presentation.

If there is an unbreakable rule, it is that the report must be self-
contained. Whoever writes it should assume that the potential readers
know absolutely nothing about the project in particular or Job Enrich-

ment in general, and that they have no familiarity with feasibility studies, interim reports, or accounts of similar projects elsewhere.

The following list is drawn from the author's acquaintance with final reports on Job Enrichment projects in client companies. We believe that by covering these areas, a report can be adequate to its mission without demanding excessive time either to write or to read.

Executive overview. This is the first section inside the cover, even before the table of contents. It should summarize the salient points of the project in no more than one or two pages: Why the project was undertaken; the major steps; the most significant results; cost savings.

Table of contents. List all material contained in the report.

Introduction. This section should outline the problems or considerations that led to the Job Enrichment trial. If there is any background material of special relevance to the industry or the work force in question, it should be filled in briefly. Explain why Job Enrichment was identified as a possible solution to the problems, and describe briefly the principles of job design for enrichment. (Some organizations split the introductory material and the description of Job Enrichment into two sections. This approach seems particularly advisable if the specialized data on the industry or the work force are on the long side.)

Description of the project. This section should make clear what changes were made to the target organization in the period of the test. Follow some logical sequence—for example, chronological or order of importance. Cover changes in the content and structure of each job affected, changes in supervisory relationships, controls, pay grades, etc. Try to link each change to a basic principle of job design. In each case, try to make clear how things worked before and how they work now. Often the best way to do this is to use simple diagrams and organization charts.

Description of results. Outline here what changes took place in the operating results, personnel measures like turnover and absenteeism, and attitudes. Explain briefly what were the bases of measurement. Point out and explain any particularly striking results. Again, use charts and graphs to clarify whatever you can.

Measurable improvements in operating results are the most important facts to line managers. However, the results cannot be limited only
to the "hard" measures. Sometimes the change in organizational tone
wrought by the Job Enrichment project can be conveyed best by describing in narrative form how certain organizational roles—particularly supervisory roles—were transformed. Another effective method
is to quote the most telling passages from employee interviews conducted before and after the project.

Conclusion. The quotations may be the most effective way to end the
report. In other cases you may want to add a page or two of evaluation. It might deal with particularly gratifying aspects of the results—
or even some disappointments. It should convey what the organization
learned through the project. And it might assess prospects for further
use of Job Enrichment.

A report that covers all these areas will be pretty complete for
most of its intended uses. Some organizations, however, like to include
more description of the survey methods, implementation techniques,
training methods, and management meetings. Provided the amount of
detail is not too great, this material can sometimes be covered in the
body of the report. Otherwise, it is often advisable to put it in a separate appendix at the end, where it will not impede the flow of the basic
story.

Finally, if the project has been preceded by a feasibility study, it
may be enough to refer readers to descriptions of study methods and
the implementation techniques which typically accompany such studies.
This short cut does not make the report less useful for most of its
audience, and does not violate the rule that the report should be
self-contained.

Who Prepares the Presentations?

The responsibility for preparing the oral presentation and the written
report can rest with the outside consultant, the internal specialist, or
the head of the project management team.

As experienced consultants, the authors strongly recommend that
the report responsibility be kept within the organization. Many con-

sultants have the capability to prepare the reports and presentations and are not unwilling to do so. Few of them, however, would claim that writing reports is the best use the client can make of their time. Besides, having the report done inside has certain positive advantages, the most important of which is that internal preparation creates more feeling of involvement and ownership. By the end of the project, a good consultant certainly has all the material he needs to write the report. If he does a good one, the consultant looks good to management. But this should not be the consultant's objective. He should be finding every possible way to get managers to demonstrate their ownership of the project and reap its rewards.

Although the authors make this situation clear to their clients— often in words nearly identical to those above—many clients still want the consultant to prepare the report. The usual reasoning is that the consultants have all the facts at their fingertips as a result of their study of the problem in the first place; and that they do such reports all the time, and can therefore do them quickly.

In fact, a consultant who has done a thorough job does have most of the facts readily at hand—but not all of them. A good many, including those on which measurements will be based, are just as readily available to internal people.

True, the consultant's experience in conceptualizing the kind of information that goes into reports probably lets him work faster. But this in itself is an argument for having the report done internally, for it's the internal personnel who need the experience, not the consultant. Especially if the internal specialist or key man is to be involved in other organization development projects as an in-house consultant, he should have the capability to prepare good reports quickly.

In practice the typical final report is a collaborative effort. Some material comes from the outside consultant, some from internal staff, and some from the managers within the project work group. What is important is to assign the responsibility for coordinating all these sources and getting the inputs all together.

The contents of the report, as outlined in the previous section, can serve as a basis for organizing and delegating the process of preparation. The consultant might be called on to provide some of the theory of Job Enrichment. The personnel function could provide special data on the work force and personnel measures. Bases of measurement of performance could come from industrial engineering or another appropriate source.

None of these delegations has to be ironclad. The point is that the work of writing the report can be shared if the responsible person does not do it all himself. It is important that the responsibility be fixed early. Then the responsible person can keep records of all the things that occur in the project, with an eye to including them in the report.

CONVEYING RESULTS TO EMPLOYEES

Once the report exists and the results are in management's hands, the Job Enrichment project is virtually finished. There is, however, another step in disseminating the project results: conveying them to the employees of the work group.

Because Job Enrichment emphasizes feedback, a well-run project is likely to have given continuing knowledge of results as it goes along. Even so, the end of the project ought to be marked by some sort of official feedback of total results—not least of all so that the workers will not suddenly feel out in the cold while the success of "their" project is celebrated elsewhere.

The exact medium and format of the feedback may differ from one organization to another. A brief meeting, even in the work area itself, may be appropriate in some organizations. A letter of appreciation from management to the individual employees may be right in another. In a few cases, the oral presentation already made to management might be adapted. Choice of medium and format will be influenced by the size of the group and the overall organization, the sophistication of the work group, and other factors. But in any case, there should be this specific form of feedback.

FIXING ACCOUNTABILITY FOR CONTINUATION

By the time the project is drawing to a close, it should be fairly obvious what the future of Job Enrichment in the organization is to be. Now is the time to fix responsibility for assuring that future. First, someone within the original project should be chosen to review all significant actions or decisions affecting the work group for their effects on job design. Second, if Job Enrichment is to be extended to other work groups, the internal key man should be picked to coordinate the effort. In practice this is often done in the early state of the original project. If so, it is still necessary to devise a fairly detailed schedule of the handing over of duties from the external consultant to the key man inside.

Since changes in job design were accomplished in a structured situation, it must be remembered that the process of Job Enrichment is never finished, and so there is really no end to it. Workers at all levels will learn the new designs, and once they have mastered these new experiences they will be looking for more. So management can never relax but must continually think of what they can do next to continuing the human learning and growing process.

REFERENCES

1. Either the Edgar Borgatta *Job Reaction Survey* or *The Job Diagnosis Survey* are appropriate. Both are available through Roy W. Walters & Associates, Inc.

chapter TWELVE

Assuring a Successful Job Enrichment Project: a Checklist

INTRODUCTION

The premise of this book is that Job Enrichment can work to solve motivation and performance problems in a variety of business and other management situations. Preceding chapters have described in detail the underlying concepts of Job Enrichment and the steps to practical application. If those steps are followed reasonably well, the project should have a high probability of success.

It is only realistic, however, to acknowledge that at each stage of a Job Enrichment project there is potential for errors of omission or commission which can weaken the project even to the point of failure.

Many of these problems have been mentioned along the way, and their solutions at least implied. We bring them up again to review them systematically and to show how they may be used as the basis of one more practical tool: the project checklist.

The errors that doom a Job Enrichment project to failure often occur through inadequate planning or oversight. Compared to other methods that are designed to ensure that all factors are considered, a checklist may seem mechanical and oversimplified. Considerable experience has demonstrated, however, that such a device, available for quick reference as the project moves through its various stages, often makes the crucial difference.

FACTORS THAT LIMIT THE SUCCESS OF JOB ENRICHMENT

The problem points of a Job Enrichment project can be numerous, and are never quite the same for any two projects. They arise in conjunction with the following matters:

- Timing of the Job Enrichment effort
- Degree of commitment
- Scope of the initial project
- Diagnostic procedures
- Communication
- The project model
- Education
- Problem solving
- Organization
- Long-term planning
- Installation
- Measuring and reporting of results
- Building an internal consulting cadre
- Expansion
- Longevity

We shall discuss briefly some problems to be avoided in each of these areas.

Timing.   There are two general cautions to keep in mind about timing. First, Job Enrichment through redesign often causes quite sweeping organizational change. Change encounters resistance. So if it can be avoided, Job Enrichment should *not* be introduced into a situation in which current or recent changes of other types have already caused anxieties among employees. Examples might include a merger or a large-scale conversion from manual methods to automation. This is not to say that Job Enrichment should *never* be attempted in such situations—but caution is advisable, since the rigors of job redesign may be too much at such a time.

Second, in any organization there is continuing competition for a finite amount of resources. Installing Job Enrichment takes resources of time, money, and manpower. It is generally not wise to undertake a Job Enrichment effort unless it can reasonably be assured a priority high enough to command the necessary resources. If you can do it better later, postpone it.

Commitment. As mention of priorities suggests, the commitment of management (at all levels, but particularly at the top) to a Job Enrichment project may vary with the urgency of other demands on resources. It can vary for other reasons as well.

A Job Enrichment initiative has to come from somewhere. The critical question, in terms of commitment, is whether the initiating individual or group finds the organization sufficiently receptive to the idea.

It should be made clear that total commitment is not vital, even from top management, nor is it common. On the other hand, outright hostility at the top is probably a hopeless climate for Job Enrichment, particularly if the hostility is likely to be acted out in policy or organization changes incompatible with Job Enrichment. Probably the minimal requirement is a pragmatic "Show me" attitude on the part of top management and a few key people lower down. Such a climate neutralizes emotional factors and emphasizes results.

Paradoxically, the other extreme can be just as troublesome—the case in which the initiative comes from top management, and Job Enrichment is forced on the rest of the organization. Again, change is threatening. Resistance can be overcome, but not very easily if employees' normal anxieties are amplified by resentment at having change imposed from too far above.

Scope. Broadside application of Job Enrichment is a more common error than is too-restrictive application. It creates three general types of problems. First, it tends to create more change than the organization can easily assimilate. Second, it strains the internal resources available. Third, it deprives management of the opportunity to evaluate job designs and shake them down before they are widely applied.

It is possible, however, to make a Job Enrichment project too narrow in scope to produce best results. For example, a Job Enrichment specialist might be asked to develop new job designs for clerical workers in a computer department, because that is where management can see the most obvious signs of poor morale and productivity. The specialist might determine quite early, however, that the best job design will result from integration of the clerk's job with that of a computer terminal operator. If he concentrates narrowly on the one type of job originally brought to his attention, he develops only a partial solution. A specialist contemplating Job Enrichment within a given context should not let his horizon be limited by someone else's concept of a single job.

Diagnostic procedures. Although the techniques for diagnosing organizational ills (and the suitability of Job Enrichment as a remedy) have recently improved dramatically, diagnosis remains one of the weakest aspects of the typical Job Enrichment project. In fact, the hot issue of whether Job Enrichment is no more than "a fad or a fraud" ultimately hinges on misuse or nonuse of the diagnostic methods.

The highly visible successes of Job Enrichment have made it a buzzword, and have created a tendency toward viewing Job Enrichment as a panacea. However, there are many cases of poor productivity in which human factors are not the major or even the contributing causes. Even when human factors are crucial, the situation may not call for job redesign. All these situations can be sorted out by increasingly sharp diagnostic tools.

The most common reason for skipping or slighting the diagnostic phase is overenthusiasm. Someone gets religion about Job Enrichment and manages to talk other converts into a premature commitment. A project then gets launched without a diagnostic effort to determine whether Job Enrichment is really appropriate.

Suppose a manufacturing company encounters low productivity and high error rates with sophisticated new machine tools. Engineers may put the blame on the operators, although the real problem is that the machines are not properly adjusted and debugged. Alternatively, it may be that the machines are suitable and properly set up, but that the operators are inadequately trained. Neither case involves a motivational root—although they could ultimately affect motivation adversely.

Finally, the technology, training, and job design may all be fine, and the poor performance be rooted in interpersonal group conflict. Team-building, conflict resolution, or some other organization development technique may be what's needed.

In none of these cases would Job Enrichment be the appropriate solution. Applying it could mean almost certain failure—a failure that could have been avoided by proper diagnosis.

Communication. The most pervasive communications problem in Job Enrichment projects is too little diffusion of information. No one, at any level, likes to be kept in the dark about changes that will affect him. Problems can start as early as the diagnostic stage. If one day an interview or written questionnaire is sprung on workers, or if they become aware that certain jobs are under special scrutiny, they are likely to become uneasy and balky unless they have been prepared with an explanation of the objectives and the possible outcomes. Poor communications can also undermine a sense of being constructively involved in the changes taking place, and thus weaken support. In addition to serving these essentially psychological functions, good communications channels also provide the organization with a flow of practical information which becomes more vital than ever when change is under way.

A particular weakness of communications in many projects is the lack of provision for dealing with the fears of middle managers. As with much organization change, Job Enrichment often has its greatest impact at the middle-management levels. Functions may be combined or split off, and tasks and responsibilities may be moved up or down. All this is threatening. A workable Job Enrichment program provides for channels of communication specifically to middle managers, to explain why and how certain changes are being made.

There is at least one respect in which there can be too much communication: overexpansive claims or forecasts. As was pointed out earlier, Job Enrichment is not a panacea. It should not be made to look like one through hard-sell statements, memos, or articles in house organs. Objectives of the project should be stated clearly and factually, and the results later allowed to speak for themselves.

There is a similar problem that arises at the earliest stages. An internal or external specialist, aware of the power of Job Enrichment to "unfreeze" organizations for massive change, may tend to play up this potential in presenting the findings of the diagnosis to management. This error creates two kinds of dangers. One is to raise hopes unrealistically high. The other is more common: to conjure up visions of change so massive and threatening that the response is "We're not ready for that." Then Job Enrichment is torpedoed before it gets started.

The project model. The two most common kinds of errors in designing a model for change through Job Enrichment concern the degree of employee participation and the relative emphasis on changing attitudes and behavior.

Employees can participate either too little or too much in job redesign. In some organizations the climate set by top management discourages employees from participating. (In such a climate it would probably be very hard to get a Job Enrichment commitment in the first place.) The more common case is that top management does not oppose participation, but through inertia lets the Job Enrichment initiative pass completely into the hands of middle management instead of staying close to the first-line supervisors.

Although Job Enrichment is characterized as a participative management technique by reason of its objectives, there have to be practical limitations. Otherwise, two practical problems arise. First, too many employees are away from their jobs in planning and implementing sessions. Second, lower-level employees, without supervisory experience, may have trouble conceiving overall objectives and will spend too much time on details.

Perhaps the clearest case for employees participating in redesign of their own jobs occurs when they have a clearer grasp than anyone else of the technical aspects of those jobs.

One of the signal advantages of Job Enrichment, compared to many other approaches to organization development, is that it has the potential of making significant changes, very quickly, in what people actually do in their daily work. The changes in structure and action cause changes in behavior, which lead to changes in attitudes. Then the sequence becomes self-reinforcing. This immediately visible change gives people a sense that things are happening. To start with attitude change and expect behavior change to follow creates a risk that people will lose interest before there are any significant results.

Education. As described in the earlier chapters, the Job Enrichment project model includes specific educational activities, for varying purposes, aimed at all levels of management. The most common error in the educational aspect of Job Enrichment is not making those activities inclusive enough, especially as regards technical personnel and middle managers.

There are many people whose work will be affected by the immediate Job Enrichment project or by the later spread of Job Enrichment to other functions. Industrial engineers, systems designers, and such should be at least briefed on Job Enrichment's objectives and potential. This briefing should help to minimize any perceptions of conflict between their methods and preoccupations and those of Job Enrichment. The result will be smoother implementation of systems redesigns, measurement systems, and other aspects of the project.

In terms of the immediate project, it is probably not essential to expose any managers but those in the target work group and those above it to the concepts of Job Enrichment. But in terms of the future it is certainly desirable to expand the education effort laterally. That is, make it include managers from departments most affected by changes in the target group, and other managers whose own operations are likely targets of future Job Enrichment efforts. It is often constructive and diplomatic to include some managers who are not in either of these categories but are particularly influential among their peers.

Problem-solving/implementation planning.   In the meetings with lower management and supervision, the education phase gives way to problem-solving. The major hazard at this point is that the greenlighting sessions, in which participants are supposed to throw on the table every conceivable job change, will become too structured, too directed, too limited by practicality. It is up to the specialist leading these sessions to encourage all suggestions, and to defer any narrowing-down of possibilities as long as the group seems able to produce more ideas. The problem-solving sessions give plenty of opportunity for weeding out low-payoff suggestions.

Organization.   After the problem-solving sessions, by contrast, structuring for action becomes extremely important. This structuring should consist of three elements: (1) determination of steps to be taken; (2) assignment of responsibility for seeing that they are taken; (3) establishment of a time range or limit for the action steps.

Every implementation meeting, from the beginning to the end of the project, should work toward this basic structuring.

Long-term planning.   At this point the project is ready to take its first substantive actions, and participants are typically full of enthusiasm and impetus to get on with implementation.

Naturally, the Job Enrichment specialist is eager to take advantage of this impetus. Before plunging ahead, however, he would be wise to stop for a day or two, review the proposed project model, anticipate possible problems (especially those likely to crop up early) and plan the overall course of installation.

Installation.   The Job Enrichment specialist and others immediately around him with a high degree of commitment all expect, if only subconsciously, that everyone is going to welcome beneficial changes in jobs. This is not necessarily true. The specialist should be prepared for resistance, and should have developed in advance at least a general strategy for dealing with it.

A second main problem that arises in installation concerns scope and speed. Even if the project is small in scale, relative to the overall organization, it may be wise to apply job changes to a few selected workers who serve as a "pilot project within a pilot project." This approach permits debugging of the new job designs and minimizes the number, cost, and impact of mistakes.

Measuring and reporting of results.   From Job Enrichment as from any other innovation, management generally desires "hard" results—measurable improvements in productivity, profitability, quality, and related measures. Some Job Enrichment specialists and organization development consultants feel more comfortable dealing with the "soft" intermediate measures—morale, attitudes, etc.

A project model should be designed to include concrete criteria by which progress or improvement will be evaluated. These criteria should be measurements that are useful and meaningful—and, if possible, familiar—to line managers.

Building an internal consulting cadre.   Like any change effort, Job Enrichment needs a certain protected status, for the good of the whole organization as well as the project. It is a common error, however, to prolong this special status, with two harmful effects. First, it presents an image of Job Enrichment as something outside the management mainstream—interesting, but not very useful. Second, the project and its staff might begin to appear as a threat to the central personnel or organization development staff. Rivalry could then set up "political" problems destructive to the Job Enrichment effort.

A serious flaw can develop if after one project no attempt is made to establish a talented staff to carry on widespread enrichment activity beyond a pilot project.

The ultimate aim of Job Enrichment should be an internal consulting staff integrated into the central personnel or human resources organization.

Expansion.   The success of a single project does not ensure the future of Job Enrichment for wider application. Three possible dangers can get in the way.

The first is that the consultant has concentrated so much on the immediate project, and done so much of the work himself, that the internal staff has not been adequately prepared to direct future efforts.

The second problem is that the results of the project are not communicated to management in such a way as to make an impressive case for further applications.

Finally—perhaps because the initial project is highly successful—a follow-on project may be carelessly chosen and implemented, and end in failure. More than one success is needed before Job Enrichment can be considered secure.

Longevity.   Job Enrichment is not self-sustaining. All too easily it can become last year's exciting management idea. There are numerous reasons why this happens.

A common one is that pay and other aspects of the reward system are not changed to share cost savings with employees, to reflect new management, supervisory, and worker responsibilities.

Another common reason is that no responsibility is fixed, in the enriched work group, for evaluating every proposed action or policy change in terms of effects on job design.

Also, while management may be pleased with the results of the project, it may settle for a one-shot effort, because it does not want to allocate the resources for a continuing internal consulting group for job redesign and other organization development activities.

And finally, the responsibility for promoting growth and development of subordinates by managers and supervisors may not be emphasized in the reward system. Those who are good at this responsibility must be recognized and rewarded. Those who neglect it must be penalized, or the spirit of enrichment, the mutual growth of company and individuals, will never become firmly rooted.

THE JOB ENRICHMENT PROJECT CHECKLIST

So far in this chapter we have summarized the kinds of problems that can arise to threaten the effectiveness of a Job Enrichment effort. Now it is time to introduce a device that the project managers can use to head off these problems: the Project Checklist.

Basically this is a list of questions to be asked—and positively answered—at several points in the project. It is organized according to the six-phase project model introduced in Chapter 6. Without going into detail, the list gives the project manager reminders of things that should be accomplished or planned for at each stage. Of course, the list itself does not assure the success of the project. But if it is used as a framework for the various actions discussed in the earlier chapters of this book, it should help to avoid the most common pitfalls.

Phase I: Data Gathering and Analysis

___ Have diagnostic methods been sufficiently broad and open-ended to establish credibly that problems of motivation do exist, and that Job Enrichment is a likely solution?

___ Has it been determined that there are no overriding reasons why a Job Enrichment effort should not be undertaken at this time?

___ Are resources of money and manpower committed at least for an agreed trial period?

___ If the project is intended as a pilot or demonstration, are the jobs typical enough of the whole organization to produce widely applicable methods and results?

___ Are the size and scope of the project manageable, yet big enough to provide convincing evidence?

___ Has a director been given clearcut responsibilities for various aspects of the project, including liaison with outside consultants and with other internal departments? Does he have adequate staff? Have other responsibilities, if any, been adjusted to allow adequate time for the Job Enrichment project?

___ Has the degree of employee participation been decided?

___ Is there an implementing plan, indicating in general, flexible terms when various aspects of the project should be accomplished?

___ Have measurements been selected or designed? Has it been established what degree of improvement will be considered "success?" Are the measurements likely to be useful and intelligible to line managers as well as to organization specialists?

Phase II: Education

___ Do the participants in the workshop include all managers and workers who might have an influence on the present Job Enrichment effort or on likely future efforts?

___ Has a top management executive agreed to introduce the workshop, and has he been briefed on his role and the function of his remarks?

___ Do the workshops for the team include all supervisors and workers whose knowledge is needed in the job design process?

___ Have the times and places for workshops been so chosen as to provide isolation and freedom from routine interruptions?

___ Have preworkshop reading materials been selected and made available to participants?

___ Have instruction methods been planned to maximize participation rather than passive instruction?

___ If the size of the project requires, have the greenlighting sessions been broken down into appropriate groups?

___ Are physical supplies on hand for each type of workshop: films, projectors, flip charts, graphics, markers, etc.?

___ Has greenlighting been allowed to run long enough to get all possible job change ideas on the table?

___ Is the final, conditioned list of greenlight items specific enough, and is it clear how each one of them would enrich the job?

Phase III: Primary Implementation

___ Is responsibility clearly assigned for the specific actions needed to implement?

___ Is there a time schedule for the implementation actions? .

___ Is the sequence of implementation logical—that is, are things being done first which will make later steps easier?

___ Is there enough significant change planned for the start to create momentum and enthusiasm?

___ Have all necessary approvals for changes been obtained?

___ Are there provisions for communicating the changes as necessary?

___ Has thought been given to ways of dealing with problems that may arise?

___ Have supervisors been briefed on how they should report imminent changes back to the work group?

___ If technical or supervisory training will be needed, has it been planned?

___ Has responsibility been fixed for gathering and reporting data on results of the changes?

Phase IV: Expanded Implementation

___ Are the measurements for the original, limited project being scanned for data that might be useful in expanding?

___ Have the major problems of the original implementation been solved, and could the experience be used in planning the expanded implementation?

___ Is an effort being made to monitor reactions to the job changes, either formally or informally?

___ Does the pace with which changes are being implemented seem to be suitable to the organization, and easily assimilated?

___ Has the need been considered for additional workshops, either to bolster management commitment or to refresh the team's command of Job Enrichment concepts and techniques?

___ Has management been adequately briefed on progress to date?

Phase V: Building Autonomy

___ Has the burden of day-to-day management of Job Enrichment matters been passed from consultants to internal personnel—line supervisors, staff specialists and workers or autonomous teams?

___ Is there provision for any special training of internal people which might be needed as this transfer takes place?

___ Has someone been given specific responsibility for reviewing future policy decisions in terms of their effect on job design and motivation?

___ Are internal personnel, rather than consultants, conducting most of the meetings (including problem-solving workshops), and preparing and presenting reports to management?

Phase VI: Final Analysis

___ Have the surveys and interviews administered at the start been repeated?

___ Have the changes in selected measurements over the course of the project been charted and analyzed?

___ Has there been a decision on the timing, content, and audience for a report to management?

___ Does the planned report include recommendations for further action, in terms of the pilot group, the larger organization, or both?

___ Does the report include estimates of savings in dollars, man-hours, or some other bottom-line measurement?

___ Has there been consideration of publicizing the project and its results to the larger organization, the press, or others who might be interested?

chapter
THIRTEEN
Case Histories: Clerical

INTRODUCTION

The main purpose of the preceding chapters has been to describe, from start to finish, the steps that must usually be taken to install Job Enrichment successfully. However specific we have tried to make the description, we have nonetheless been dealing with a general methodology of Job Enrichment. Now it is time to demonstrate through case histories how the methodology has worked in individual, concrete instances.

Just as the methodology we described was drawn largely from our own experience in applying Job Enrichment, so most of the case histories that follow describe projects in which we were involved. Far from illustrating a single "best" approach to implementation, however, the cases make clear that flexibility is good and even necessary. Even the projects involving the authors vary in style and approach. Those from other sources are included to show that many techniques can serve the same general principles and produce valid results. A pragmatic attitude of this kind is more valid than any strict party line.

In describing theory or methodology, we usually dealt with the steps of Job Enrichment one by one, in the interests of clarity. In practice some of the steps may be telescoped, so that two or more are implemented simultaneously, or one may serve the purposes of several implementing concepts.

In the case histories we have made no consistent attempt to relate each specific step to an objective or principle. Doing so would have resulted in an unsuccessful attempt to impose on the cases a uniformity they do not have. It would have led also to a great deal of repetition. We are convinced that the rationale will usually be clear in the light of the preceding chapters, and we shall add some minimal explanation where it seems necessary.

We have sought to describe in a clear narrative flow the problems to be solved, the actions that were taken, and the results achieved. Beyond this objective, we have sought only to classify the cases into two broad categories: clerical (in this chapter) and manufacturing/production (in Chapter 14). The classification was chosen not because Job Enrichment requires two different approaches in these contexts, but because most readers will probably be more interested in one than in the other. All of them, however, are likely to have at least some value for most readers.

THE TRAVELERS INSURANCE COMPANY

The first case histories are drawn from projects in two different operations in The Travelers Insurance Company, Hartford, Connecticut. Besides the intrinsic interest of both cases, they illustrate how an initial Job Enrichment project, if successful, leads to applications elsewhere in an organization.

Keypunch Operations

Many managers believe that Job Enrichment has limited power to improve jobs that are determined by machinery or some other aspect of technology. If this were true, then a vast number of jobs would be beyond hope—not only on the factory floor, but also in many clerical operations, which are increasingly dominated by computers and input channels.

This case history shows how it was possible to enrich highly machine-bound and routine jobs in just such a context: keypunching.

The impetus for the project came from problems that seemed to affect all the keypunch operations in the company. In general, they did not meet the performance criteria management thought reasonable in terms of standard work-measurement methods. Since this substandard performance was also coupled with high absenteeism and turnover, a motivational root was suspected.

The purpose was to test the potential of Job Enrichment for improving performance in various jobs throughout the company, as well as in the initial group. It was decided that two similar work groups would be chosen, one for experimental Job Enrichment, the other for control. Both the groups were part of a data input division, and were similar both in demographics and organization.

All employees below the level of assistant supervisor were women; 49% were 40 or older, and 52% had been in keypunching at least five years.

The experimental group consisted of a supervisor, assistant supervisor, and 75 other employees. There were 42 keypunch operators and verifiers, organized into units of varying numbers. There were also 11 unit leaders, 9 alternate leaders, 4 tabulating machine operators, and 9 service clerks.

The basic task was to punch into tabulating cards information on a variety of policy transactions, which came from branch offices or agencies in typed or handwritten documents. Individual batches varied from a few cards to as many as 2,500; some had due dates specified, while others, of a recurring nature, got routine service by a preset schedule.

The service clerks reviewed the incoming jobs for obvious errors or other problems, then parceled them out at random in batches estimated to provide an hour's work. Any job found by a clerk to be unsuitable for punching went to the supervisor, who either returned it unpunched to the originating department or cleared up the problem by phone.

After punching, all work had to be 100% verified—a task taking nearly as much time as the punching itself. Completed work went to the supervisor. If verification had revealed any errors, the supervisor gave the work of correction at random to any operator. Correct work went to the computer room.

The printout generated by the cards went to the originating department. Any erroneous cards that remained went back to the supervisor, who assigned them for correction—again at random.

The greenlighting process produced a list of 73 possible changes that could be made to enrich the job. Problem-solving reduced the list to 25. These changes can be conveniently described in terms of the implementing concepts explained in Chapter 5.

Natural work units. The batch system of assigning work meant that there was no continuity in an operator's job from hour to hour. To correct the situation, each operator was given continuing responsibility for handling all work from certain departments. These "accounts" were assigned in such a way that the workload was about evenly distributed.

Client relationships. When each operator had continuing responsibility for certain segments of work, it also became practical to give them direct contact with their "clients" in other departments. Operators, not assignment clerks, were given the task of checking incoming work for correctness and legibility. The operators, not their supervisors, were given the task of clearing up any of these problems with clients.

Vertical loading. The *unenriched* jobs had been totally lacking in autonomy. For example, some documents came to the operators with obvious coding errors—inconsistencies between the verbal information and the numerical code to be punched. The operators were told that under any circumstances they must punch only what they saw—even though they knew coding very well and could recognize an error when they saw it. In effect, they were told to make avoidable errors—a frustrating and demeaning situation. They were also deprived of autonomy by the work assignment system, which gave them no control over planning their own work day.

The *enrichment* process improved autonomy in several ways: The operators were allowed to correct coding errors; they were allowed to set their own schedules, provided that they met their own commitments to clients; and some highly experienced operators were given the option to send their work directly to the computer room without verification. As error rates began to decline, other operators were given the same option.

Feedback. So that operators might have knowledge of results, several channels of feedback were built into the job. One already mentioned was the direct contact with their client departments. In addition, when incorrect cards came back from the computer room, they were corrected by the operator who punched them, not by random assignment. Each operator kept a file of copies of her errors, and could refer to them to check trends in her error pattern.

Task advancement. As formerly structured, the keypunch operator's job provided no sense of personal growth and advancement. To enrich the job in this respect, several changes were made. First, measurements of operator output and proficiency were made available to the operators themselves, so that they could see evidence of improvement. As they improved, they were given greater autonomy in scheduling and deciding whether to verify. Finally, the new relationships with client departments led in some cases to promotions to better jobs in those departments.

When the operating results in the experimental group were compared with those in the unenriched control group, they showed clearly that Job Enrichment was effective. To summarize briefly:

- *Quantity of work.* The group whose jobs were enriched increased the average number of cards it punched and verified per hour by 39.6%. In the unchanged control group there was an 8.1% improvement. The effectiveness ratio (based on the number of hours needed to process a given number of cards plotted against the hours estimated by work measurement standards) improved from 78% of standard before the trial to 104% thereafter. In the control group there was no significant change from a standard of 94%.

- *Error rates and quality.* For a group of experienced operators evaluated before and after the Job Enrichment trial, average error rate dropped from 1.53% to 0.99%. Concurrently, the number of operators with outstanding error rates (less than 0.5%) rose from 20% of the group to 50%.

- *Personnel measures.* Absenteeism dropped 24.1% during the Job Enrichment trial, while it actually increased 20% in the control group. There was no appreciable change in turnover in the experimental group—which was lower than company average in turnover, probably because of its age composition. The saving in work through selective elimination of control activities was estimated to be the equivalent of adding seven operators.

- *Cost savings.* The improvements listed led to estimated savings of $65,000 in the year of the trial, and additional potential savings estimated at $90,000 a year.

- *Supervisors' behavior.* The shift of many responsibilities from supervisors to operators meant that the supervisors were freed to devote more attention to planning, organization, and control, rather than constantly dealing with crises.

• *Attitudes.* Job reaction surveys administered before the Job Enrichment trial found the control and the experimental group just about identical in attitudes toward the job, and about average by the norms of the survey. After the trial, the control group showed no significant change in attitude, while the experimental group's overall score rose 16.5%. The improved attitudes also showed up in interviews held after the trial. Operators generally felt pride in their work and increased responsibility, and a new sense of value to the company. Frustration and boredom that formerly characterized attitudes disappeared in many cases.

Life, Health, and Financial Services Department

The success of Job Enrichment in the keypunch case led to another application within the same company. The area was the Statement Billed Accounting Section. The twin problems were poor service and overspending on the manpower budget.

The section consisted of six units: combined billing, national accounts, special cases, government allotment-fund services, report-Plan I, and mail. Initial workshops produced a greenlight list of more than 100 items affecting all these units. The most significant changes were concentrated in combined billing and national accounts; so, we shall concentrate on those changes.

The core job in both units was that of registration desk operator (RDO) who is concerned with billing and collecting premiums. Before the Job Enrichment project, the work flow was like this:

The mail unit distributed incoming mail to RDO's or to correspondents (specialists in customer contact in certain areas). The RDO read the correspondence to determine whether she could respond herself. If she could not, she referred it to the correspondent. In case of delays, the unit supervisor and manager handled some cases. After processing, the correspondence was filed and eventually destroyed.

The objective of the Job Enrichment project was to make the RDO's job as complete as she was capable of handling, and particularly to include higher levels of responsibility. Accordingly, RDO's were given responsibility for:

- Balancing paid statements with the remittance and posting payments to the computer
- Processing even complex and "problem" cases
- Contacting clients directly when necessary
- Correcting their own errors

Since the restructuring, each RDO receives correspondence directly from the mail unit, handles the request from start to finish, and destroys the original request. Correcting her own errors gives the RDO objective feedback on her productivity and quality.

The change in job structure produced the desired improvements in service and manpower. The number of statements processed remained about the same, but the monthly number of statements unprocessed within five days of receipt dropped from about 5% to less than 0.75%. Statements rejected by the computer for errors dropped from an average 4,000 a month to less than 400. Another type of error, involving incorrect dollar amounts, declined more than 50%.

These improvements in productivity enabled the manpower level of the whole section to be reduced from 135 to 103 employees, and overtime dropped by 80%. Although the workload remained constant, Job Enrichment led to manpower savings estimated at $104,000 a year.

One significant result in this project, as in many, was the change that occurred in the supervisor's role. The best way to understand the change is to compare distributions of supervisors' time before and after Job Enrichment:

Function	How time was spent	
	Before JE	One Year Later
Production work	45%	10%
Answering questions	35	15
Training and development	8	25
Record keeping	5	20
Planning, organizing, control	5	25
Distributing work	2	5

Ideally, strong management should be able to count on plenty of support from supervisors in the central managerial functions of training and development and in planning and organizing. In this organization, Job Enrichment made it possible for supervisors to devote about 50% of their time to these vital functions, instead of 13%. They were transformed from superclerks to genuine first-line managers.

HARRIS TRUST AND SAVINGS BANK, CHICAGO

The banking industry shares with the insurance industry a problem in personnel utilization that is particularly challenging to Job Enrichment, and yet particularly responsive to it. The situation is that clerical operations are on a large scale, but characterized by multiplicity. There are many different kinds of operations, and only a few employees—maybe only one—engaged in each one.

The dilemma is that with such specialization turnover becomes critical. If one of the specialists quits, production has to suffer until a replacement can be trained. Yet because of the specialization, these very jobs are likely to be highly repetitive and controlled—conditions that are highly conducive to job dissatisfaction and turnover.

The challenge of the situation in terms of Job Enrichment is that numerous jobs, perhaps dozens, have to be redesigned to make significant impact. Very often, the individual job changes make necessary extensive reorganization. Success in handling both these aspects is a true test of management's understanding of Job Enrichment skills and implications.

Such a situation was treated in a Job Enrichment program for the Corporate Trust Securities Division of Harris Trust. The division consists of a number of units, each dealing with a special type of transaction. The transactions, in turn, were broken down into many separate activities, each performed by only a few employees.

Job Enrichment was tried as a possible solution to a number of problems: low productivity, backlogged work, poor quality, high absence and turnover, high overtime, and signs of low morale. Workshops produced 130 greenlight items, of which 40 were implemented in a six-month period. Some of these changes, and the results they produced, are discussed here.

Bond Transfer Unit

The unit consisted of three tellers and three typists. Bonds to be transferred were assigned randomly to two of the tellers, who prepared them for any one of the three typists. After typing, the third teller checked the items for accuracy, with assistance as necessary from the other two. The bonds were then signed and sent to customers.

Just before the Job Enrichment program began, one teller and one typist quit, so the remaining four were divided into two teams—each consisting of a teller and a typist. Each team had its own continuing responsibility for all functions in transactions involving certain accounts.

The result was that the four remaining employees were more productive than six had been before. Overtime was reduced and backlogged work was nearly eliminated. Bonds are now typically processed within five days, instead of two or three weeks.

Securities Transfer Unit

This unit is similar in function to Bond Transfer, and was organized on a similarly random assignment of work. Tellers rotated among various functions on a daily basis. Each complete securities transaction passed through several tellers, as if on a conveyor belt. Although the rotation might be thought to add an element of variety to the job, it did not lead to continuing accountability.

The Job Enrichment program called for dividing the tellers into small teams, each with continuing responsibility for specific accounts. The team did the job from beginning to end, including transferring, checking, balancing, matching, and mailing. They also handled research on their accounts, and provided special handling for accounts that needed it.

The unit's supervisor was particularly impressed by the improvement in the employees' attitudes toward their work—an improvement reflected in quantitative measures as well. Although work volume has remained stable, it has not been necessary to replace an employee who left the unit. During the first six months of the program, overtime was 50% below a year earlier, and absences were down 30%.

The individual error rates averaged 0.5% after Job Enrichment.

While this is good in absolute terms, no comparison with earlier rates is possible, since under the old organization it was impossible to determine who was responsible for errors.

The supervisor also reported that the new arrangement of jobs have given vastly improved control over documents. Instead of possibly having to query ten different tellers to find the status of a given account, it was necessary to ask only one. The supervisor believed this change alone had saved him about one hour a day formerly spent in researching transfers.

Division results. The specific results cited above are reflected in the operating figures for the division as a whole. The units most affected by Job Enrichment increased productivity 21% compared to a year earlier, and overtime was reduced 44%. The same amount of work, or more, is being done with fewer people. Changes made in four units of the division saved or freed up nine employees in the six months of the trial. These people have been reassigned elsewhere in the division. Another three employees left through normal attrition, and it has not been necessary to replace them. Overall, the project is estimated to have saved the bank $75,000 a year in salaries and overtime.

A MAJOR NEW YORK BANK

Job Enrichment does not operate alone as a means of improving organizational effectiveness. The Stock Transfer Division of a major New York Bank undertook a program of Job Enrichment to help attain the goals of a related program of management by objectives. The division's experience illustrates various elements usually thought of in connection with broader forms of Organization Development—not simply Job Enrichment. Whatever the label, however, the case demonstrates the value of a commitment to combine the methods of the behavioral sciences with the experience of line managers and employees.

The total project sought to change five basic variables: Job design; feedback systems; work flow; organization structure; and management style, as reflected in communications, participation, and planning. While the first two of the five are central to Job Enrichment, the others are more typically associated with OD.

Before the project began, both work flow and organization structure were fractionalized along functional lines. Work flowed from section to section, and each section performed a small part of the total work process. Within each section, in turn, the work was further specialized, with some employees performing the basic task while others did support work. Most jobs were routine and required little judgment. Since work was distributed at random, employees had no ongoing responsibility, little feedback, and little incentive to maintain high quality.

The system satisfied no one. Management found costs too high and manpower used wastefully. Employees were unhappy about the lack of opportunity for meaningful work. This attitude showed up clearly on a job reaction survey.

A basic change in the division was the conversion of the sections from a functional specialization to an accounts orientation. Reorganization was begun so that each section would include all capabilities necessary to process completely the transactions of specified clients.

A first step in reorganizing the work flow was to have all incoming items sorted as the first stage of processing. Previously the incoming work went through several of the first processing steps in random batches.

Although all the changes contemplated for the division were planned for completion over several years, significant results were soon available from two areas of operation.

Evening and Night Electronic Stock Transfer

This department formerly comprised four sections: account files, typing, certificate allocation and computer proof, and checking.

The first step in reorganization was to eliminate the checking section and give the typing and account-files sections the responsibility for checking their own work. In addition, each section was organized into three units, each responsible for one-third of the total volume.

To provide for natural units of work and feedback, the work flow was changed so that the allocation section received debits arranged by company and security code and processed by the unit responsible for the particular codes. Since the flow of work from allocation to typing to files is all within one section, there is less handling of the work.

Within each allocation unit, furthermore, one operator performed all the allocation functions for given accounts.

In account files and typing, checkers were then cross trained and given the responsibility of notifying operators immediately of any errors discovered. As another means of feedback, each operator received weekly a form listing volume and errors by individual, unit, and section.

Following these changes it became possible to reduce the amount of checking by 50% with no increase in errors. It was anticipated that as operators' proficiency improved, it would be possible to reduce checking still further.

After a few months under the new setup there were indications of immediate improvement in productivity and quality. Individual employees averaged about one-third greater productivity than at the start of the project. As for quality, the average number of documents processed without error increased as follows:

Function	Start	Six Months Later
Certificate allocation	220	330
Account files	1000	3300
Typing	28	52

Improved quality was also indicated by the drop in the number of cancellations—a replacement for an improperly processed certificate. Here are figures for the first quarter after Job Enrichment was implemented:

Month	Cancellations	Volume
July	136	261,686
August	93	293,000
September	55	243,350

Keypunching

Before Job Enrichment, the keypunch operation consisted of one punching section and one verification section, with work assigned to operators at random.

The Job Enrichment program set up three units, each including both punching and verification. Within the units work was assigned by security code to units with continuing responsibility for those codes. Special jobs were scheduled on the basis of workloads in the units.

Employees rotated the positions of operator and verifier. Operators were responsible for processing all the source documents that entered the keypunch section.

For feedback purposes, each completed batch was accompanied by a card indicating the number of cards punched and the number of errors in the course of processing. Total results were fed back to operators monthly.

As a result of the new setup, average monthly productivity increased about one-third. Errors decreased from one per 59 certificates to one error in every 64. Since this quality improvement occurred concurrently with elimination of half the checking, it was possible to reduce personnel from 67 to 49.

Besides these measurable improvements in performance, there was evidence from anecdotal data that employees' job satisfaction had also improved.

BANKERS TRUST COMPANY

A year-long project in the stock transfer department focused on changes in the job of production typist. There were about 100 such jobs on each of two shifts. The typists' job was to type and record stock transfer data into many blocks on large forms. Because of the serious problems created by errors, there was one checker per typist, with few exceptions. Every typed form was verified, and any errors were corrected by special typists. After certification by another checker, the information was keyed into magnetic tape for computer input. Figure 13.1a shows in more detail the work flow in this process, and the position of the production typist.

The whole operation was a serious problem to management. Production was low and quality was poor. Employees considered their jobs routine, repetitive, and devoid of interest. Interviews with employees drew such comments as: "I don't see anything good in the job—not anything. What could you learn from typing names and addresses?" "The same sheeting every day. You don't know when you make errors." "I

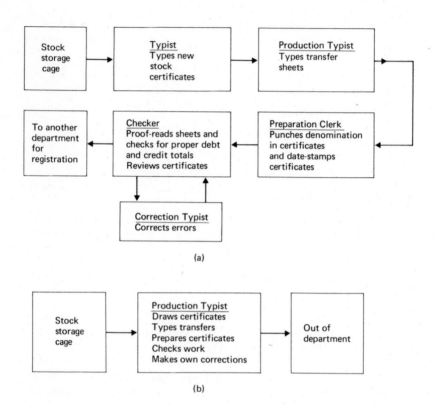

(a)

(b)

FIG. 13.1   (a) Pre-Job Enrichment work flow   (b) New modular design

have five bosses to account to. It's ridiculous. I like to be treated like an adult." Not surprisingly, absenteeism and turnover were high.

Greenlighting sessions produced a list of 52 possible changes. About a dozen were ultimately implemented. The first change was to allow certain typists to change their own computer input tapes. Group leaders had been responsible for this, because higher management feared increasing risk of losing information. Although supervisors considered the change inconsequential and were eager to push on and implement "more important" changes, the typists reacted highly favorably. The feeling that they were receiving new degrees of trust was important in the success of the project.

Essentially, Job Enrichment telescoped the multipart job of the stock transfer function into one job, as shown in Fig. 13.1b. Early in the project, the management team recognized that almost none of the employees felt a sense of responsibility for their own work. Many of the subsequent changes were aimed directly at this widespread problem.

The work was rearranged so that instead of being assigned work at random by a supervisor, typists drew new certificates from the vault. They prepared the certificates, typed in shareowner's name and address, entered the information on transfer sheets, checked the work, and corrected errors. Each typist did this entire sequence for certain corporations for which she had continuing responsibility.

Since experience of the various typists differed, not all were considered capable of immediately taking full charge of a customer group. So that even these typists could assume larger responsibilities, they were assigned to teams with continuing responsibility. Typists and checkers together scheduled their work, checked and corrected errors, and kept production counts and quality records. Some of these teams consisted of only two people, a typist and a checker, and all errors were corrected within the team.

In one such team, the typist had been considered an attitude problem case. She was late and absent frequently, and resented criticism. After Job Enrichment, she became one of the most dependable typists in the section. She frequently suggested ways to improve the work, and in an interview said that for the first time she was enjoying the work.

Typists of demonstrated accuracy were checked with less frequency.

As checking declined, so did errors. There was a far greater concern for quality.

Before Job Enrichment only a few typists were assigned "specials" —transfers involving highly complicated and diverse entries. As part of the enrichment process, the typists experienced in specials trained most of the other typists, who showed great proficiency. The newly trained typists found the new work more interesting, and the experienced typists found satisfaction in their role as trainers.

Before Job Enrichment, quality had never been consistently measured. Errors were rarely discussed with the employee responsible—if, in fact, it was possible to fix responsibility in so fragmented a work situation. As a remedy, the management team had a computer program developed to detect the most common errors before the stock certificate was issued. It was then possible to return the errors daily to the responsible typist for correction. This, of course, provided the typists with immediate feedback on their performance.

Since the primary objective of the project was to improve productivity, supervisors were somewhat reluctant to implement items that might cause production to drop. In fact, their fears were not groundless. During the early phases of implementation there was a drop in the output of those typists whose work was no longer checked. The reason was that with the greater responsibility, each typist was paying more attention to quality.

Overall, however, time saved in clearing delays and eliminating or combining functions increased output dramatically. In two of three sections, average transactions completed per hour more than doubled. In the third, it nearly doubled.

As a result of such productivity and quality increases, the section was eventually able to eliminate about half its checkers—for a saving of $300,000 a year in salaries.

Attitudes changed dramatically from those expressed at the start of the project, the change being shown by such comments as:

"I have had more duties added to me, which I appreciate. More work, but I enjoy it."

"I feel I am responsible for something. I know if anything happens it's going to come back to me and I'm going to feel bad about it."

"My absence and lateness were terrible. But now I say, 'If I don't come in, who is going to do my work?' I can't stay out."

CHEMICAL BANK, NEW YORK: LOCKBOX DEPARTMENT

This department consisted of a number of different sections, each performing a specialized clerical function. The department as a whole was experiencing abnormally high turnover and absenteeism, and there were signs of generally low morale. In addition, some sections were plagued by low productivity and high error rates.

Following a Job Enrichment feasibility study, management decided to implement Job Enrichment in several sections. Our report concerns the changes and results that occurred in just one, the Electronic Customer Services section.

Before Job Enrichment the work proceeded in the following manner: Each clerk was given a batch of envelopes containing bills and customers' checks in payment of them, and was responsible for inspecting the contents and separated the bills from the checks. Then the checks, arranged by account, were given to other clerks for final inspection of payee, signature, and date.

Both checks and bills then went out of the section for encoding, listing, and balancing. In the meantime the clerks were kept busy by being loaned out to other sections or by being given work brought in. When the balanced checks and bills were returned, each clerk received a batch of accounts, randomly assigned, for closing out. This process consisted of writing up the tape listing, creating a customer advice and credit, forwarding checks to the microfilm area, and mailing out all detail work and information. If customer contact was necessary, the supervisor handled it.

To enrich the job, each clerk was given full responsibility for a number of accounts and processed them from start to finish. This meant pulling and reviewing bills and checks, creating adding machine listings, encoding checks and creating a check tape for balancing, reconciling out-of-balance accounts, and closing out accounts. In some cases the clerk was given the authority to make simple changes and adjustments and to contact customers directly.

The changes in job design had a marked effect. Productivity increased nearly 50% in six months, and individual error rates dropped, on the average, from 65 to 30 per week. The most obvious reason for the quality improvement was that each clerk, now handling the whole account, could recognize errors more easily. Under the old setup, individuals who made errors could never be sure of seeing them again.

Department Results

Job Enrichment was applied similarly to other sections in the Lockbox Department. Although we shall not describe these changes, it is instructive to look at some of the operational improvements they brought about:

Turnover.   This was one of the most serious problems to be attacked through Job Enrichment. In the four years preceding the Job Enrichment project, turnover in the Lockbox Department had averaged 59%, roughly double the average for the bank as a whole. After Job Enrichment, turnover dropped to 24%.

Absenteeism.   Average absence in the department dropped from 11.2 days to 9.3 days during the period of Job Enrichment implementation. The bank's average also dropped, from 11.0 to 9.9 days. Thus the Lockbox Department's improvement was significantly greater—about 17% versus the bank's 10%.

Attitudes.   "Before" and "after" job reaction surveys showed improved attitudes in seven out of nine possible categories. One remained unchanged, and one deteriorated slightly.

chapter
FOURTEEN
Case Histories: Manufacturing

Because of the tremendous capital investment typical of production equipment, enrichment of manufacturing and production jobs is often said to be harder than enrichment of clerical jobs. We are not sure that this differential is always clear-cut. More and more clerical operations require computers and other equipment that approaches the costs, say, of typical machine tools.

In terms of Job Enrichment potential, manufacturing/processing jobs have the advantage that the tasks themselves are often highly interesting and challenging. Thus a good deal can be accomplished merely by restructuring, with no change in technology. This is particularly clear in the first of the following case histories.

AMERICAN PROFESSIONAL COLOR
CORPORATION: ART DEPARTMENT

APC processes films and prints for commercial, industrial, and portrait photographers. Its entire plant consists of 70 employees, including 10 working supervisors.

The Art Department consists of 12 employees—all women—and one supervisor. It was picked as a first site for Job Enrichment because it exhibited several problems of a type often associated with poor job design.

First, turnover was high—so high that at the start of the project nearly half the department's employees had less than three months' experience. Second, in interviews and job reaction surveys, the women said that the work itself was potentially quite interesting and worth putting effort into; but that they were dissatisfied by the way the job was structured. They felt that they had little responsibility or control over the

way the work was done and received little feedback on their performance.

These attitude problems were reflected in performance. Quality was
generally poor and much of the work had to be redone. Customers were
unhappy because of missed deadlines.

The Art Department's basic job is to perform retouching, spotting,
texturing, or airbrushing as needed on prints. Typical tasks included
removing blemishes from portraits, filling in white or blank spots in
backgrounds, correcting eye color, etc.

Before Job Enrichment began, the department was organized as follows. The supervisor received all incoming work. She sorted, scheduled,
and assigned the work according to due dates and the skills of various
workers. When the workload was heavy she also did some of the work
herself.

When the work was finished, the supervisor checked it. If it was acceptable it went to the Print Department for final inspection. If unac-
ceptable, it went into the repair file.

This file seemed bottomless to the supervisor. It was always backlogged, often to the point where the supervisor would have to redis-
tribute the whole file to various workers for reworking. This step, of
course, interrupted the entire schedule.

The supervisor handled all contacts with the Print Department, and
all customer contact related to finished work. She also ordered all supplies for the department. Not surprisingly, she had almost no time for
training new workers, although she was eager to do so.

For this reason, and because the workload was heavy, new employees were given nothing to do but backgrounds—filling in spots.
More experienced workers did the more difficult tasks, such as removing
blemishes. There was only one worker experienced in each of the specialized functions, such as airbrushing or texturing, and they handled
all of this kind of work.

The compensation system aggravated the problem situation. All employees were paid a piecework incentive based on production. Since the
newer employees were assigned the easier jobs, they were typically able
to turn out more items of work. Therefore, they got the bonuses while
the more experienced workers did not.

One final item of hygiene. The workers were not allowed to talk with one another as they worked. Coupled with the lack of say in how the job was done, this rule made them feel, as one worker put it, that they were "treated like kindergarteners."

The job redesign that emerged from Job Enrichment workshops centered on creation of teams. Three experienced workers who could handle all or most of the separate functions were designated as technical experts in each of three main categories: commercial prints, industrial prints, and weddings and portraits. The other employees were assigned to these teams to produce a balance of skills. The technical experts became, in effect, team leaders. They were responsible for sorting and assigning work and for training new employees in the more demanding functions. Each new worker was to be trained quickly to be able to do an entire retouching job, rather than just the backgrounds.

Thereafter the inexperienced workers discussed problems with their team leaders rather than with the supervisor. If the problem arose from work done by another department, the worker was encouraged to discuss it directly with that department.

The supervisor no longer inspected finished work. Any inspection within the department was done by the team leaders. However, only the work of the most inexperienced workers was inspected. The departmental repair file was abolished. Each worker was given responsibility for handling her own repairs along with her scheduled workload.

All feedback, good or bad, went directly to the woman who did the work. Workers were expected to phone directly to customers with questions about work in progress, set their own schedules to meet due dates, and order their own supplies without going through the supervisor.

The results of these changes have been impressive. Although the workload increased, the work backlog disappeared entirely within one month of the job design changes. Monthly output increased about 35%, with no increase in number of employees. Much of this productivity improvement directly reflected better quality—getting it right the first time.

Changes in the core of the job itself were supported by wider-ranging changes, which have done a lot to improve employees' satisfaction. The old incentive system was replaced by straight hourly increases reflecting increased productivity. One result was much greater cooperation among workers when workloads were heavy in some specialties and light in others.

Greater customer contact was also a source of satisfaction. Employees were frequently asked to escort visiting customers or photographers on tours of the operation—a responsibility which had previously fallen to the sales manager.

The supervisor's job changed substantially. She was able to devote much of her time to training and development. She set up internal and outside programs for improving workers' skills. She also had time to devise new kinds of services to be offered to customers.

KAISER ALUMINUM AND CHEMICAL CORPORATION: MAINTENANCE WORKERS[1]

To practitioners of Job Enrichment in a manufacturing or production context, maintenance jobs are almost always intriguing and challenging. The job itself typically demands the high skills of a craft. Maintenance personnel usually say they are highly satisfied in their work. In many cases the maintenance function operates with a high degree of autonomy.

Nonetheless, maintenance often seems to perform poorly its basic mission, which is to keep productive equipment operating at the highest possible efficiency and reduce downtime to a minimum.

An almost universal symptom of poor performance is poor communication, indifference, or outright friction between maintenance and the production function it is supposed to support.

Thus, in applying Job Enrichment to maintenance jobs, it is often a central problem to establish better liaison between maintenance and production, so that control and communication support the mission, rather than undermine it. If morale in maintenance is poor, as well as its productivity, the challenge is even greater.

There are several basic approaches to a remedy. One common one is to integrate certain basic maintenance functions into the production job module. A second is to eliminate the separate maintenance function entirely, and make maintenance personnel part of production teams. A third solution was applied by Kaiser Aluminum and Chemical at its Ravenswood (W. Va.) works. The corporation made maintenance the focus of a Job Enrichment effort, kept the function intact, and strengthened it.

The case involved about 60 workers who maintained the aluminum reduction potlines. The potlines normally operated around the clock in three shifts. Before Job Enrichment, maintenance also operated on three shifts. Among the problems of the plant were maintenance jobs frequently left incomplete at the end of a shift, chronic walkouts and slowdowns, and productivity problems which maintenance blamed on production and production blamed on maintenance.

These problems were not surprising, given the way the work was organized. There were two basic kinds of jobs. In one, workers did routine maintenance on the line. In the other, they worked on equipment that had been removed to the rebuild shop for more drastic repair. Workers were assigned to these jobs without regard to their skills, interests, or craft. They were shifted from one area of the plant to another. They might work on one job for one day, and be shifted to another the next day, even if the job was not finished.

Kaiser took a basic gamble that Job Enrichment could increase maintenance productivity so much that all maintenance could be accomplished in one shift a day. So, three shifts were replaced by a single day shift, staggered in five-day turns so that there would be seven-day coverage.

Workers were allowed to bid for assignment to the rebuild shop or to line maintenance. In either case, they worked without supervision, kept their own time records, and used their own judgment on priorities.

The workers on the lines were assigned continuing responsibility for specific potlines. They decided what maintenance should be done and in what order. Each of these workers got a monthly report of maintenance costs for the lines he serviced.

Kaiser's gamble paid off handsomely. Results in the first year under Job Enrichment included the following:

- Maintenance costs (labor and materials) decreased 5.5%, despite higher wages and benefits negotiated in a new labor contract.

- Four supervisory posts were eliminated—an additional saving not included in the maintenance cost savings.

- Uptime rose to about 99%. Although comparable figures for earlier periods were not available, the manager of reduction operations reported that there was "no question that maintenance is better by far."

- At last report, there have been no grievances filed by maintenance workers since the Job Enrichment program began.

Besides these concrete results, management and employees alike reported improvements in morale and pride of workmanship, which led to the improvements in quantity and quality of work. There is no doubt that by making production workers the "customers" of the maintenance workers, Job Enrichment increased the sense of interdependence necessary for teamwork. As one maintenance worker put it: "Keeping the good will of those guys on the line is our most valuable asset. They could really tear things up if they wanted to. If I make their job easier, they'll make mine easier."

One rewarding aspect of this case is that the Job Enrichment improvements were accomplished entirely within the terms of a union contract, with no resistance from union members or officials. On the management side, the program was so satisfactory that it served as a pilot project for other applications within the company. As so frequently happens, Job Enrichment created greater awareness of the areas in which management and labor interests coincide, and provided a structure that could take advantage of this overlap.

VOLVO AB

No innovations in job design are more widely known than those of Volvo AB, the Swedish car manufacturer. Volvo's experiments in job design are unique, particularly in comprehensiveness. They developed in a tradition quite different from that which underlies most of this book. At least partially for this reason, they involve many specific techniques or innovations that are not, strictly speaking, "Job Enrichment" as we have been considering it.

Our purpose in considering Volvo here, then, is to put into a specifically Job Enrichment perspective activities which are significant for the quality of working life, no matter what the activities are labeled. We shall also see just how broad a scope, both technological and social, Job Enrichment may eventually embrace, and how generally applicable its principles are.

Automobile manufacturing is virtually synonymous with the assembly line; and the assembly line is virtually synonymous with fragmented and repetitive jobs. To varying degrees, all the major car makers have tried to counter the resulting boredom through changes in job design. Very soon in the process, however, these efforts come up against the tremendous commitment of capital to the established technology. You don't simply tear down the assembly line to improve workers' job satisfaction.

With proper long-range planning, however, you can gradually introduce modifications to the established job design. Eventually you can incorporate Job Enrichment principles into the design of new plants or the modernization of old ones. This is the course Volvo has followed.

Volvo has been experimenting with enriched job designs since the Sixties. It began to do so because top management accepted the idea that workers had a basic need for control and influence over their work situation, and for variety and interest in their jobs. Without these attractions, the company believed, it would have trouble recruiting and holding employees and motivating them to perform well. The problem would increase, the company felt, as the educational level of the workforce continued its steady rise.

Volvo already had a mechanism through which workers could influence many aspects of the job. Every company in Sweden with more than 50 employees is required by law to have workers' councils. As explained by Pehr Gyllenhammar, president of Volvo, these councils are media "for information and joint consultation between management and employees through their trade union organizations within the company." In many plants, including Volvo's, the council is supplemented by joint committees on various matters of mutual interest to management and workers.

These councils provide, to a degree quite unlike the typical U.S. organization, at least two basic components of an enriched work situation. One is a large influence over the way the job is done (and over the hygiene aspects of the job). The other is an effective channel of feedback both on production performance and on larger questions of company policy, such as marketing, investments, and financial reports.

This high degree of participation is an essential and characteristic part of Volvo's variations on job design.

As a basic means of introducing variety and interest into jobs,

Volvo established a system of job rotation. For example, at the passenger-car assembly plant in Gothenburg, about 1,400 out of 7,000 employees rotate jobs on a voluntary basis. The schedule of rotation is drawn up by the employees themselves.

In general it is important to distinguish between job rotation, which adds variety to a worker's activities, and Job Enrichment, which connotes broader responsibilities as well. The Volvo rotation arrangement adds variety. Since the workers have considerable control over the arrangement, it might be considered almost a form of enrichment. In addition, by familiarizing each worker with a wide variety of skills, it serves as an underpinning of the work organization usually considered typical of Volvo's enrichment efforts. That is the team assembly concept.

At the Gothenburg truck plant the assembly process is organized into 20 teams, each assigned a basic assembly job. Teams include anywhere from three to nine workers. The team itself chooses one of their number to act as its spokesman to the foreman: usually the spokesmanship rotates among the various team members.

The work to be accomplished by the team is assigned in periods of a week or so, and the team members decide how they shall divide it. Pay is related to the performance of the team as a whole.

When new members are assigned to the team, they receive considerable skills training, which demands about 130 hours spread out over the first 16 weeks on the job. To offset the possible drop in the team's productivity during this period, the team is allotted a so-called instructor's fee so that earnings do not suffer.

At least once a month there is a meeting that includes the current team spokesman, another member, the supervisor, and the production engineer. These meetings cover a variety of matters. According to Volvo, they frequently produce solutions to operating problems, such as choice of tooling, which could not have occurred any other way. They are a vital channel of worker participation.

Obviously the fragmented, linear sequence of typical assembly operations is at odds with the kinds of work organization concepts Volvo has been applying. The ideal is the small craft shop, not the massive assembly line. This implication is being carried out in the design of Volvo's latest plants. Perhaps the most dramatic illustration of the impact of Job Enrichment on plant design is the passenger-car assembly plant at Kalmar.

The Kalmar plant, with a capacity to turn out 60,000 cars a year, was designed around the concept of building a number of team workshops into a large plant. The workshops are ranged along the perimeter of the plant. Each team, consisting of from 15 to 25 workers, has its own entrance, locker room, washroom, and facilities for work breaks. Each team has responsibility for a certain section of the car: electrical system, steering and controls, brakes and wheels, etc.

The stores of parts for all the teams are in the center of the plant. Buffer stocks of work pieces are placed between individual operations and between various teams, so that workers have considerable freedom in varying the pace of the work. A team can decide, for instance, to speed up its work pace in short bursts and then take a coffee break. The break room has a view of the work bay, so workers can see when they have to return.

The work itself is organized in two basic ways. In the first, work stations are in series. Two or three workers at each station can rotate jobs if they wish. They follow the work as it moves along a line.

The second setup has teams of two or three workers doing an entire task on a stationary car body.

Plant equipment is designed to help the teams handle as wide a variety of tasks as possible—including maintenance, material handling, tool changes, etc. Car bodies move within and between work areas on self-propelled carriages. Tipping devices permit turning the body for comfortable work on all sides.

This effort to design facilities and work systems so that workers have variety, control over the pace of work, and opportunities to learn new tasks instead of being locked into rigid classifications, is very recent. Data on economic performance is not available as of this date. However the Kalmar people can report a decrease in turnover, a decrease in absenteeism, and an improvement in quality.

Obviously, this new plant design built around a concern for the quality of work life is the wave of the future. It presages exciting new things to come in the manufacturing world.

HEAVY MACHINERY REMANUFACTURING

The organization in this case overhauls diesel engines. Usually when an engine is returned to the shop, it is replaced immediately with a rebuilt engine. The customer is billed on the basis of work done to rebuild his own engine, although he may never see it again. At many points during the rebuilding, parts are inspected to determine which can be recycled and which must be scrapped. These determinations are recorded on a packet of documents which follows the engine through the cycle and serves as a basis for billing.

The cycle has five stages. In *teardown,* three men disassemble a returned engine and inspect parts for a preliminary decision on scrap or reclaim. In *small-parts cleaning,* reclaimable parts are cleaned by steam, abrasives, etc., and inspected again for disposition. In *rework,* machining brings parts up to various specifications, and they are inspected for conformance. In *assembly,* the reconditioned parts and any new ones required are reassembled into a complete engine. In *engine test,* the rebuilt engine is run in a test cell that duplicates conditions of use. Final adjustments or changes are made before shipment.

Before jobs were redesigned, the cycle was full of worker complaints and production bottlenecks. Engine teardown began on one shift and finished on another. Conflict arose because one shift thought the other had made too little progress, given insufficient briefing on potential problems, or broken or twisted parts.

In small-parts cleaning, workers complained that they lost too much time waiting around for inspectors. The physical layout was inconvenient, and workers had specific complaints about certain equipment. Parts were cleaned in order of arrival, not by priority. As a consequence, assembly workers lost time in constantly running to the foreman of the small-parts area for parts that were not on hand. They also had to make frequent trips to the toolroom for equipment that was not at the work stations.

In the rebuilding operation as a whole, there was no training that gave employees an opportunity to see how the individual part and the individual job fitted into the whole process. Training was not given as trainees required it, but according to the supervisors' decision about "the next job I want to teach them."

How Jobs Were Redesigned

The natural unit of work, the individual engine, was made the basis of a genuine team. Only one shift worked on tearing down any one engine, taking as many work turns as necessary. Assembly was organized the same way.

Autonomy was increased in several ways. In teardown and in small-parts cleaning, the lead man on each shift was given authority to determine disposition of parts.

The average worker's involvement in the total task was increased considerably. In teardown and assembly, tooling was made available at work stations, and a production employee made responsible for it. In small-parts cleaning, workers were given a voice in choosing equipment they would have to use. They also went into the field with purchasing representatives to check out the use and performance of potential equipment.

One worker's job was expanded so that he made some items of tooling and fixtures in the shop—including the design work—instead of having it supplied from outside. A quick-disconnect device reduced test-cell time considerably.

Each assembly team was provided with a small-parts accumulator, whose job was to make sure the parts were on hand as needed. A day ahead, he received from the team a list of parts that would be needed for the next job. If they were not available when he checked the list, he expedited them with the coordinator in the small-parts area.

How the Changes Improved Productivity

A few of the improvements that occurred after the changes described are listed here:

- Average time for tearing down an engine dropped from 55 man-hours to 48.

- Giving operators responsibility for part inspection virtually eliminated the need for a separate inspection effort in the teardown area.

- A similar change in small parts eliminated duplicate inspection, reduced the average time for cleaning parts, and freed inspectors for greater attention to quality control problems and reduced material losses.

- Tool usage was reduced by better control, but tool availability was improved with no increase in toolroom staffing.

- Making some tooling and fixtures in house reduced costs of purchase from outside suppliers.

- A quick-connect device designed by workers reduced average time for test-cell hookup from 45 to 15 minutes.

- Overall assembly time was drastically reduced by elimination of chronic unavailability of parts.

- Creation of the accumulator's job in small parts filled a training need. It was essentially a training position for the next available spot on the assembly team, and in filling it the trainee got to know the parts required.

The aggregate initial-year savings from these changes amounted to $129,000.

A WEAVING PLANT

This plant is operated by a division of a major textile corporation. With Walters & Associates as consultants the company undertook several projects to improve the quality of working life. Each project dealt with some specific weaknesses or problems in productivity. All of them, however, were meant to deal also with a problem increasingly serious for the textile industry: How to attract, retain, and motivate a work force for jobs that are mainly repetitive, nerve-wracking, and exhausting. The labor supply in the South was once plentiful, and it was easy to recruit mill workers from a predominantly rural population. As the South developed economically, other industries moved in to compete with textiles for the labor force—often with higher wages, and almost always with jobs that were physically more tolerable.

In this case, Walters & Associates found that overspecialization, inappropriate incentives, lack of shared goals, inadequate supervision and training, and insufficient worker participation in operating decisions were interfering with the mission of the plant: to weave sheeting and other textiles with maximum output and quality.

Work groups consisted of *weavers*, who attended to the basic operation of the looms; *loom fixers*—a higher pay category—who made fine adjustments and repairs and who troubleshoot; and five other support positions, whose duties included oiling, hauling quills of yarn, taking off cloth, and doing "smash" work on badly fouled looms.

Walters & Associates found that the weaving operation was organized to produce "conflict, not cooperation." Despite the number of separate job categories, all the pressure for efficiency was on the weavers. They were paid on an incentive basis, and thus were directly penalized for downtime or rewarded for productivity. However, the other workers, especially the loom fixers, had an influence on the operation of the looms as well. They were all paid a flat hourly rate, and would get it even if the looms were down. As a result there were many instances of bad feeling between weavers and loom fixers.

The reward system also paid off for different fragments of the total mission. Weavers' pay was based on production. The loom fixer was supposed to be responsible for quality. No member of the group was encouraged to feel responsible for the complete mission.

Too many decisions were concentrated in the shift supervisor. Rank-and-file workers had no voice at all even in decisions that affected their jobs and their performance.

Looms in the plant were connected to a computer that provided instant readout on the percentage of looms operating at a given time. Weavers and supervisors—but not the other workers—felt under tremendous pressure from the hourly postings of readouts on each battery of looms. The posted figures were the weavers' only feedback on whether or not the supervisor was satisfied. If the efficiency figure slipped, the weaver got a complaint or reprimand. Feedback on quality, however, went to the loom fixer.

In short, feedback was not being used to further the total mission. There was little chance for workers in the weaving plant to develop commitment to the total mission of the plant—much less that of the division or corporation.

How Jobs Were Redesigned

The central concept of the changes undertaken was to replace the *work group*, with its high specialization and internal conflicts, by a *work team*—a group of workers pooling their skills to accomplish common goals to which they were committed.

A key idea was to strengthen the "core job" of the weaver by including in it some activities of loom fixer and other support workers. This step not only increased the variety of the weaver's job; it reduced loom downtime by letting weavers perform some maintenance and adjustment tasks themselves, instead of waiting until a loom fixer was available.

The jobs of oiler, quill hauler, and cloth takeoff man were combined. The job of smash hand was eliminated, and all members of the team were trained to do smash work.

This despecialization increased the variety of skills most workers used on the job. It provided a better basis for each worker to identify with the whole team task.

Restructuring of the reward system was one of the most important steps toward a true team. Instead of incentive pay for weavers and flat rate for all other workers, the whole team was paid by an incentive based on total performance. Cooperation to accomplish the entire mission was what paid off.

The effect of these changes on workers' attitudes can best be shown by their comments:

A loom fixer: "Before, I didn't care much about production. Now I feel good when I pitch in and get production up. It's not just the money, but the feeling that you yourself did something that helped the team figure. My job just means more to me now."

A weaver: "We are working more together now. People are helping out when they can; instead of leaning or standing around when someone else's looms are down, you try to help. They will do the same for you."

How the Changes Improved Productivity

However much worker attitudes improve, the real test of success is in the operating figures and other measures that contribute to productivity. Here they are in summary:

- Efficiency (essentially a measure of the average percentage of all looms operating): Efficiency averaged for all three shifts was up to more than 90% within the first five weeks of the trial, compared to an average 85% during the base period before the changes were made.

- Seconds as a percentage of total output: The incentive system was based on an estimated 3% seconds. Actual percentages were consistently below 1%, and as low as one-fifth of 1%.

- Absenteeism for the base period averaged about 8%. Since the team concept was implemented, absenteeism has been halved.

The aggregate initial-year savings from these changes amount to more than $100,000.

REFERENCES

1. Material in this case history is adapted from article by Donald B. Thompson: "Enrichment in Action Convinces Skeptics," *Industry Week*, (February 14, 1972); and from *Job Enrichment Newsletter* (April, 1972).

chapter FIFTEEN

A Pebble in the Pond:
A Job Enrichment Model
of Organizational Change
and Development

Our presentation so far has focused on the use of Job Enrichment as a means of solving specific, well-defined problems. In the interest of clarity we have emphasized a straight-line sequence from recognition of a problem or problems (turnover, absenteeism, low productivity, etc.) through diagnosis, implementation, and results.

The impression of Job Enrichment thus created is true so far as it goes, but it is not complete. In their consulting practice the authors have often had the experience of seeing the initial impetus of a successful Job Enrichment project broaden beyond the target jobs until the entire organization teems with change and vitality.

This process can be visualized through a simple and familiar image. Dropping a pebble into a still pond releases energy that sends waves radiating out from a single point in ever-widening rings. Each ring merges inevitably and naturally into the next, and ultimately no part of the calm surface is left unmoved or unchanged.

In the case of Job Enrichment, the "pebble" is the actual change in work content. The "pond" is the organization. The "widening rings" are all the changes in structures and relationships that follow naturally from the job redesign, and finally result in true changes of management style.

In this chapter we shall outline how this process occurs, and suggest what management might expect along the way. Our aim is to construct a general model of organizational development with Job Enrichment at its core.

HOW ARE JOB ENRICHMENT AND ORGANIZATION DEVELOPMENT RELATED?

A recent survey of corporate Organization Development (OD) practices found virtually no agreement on what OD actually is—even among corporations and consultants that claim to be using it. On one hand, many are careless about defining what they mean or do not mean when they use the term "Organization Development." On the other, some define OD so carefully that it means only what they themselves practice. Then, because there is confusion, practitioners and theorists periodically joust over "what OD really means."

This kind of debate over theory deserves little space in a book designed to be practical. Above all, we have no intention of defining OD so narrowly as to exclude everything but Job Enrichment.

Perhaps the simplest way to approach a definition of OD is to consider briefly what gives rise to organizations in the first place. An organization exists to pursue goals that its members cannot achieve—or cannot achieve easily—by individual action. The organization is a network of relationships among the individual members and their activities in support of these goals. The particular organization succeeds to the extent to which the network conveys:

- Awareness of the overall goals.
- The relevance of the individual's person and activities to pursuit of the overall goals.
- The information that will enable the individual to further the organization's goals.
- The rewards—in pay, fringe benefits, inherent work satisfaction, and social payoffs—that motivate the individual to work toward the organization's goals.

Let's think of two basic kinds of organizations. The first is characterized by spontaneous commitment to shared values. It may also attempt to accomplish goals outside the organization, but the primary reward of the organization to its individual members is often just the satisfaction of belonging. This type of organization is usually quite informal.

The second basic type of organization exists primarily to accomplish

external goals. To do so, it must include as members some individuals
—perhaps many of them—who have little or no inherent commitment
to the goals. To prosper, such an organization must provide its members
with other kinds of rewards. If, along the way, it can increase members'
identification with organization goals, so much the better.

Of course, in this category we are talking about business corporations as well as governmental, educational, and religious organizations.
It is in this context that we shall define OD.

Organization Development, as we use it here, is a process of change
in the behavior of an organization or its components, initiated and
directed to make the organization better able to achieve its goals. Principal purposes of the change process include increasing identification
with organizational goals, rewarding behavior that furthers them, and
reducing nonproductive conflict among subordinate goals. The process
of OD can be accomplished by varied methods of analysis, training,
structural change, and other actions and interventions. The process as a
whole draws heavily on the insights and methods of the behavioral
sciences.

This definition is fairly neutral and inclusive. In fact, it may include
more territory than OD has commonly come to connote. In many minds,
that connotation includes these ideas about the mainstream of OD:

- It concentrates first on changing attitudes, in the belief that behavior
  changes will follow.

- It often (not always) concentrates on changing attitudes at the upper levels of the organization, in the belief that the attitude changes
  will filter down.

- It is frequently directed at better "morale" or "interpersonal relationships," rather than measurable operating results.

- It relies heavily on sensitivity training, role playing, encounter
  groups, transactional analysis, and similar approaches that are generally attitude-oriented.

- It takes a long time—at least three years is a common figure.

It is often a tossup whether a given organization consultant will
concede that Job Enrichment qualifies as Organization Development.
We consider it so, and our definition of OD is certainly broad enough

to embrace it. If Job Enrichment did no more than increase the satisfaction and motivation of the individual worker with his or her job, it would deserve recognition as a form of Organization Development.

Ultimately, however, Job Enrichment does much more. In fact, much of its strength as a change catalyst stems from the ways it differs from the popular conception of OD. For example:

- Job Enrichment produces concrete changes in employees' behavior soon after it is implemented.
- It typically begins no higher than the middle-management levels of an organization—most frequently at the lower operational levels.
- Properly implemented, it sets and achieves specific, measurable changes in operating results and productive use of manpower.
- It uses attitude-oriented training methods to support the central behavior changes.
- A typical project can be set up, implemented, and evaluated within one year.

Change and Resistance

Attempts at significant change almost always encounter resistance. Thus a usable approach to Organization Development must provide ways of minimizing resistance and of dealing with it when it arises.

Job Enrichment is no more immune to resistance than any other OD intervention, but it does have several advantages.

- It can be introduced into the organization on neutral ground, with minimal perceived threat to individuals or groups. Job Enrichment deals not with individuals or their attitudes, but with their jobs.
- Since changes in daily activities take place immediately, it is impossible for employees to reject the change without first experiencing it. Where behavior change is to follow attitude change, by contrast, there is ample time to nurse ungrounded fears about the change and reject it on emotional grounds before it has been tried.
- Just as the behavior change is immediate, so measurable improvements in operating results—the first signs of success—are usually available either immediately or within a few months.

- The changes stemming from job redesign make clear that additional changes are needed, and what they are.

This last point leads us directly into presentation of the Job Enrichment model of organizational change and development.

AN ORGANIC MODEL

Figure 15.1 conceptualizes the stage of spreading influence from the central job redesign through the entire organization. Although it has the weaknesses of all schematic diagrams of abstract concepts, it should be useful as a quick visual description.

The stages of the change process are:

- Redesign of target jobs affects intrinsic motivators.

- The resulting changes in job content and distribution of work and in supervisory behavior lead to changes in reporting relationships and overall organization structure.

- As the shape of the organization changes, it becomes necessary to form new management teams and engage in team-building activities.

- The realignment of duties requires a clear definition of accountability.

- As accountabilities are defined, the managers of different accountability areas begin the continuing process of joint goal-setting and review.

- The goal-setting process provides a firm basis for appraisal of management performance by objectives.

- The cumulative effect of changes in specific management behaviors is a genuine and lasting change in management style.

The order of these events is not immutable, nor will every part of an organization reach the same stage at the same time. Certain kinds of intervention may be needed at a stage other than that which we shall indicate here. Changes in hygiene factors and in extrinsic motivators such as pay, supervisory feedback, etc., are likely to occur at many points. Changes in management attitudes and behavior should appear all along the way.

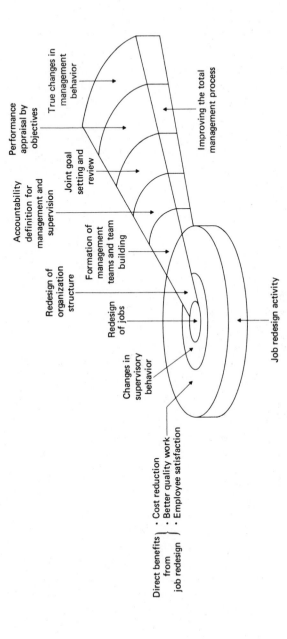

FIG. 15.1 An organic model for Organization Development

Intrinsic and Extrinsic Motivators

Herzberg's formulation of the Motivation-Hygiene theory made a clear
distinction between the aspects of a job which are capable of producing
satisfaction and motivation and those which at best can only prevent dissatisfaction. For almost as long as the theory has been around, motivation researchers have suspected that it may be somewhat too rigid to fit
the facts. Even though its value in focusing attention on task content as
the principal key to motivation is widely conceded, consulting experience tends to confirm these suspicions. Certainly, for a work force with
normally high growth needs, the core transaction between the worker
and the task is the greatest source of long-lasting motivation. Just em-
pirically, however, it is sometimes obvious that a good relationship with
a supervisor can be seen as a motivator, especially as it is a source of
additional feedback on performance. Pay systems and performance appraisal can do the same if they are genuinely task oriented.

Thus it is possible to talk of two types of motivators, intrinsic and
extrinsic. Both can produce motivation, and they both should be dis-
tinguished from hygiene factors.

As far as implementation is concerned, it is probably not too important to distinguish between hygiene factors and extrinsic motivators.
However, it is useful to keep in mind that it is the changes in job content, affecting the intrinsic motivators, that lead directly to the second
stage of development.

ORGANIZATION STRUCTURAL CHANGE

Job Enrichment directly leads to organization structural changes in two
basic ways. They are related to the two dominant patterns of enrichment, as described earlier (Chapter 11): task combination–client relationships, and autonomy–vertical loading.

If Job Enrichment in a particular instance consists principally of
the task combination complex, changes in both work group structure
and reporting relationships are almost sure to be involved. Sequences of
operations within a work group may be telescoped. Formerly separate
functions may be abolished. Two or more work groups may be combined. One—or all—of them may suddenly have a new boss.

Even if no task combination is involved, however, it may be necessary at least to examine reporting relationships and the supervisory hierarchy. Vertical loading involves taking responsibilities from higher-level jobs and adding them to the lower level. This process generates a good deal of churning of responsibilities. The organization must then face an important question: Have the higher-level jobs been so emasculated that a whole supervisory level should be abolished, or is it now appropriate to apply what Robert N. Ford calls "tandem enrichment"— which consists of enriching Job A by loading onto it responsibilities from Job B, one level higher, then pulling new responsibilities down from a still higher level to enrich Job B.

One of the most common effects of Job Enrichment on organization structure is to initiate an evolution from functional to client-oriented work organizations. This change is the exact opposite of a trend almost universally observed in industry. If "the natural history of jobs is to get worse," it is also their natural history to become more specialized and fragmented.

As we have conceded several times, there are usually plausible reasons for this specialization. The most common are (1) the simple inability of one worker to master all the skills or operate all the equipment needed to do a whole job, (2) the high cost of training one person to do it all, even if it is possible, and (3) the demands of "efficiency." Particularly as technology and its products get more complex, these arguments seem to become more compelling. So the trend accelerates, splitting what was once a single job into several.

The organization that emerges is work oriented rather than results oriented, and however reasonable that form of organization may have seemed, it has its problems. It is prone to delays and schedule distortions as the work is passed from one function to the next. Each function has its own management hierarchy, oriented toward its own objectives, and interfunctional conflicts are common. Finally, the greater the functionalization of work, the less ownership or identification the individual worker can feel with a complete end product and its user. The negative effect on motivation we have already discussed.

In the name of better motivation, Job Enrichment attempts to approach, so far as possible, the condition of the original whole job that was split up.

Suppose, for example, that a sequence of clerical operations—of the kind commonly found in banks, insurance companies, etc.—consists of steps A, B, C, and D. All documents to be processed go through each step in a separate department, and in each one the documents must be batched and distributed, given their basic processing, checked, and passed on to the next department.

In such a situation no department or individual worker can have much sense of identification with the end product. Moreover, problems of quality or throughput in one department are likely to cause friction between its manager and the manager of the next department.

Through Job Enrichment, the work flow is often reorganized. The total workload could be broken down by regions, types of accounts, distinct products or services, or some other logical grouping. Then teams would be assembled for each category; the new work groups include workers from each of the former work groups. But they are oriented toward clients or end products, not functions, and since each manager has a cross-functional module, opportunities for conflict among managers of functions are largely reduced.

The basic change in organizational focus raises the question of what kind of manager should be managing these activities—and thus has some implications for management development. To manage a cross-functional module well, a manager must have (or develop) multiple skills and areas of knowledge. Equally important, he must learn to balance a wider variety of concerns than a functional manager. He must be a general manager.

BUILDING THE MANAGEMENT TEAM

However broad and deep a manager's skills and knowledge, he or she rarely has all that are needed. Unfortunately, the ability to tap the skills and knowledge of others, and to use synergy to amplify them, is one of the most universally weak areas of management. In the development process we have been describing, as the manager's role becomes more cross-functional, this ability becomes more crucial.

This is the time to develop a new interpersonal management process. The functional approach to management tends to produce specialized managers just as it produces specialized employees. Each manager is exposed primarily to a single aspect of the overall objective. Rarely are there joint problem-solving efforts through which objectives can be harmonized and fresh perspectives provided.

Setting up a sound structure for joint problem-solving is the heart of the team-building effort. There should be regular meetings of the officer-in-charge/general manager with the management team for just this purpose.

A team is not created by fiat, of course. At this stage, especially since many of the team members may be working together closely for the first time, it is often advisable to foster the growth of team identity, and smooth out conflicts, by various kinds of training in interaction. These might include formal team-building training, role negotiation, team-effectiveness critique, or other similar experiences.

It was noted earlier that organizational change need not always follow the general sequence we are outlining here. As regards interpersonal skills training, it may be appropriate at almost any stage. For example, we have seen cases in which an organization was obviously in need of basic Job Enrichment, but the conflict among members of the implementing team was so destructive that enrichment was completely stymied until they went through some team-building exercises.

The management team structure can and should be reflected at lower levels as well. The general manager has a team of subordinate cross-functional managers. Each of them, in turn, serves (in Likert's words) as a "linking pin" to a similar structure at the supervisory level. The unit manager and his or her supervisors also meet for joint problem-solving, and the same principle applies here as at the higher level.

The structure that results is visualized in Fig. 15.2. The process that takes place within that structure is the basic dynamics of participative management.

ACCOUNTABILITY MANAGEMENT: WHERE JE AND MANAGEMENT BY OBJECTIVES MEET

One of the perennial questions about Job Enrichment is how, if at all, does it fit in with Management by Objectives (MBO). There is a definite relationship, and it becomes increasingly clear in the remaining stages of development we shall discuss. As a beginning, let's say that Job En-

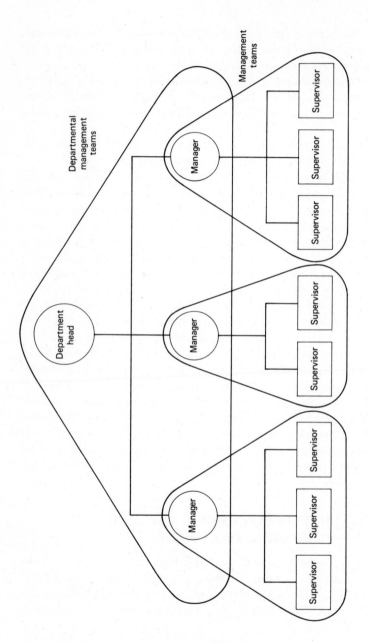

FIG. 15.2   Formation of management teams for participative management and team building

richment and MBO are branches of the same tree, and that tree is rooted in the soil of accountability.

Organizations can harness different types of power to achieve their goals. At one extreme are organizations that run on boss power—the power of the boss to enforce behavior that furthers organizational goals by various combinations of reward, punishment, control, personality, etc. Such organizations, in general, are distinctly nonparticipative. It is the boss who decides what employees' goals should be, and sees that they are achieved.

In the middle ground, as far as participation is concerned, are peer power and system power. Again, the boss largely sets the goals for the employees to pursue. But the power to get employees to pursue them is exerted through rigid adherence to a system designed for the purpose, or through forms of organization that make each worker the object of pressure from his or her peers to pursue organization goals.

The most participative organizations rely heavily on goal power. Top management still sets overall organization goals. However, there is no question of "enforcing" them. Instead, management relies, for achievement of overall goals, on each employee's commitment to goals he sets for himself. This is the process that has come to be known as Management by Objectives.

If the goals are to be met, though, there must be accountability, and accountability can exist only when there is both responsibility and authority. In the process of Job Enrichment, by setting up natural units of work, establishing client relationships, and loading into a job higher levels of authority, we enrich its accountability.

Job Enrichment and MBO share considerable territory—so much, in fact, that we can make these two general statements:

- If an organization has a working program in MBO, management jobs are inevitably being enriched.

- If the content of managers' jobs is inadequate in terms of filling their growth needs, then the lack may completely negate attempts at MBO. MBO cannot simply be imposed.

Precisely because there is still some confusion over whether Job Enrichment and MBO ever coincide, it may be helpful to identify the

territory they share, and to label it "accountability management." It
has the following aspects:

- Definition of the accountability of every manager's job.
- Mutual establishment of appropriate job objectives for limited
  periods.
- Implementation of the objectives.
- Evaluation of performance in terms of objectives.

Accountability Definition

The first step in managing accountabilities is to define them. This is a
demanding process. It is similar in some ways to preparation of job
descriptions, but it is oriented toward objectives rather than activities.

Many of the managers suddenly confronted with the task of defining their accountabilities may have had no similar experience—no
setting of objectives, or even preparation of job descriptions. Some
guidelines, therefore, may be appreciated.

Since accountability embraces responsibility and authority, these
should be the two things on which the definition focuses. Managers
should be clear on what they are expected to accomplish, in general
terms, and on the authority granted to them to do it. It is usually preferable to define both responsibility and authority positively, by what
they include. However, there are some cases in which the accountability
definition appropriately contains some explicit limitations. This is
especially true in the case of authority. Particularly in a state of transition, the amount of authority granted to individual managers may be
gradually increased. The definition should make the starting point clear,
and be revised as necessary.

The purpose of accountability definition is to clarify changing roles.
The individual doing the defining should ask himself or herself all along
the way: What is the responsibility (authority) of my new job role?
How does it differ from the old?

Establishing Objectives

The next phase of accountability management is closest to what is usually meant by "Management By Objectives." It is also most often the

crucial phase in determining whether the twin purposes of MBO—the growth of the individual manager and the attainment of organizational goals—are compatible.

Many managers and organizations find, to their surprise, that they can first conceive possible objectives clearly only after a round of job redesign. The effort to establish or strengthen feedback in the job often makes clear for the first time the possibility of measuring certain job parameters and of evaluating performance by them.

In itself, this potential for measurement is only a *basis* for setting objectives; it is not the actual process of setting them. In fact, unless the process can be taken further, there is a genuine risk of falling into the "activity trap"—being so satisfied by the greater information available that one attempts to use all of it.

In the definition stage of accountability management, managers may have to depend on their superiors for guidance about organization goals. In setting short-range goals, however, the balance of involvement shifts clearly toward the subordinate managers, for they possess the most thorough knowledge of the job.

As described earlier, the process of enriching jobs typically brings about greater client orientation. Managers should draw on this when setting their objectives. If they understand clearly what service or end product they are providing to their clients, they can use the clients' projected needs over a quarter, six months, or a year as guides to their own objectives. They can then adapt their managerial behavior to client-oriented ends, and use the appropriate forms of feedback to track their own progress.

Finally, if accountability management is to support the experienced meaningfulness that is an aim of Job Enrichment, then the objectives managers set for themselves, and the process by which those objectives are set, must contribute to the managers' own personal growth.

Implementing Objectives

The success with which all these requirements are met may depend on the mechanics set up to handle implementation. These vary from one situation to another, and usually involve meetings between the manager and his or her boss, plus a varying amount of documentation.

As is true of all other aspects of accountability, these mechanics must contribute to the achievement of organization objectives as well as the growth of the individual manager. As Peter Drucker has said in a basic statement of MBO: "Each manager's job must be focused on the success of the whole. The performance that is expected of the manager must be derived from the performance goals of the business. His results must be measured by the contribution they make to the success of the enterprise." [1]

Most MBO programs use some variant of the basic document suggested years ago by Drucker, the manager's letter. Vastly simplified, the letter works this way: The manager prepares a "letter" to his or her superior, describing the objectives of the job. The two discuss the objectives until they agree. The agreement must be real, not the superior's imposition on the subordinate of the goals the superior thinks appropriate. Finally, the manager proposes specific objectives on the way to the overall goals.

Years of experience with MBO have shown that this process of harmonizing individual and organizational objectives can go wrong at many points. There is a tendency to treat the agreed-on objectives as if they were carved on stone, and to leave managers very much on their own in pursuing them. If accountability management differs from MBO as usually practiced, it is probably in a greater commitment to flexibility. With the greater feedback that comes from Job Enrichment, there is a greater capacity for self-correction.

In many cases the manager can make the correction independently. But especially in the case of newly assumed accountabilities, the manager may feel a need for guidance from his or her superior, and should feel free to seek it. Again, this need not be an imposed solution. Most appropriately the superior acts as a consultant or resource person, helping to define the problem and the issue so that the subordinate manager sees the solutions without further help.

Evaluation

If the structure and content of the manager's job are right, and if the mechanics of MBO/accountability management are right, the manager should be making constant self-evaluations. The criteria of those evaluations should be exactly in phase with those of the organization.

At this point the organization has the final prerequisite for lasting effects on managerial behavior: an appraisal system genuinely based on performance. Most organizations would claim that they appraise performance and nothing else. But in fact most of those who do appraise performance (results) do so unsystematically. Furthermore, appraisal becomes contaminated too easily by personality, longevity, and just plain inertia. The result is that the organization gets far less of the behavior it wants, and much it does not want, because is does not consistently reward results.

To the extent that factors other than results enter into appraisal of managers, there is room for less effective managers to hide. If there may or may not be a reward for results, why take the risks needed to get them? Why set challenging objectives and strive for them?

The kind of organization that evolves through the process discussed in this book leaves the managers exposed and makes them deliver. But in the course of the evolution they learn the exhilaration of the challenge, and acquire the know-how that enables them to deliver. The behavior of individual managers is transformed, and so ultimately is the style of the organization.

SOME WORDS OF CAUTION

As noted early in this chapter, we have tried to construct a model of organization development which seems natural and workable, generalizing it from the processes we have seen countless times in the wake of Job Enrichment.

We have tried to make the model broadly inclusive—partly as a reaction to excessively narrow models put forth by some OD practitioners. Just as we have avoided calling Job Enrichment the panacea for problems of motivation, productivity, turnover, etc., so we insist that the sequence presented here need not always be applicable. Why?

For one thing, it operates in a long time frame. Thus it is not suitable for "crisis therapy." Starting as it does from a core of immediate job design change, the model starts producing results rather quickly. But if the critical problem of an organization is in an area that will be affected only at a later stage of the program, the organization may not have time to wait.

The alternatives are to start with an OD intervention aimed more specifically at the most urgent problem, or to use the basic model as outlined but speed up its action by means of additional consultants or change agents.

It is also possible for the model to be simply inappropriate. For example, if the organization's weaknesses are largely the result of conflicts of interpersonal relations at the very top, it may be useless to try and initiate widespread change until there is a change in management.

THE ACORN: AN IMAGE OF GERMINATION AND GROWTH

Despite these reservations, our experience has shown that the model of change outlined here is one highly capable of generating significant and lasting changes in management behavior in the largest number of organizations. Because it is an inclusive model, it sets aside the troublesome but false issue, "What does the organization need most?" and replaces it with the useful question, "What is the most productive combination of intervention techniques?"

This chapter began with an image from nature—the pebble in the pond. In recapitulating the advantages of the Job Enrichment model, we shall draw on another image: the germination and growth of an organism from a seed—the acorn.

This biological image is particularly apt for two reasons: Like the seed or acorn, the core activities of job redesign contain in themselves all the characteristics of the later stages of development. And like the seed or acorn, the core activities provide a source of sustenance for the later stages of growth.

The small but definite changes due to job redesign unleash tremendous forces, like the strength that enables a young tree to break through rock. It will be useful to summarize once again the particular strength of the Job Enrichment model as an initiator of change:

- Job Enrichment is introduced into the organization on as neutral a ground as it is possible to find. Nothing is "wrong" with either management or rank-and-file employees. The trouble is in an impersonal factor of job design. It is a far less threatening starting point than a wholesale restructuring of the organization chart, which provides people with a whole set of fears before they see any results. True, by the end of the process the organization chart may be restructured. But the change is merely descriptive of things people are already living with.

- Job Enrichment introduces quick change and results. The management team involved in Job Enrichment goes through a learning experience. They emerge primed and motivated to follow the change agent.

- The step from one stage to the next seems natural and inevitable in the interest of promoting growth. Accountability management comes easier if you have dealt successfully with vertical loading. If resistance emerges at any state, the management team draws a sense of support from its early team-building and problem-solving. The substance and spirit of change established in Job Enrichment should sustain the effort and serve as a touchstone for the later stages.

REFERENCES

1. Peter F. Drucker, *The Practice of Management*, New York, Harper and Brothers (1954).

chapter
SIXTEEN
Toward Enlightened
Systems Design

Tony Connole, a vice-president of the UAW, has noted that a bank of industrial robots used on an auto assembly line requires the line to stop long enough for automated welding heads to snake their way into the car body, perform their spot welds, and retract. "For robots they stop the line," he comments. "I never saw them stop it for a man."

This situation represents a long tradition of meeting technical needs at the expense of human needs, and Job Enrichment is a strategy for changing this practice. Most practitioners of Job Enrichment work within existing systems, trying to remedy situations created by this imbalance. It is not surprising, then, if they sometimes view as opponents the industrial engineers responsible for the systems.

Industrial engineers sometimes reciprocate, and look on Job Enrichment as a threat to the whole basis of productivity. The result is a controversy, alternately flaring and smoldering, over just which approach is the key to productivity. We believe the controversy is spurious and unproductive, yet we discuss it briefly here for several reasons:

- To put the controversy in a Job Enrichment perspective
- To map out some territory which we think Job Enrichment and industrial engineering legitimately share.
- To suggest how each of the disciplines can aid and supplement the other in the design of balanced systems.

THE INDUSTRIAL ENGINEERING/JOB ENRICHMENT CONTROVERSY

Current definitions of industrial engineering are overtly quite neutral. They generally boil down to something like this: "Industrial engineering is the discipline concerned with the design and management of integrated systems of men and machinery for the processing of materials."

If the practice of industrial engineering was always as evenhanded as this definition, there would be no room for disagreement between industrial engineers and Job Enrichment specialists. But as Sharon L. Lieder and John H. Zenger have noted (in an article, incidentally, that urges greater use of behavioral sciences methods in the industrial engineering context) : "The importance of 'man' and 'social sciences' is recognized in this definition, but conventional industrial engineering programs have given little emphasis to the human dimension." [1]

Both industrial engineering and Job Enrichment pursue the goal of productivity. Their differing methods reflect different assumptions about the role of workers in achieving productivity. Industrial engineering has its roots in the work of F. W. Taylor. It was Taylor's central idea that the typical worker did not want to think or make complicated decisions on the job; therefore, the work should be designed in such a way that it minimized the thinking the worker had to do. Each process should be broken down into tiny steps, and each worker assigned to repeat the same step over and over throughout the work day.

Taylor's assumption may have been valid for the work force of his time—a work force which, for the most part, had little education, little experience of economic security, and a limited sense of opportunities for personal growth. If we grant this, there still remains the question of whether the assumption is valid for today's work force, and whether the methods derived from it are not literally counterproductive in many instances.

"Taylorism" arose in an economy just starting to recognize the productive advantages of mass processing and assembly of goods. Now we are in an era known variously as "post-industrial society," "service economy," and the time of "knowledge industries." According to some estimates, true assembly jobs of the kind Taylor might have worked with make up less than 2% of the total activity of the workforce.

Notions like these may tempt us to say that Taylorism is a dead issue. If it were, there would be little profit in examining differences between industrial engineering and Job Enrichment. But in fact much of the spirit of Taylor is still very much alive in the attitudes and methods of industrial engineering.

This fact has positive as well as negative implications. An overwhelmingly positive aspect is simply the capability of making precise measurements of work accomplished, of setting valid standards, and of relating output to work inputs.

Work measurement, of course, is not the whole of industrial engineering. But it is the aspect most often identified in broad-brush descriptions of what industrial engineers do.

However, the role of the industrial engineer is changing. Writing in 1972, Robert W. Newsom, Jr., Vice-President of Operations for Lorrilard Co., said: "Although the industrial engineer's main task for years had been to design work measurement systems, his ability to design *any* system that utilizes concepts and man, in addition to systems for materials and manpower, has helped him to expand his areas of involvement and of responsibility rapidly. The result is that 36% of the American Institute of Industrial Engineers' membership are performing jobs that five years ago could not be classified even remotely as IE functions, according to the AIEE." [2]

It is in the role of systems designer that the industrial engineer and the Job Enrichment practitioner most often discover common territory. Whether they share it peaceably or dispute it depends on many factors.

Oddly enough, the very precision of the measurement capabilities of industrial engineering can often lead to conflict—by way of what Daniel Yankelovich has called the "McNamara fallacy," and described as follows:

"The first step is to measure whatever can be easily measured. This is okay as far as it goes. The second step is to disregard that which can't be easily measured or give it an arbitrary quantitative value. This is artificial and misleading. The third step is to presume that what can't be measured easily really isn't important. This is blindness. The fourth step is to say that what can't be easily measured really doesn't exist. This is suicide." [3]

Wherever the McNamara fallacy prevails, the Job Enrichment practitioner is almost sure to encounter trouble. The reasons are quite obvious. The industrial engineer can measure and talk about highly concrete phenomena—parts processed per hour, conveyor speeds in feet per minute, man-hours, etc. By contrast, the Job Enrichment practitioner has to convince management that equal attention must be paid to such vague-sounding abstractions as "job satisfaction," "meaningful work," and "client relationships."

In some cases unwary Job Enrichment practitioners add to their troubles by performing their own variation on the McNamara fallacy. They concede that they are working mainly with variables that cannot be measured very precisely, or perhaps at all. Therefore, they set up no criteria, no hard results, by which management could judge the value of Job Enrichment's contribution to organizational effectiveness and productivity.

The Job Enrichment practitioner going into an organization is quite likely to find one of the following troublesome situations involving work measurement:

- The capability for work measurement is used as a basis for a systems design that works against motivation and is actually counterproductive.

- Work measurement is highly developed, but it is not used either to give management a useful picture of productivity or to give individual workers feedback on their performance.

- Work measurement is inadequately developed and applied, so that individual units or whole organizations have little idea of their actual output or potential.

SHORT INTERVAL SCHEDULING

In many cases the Job Enrichment practitioner walks into a situation where, although work is organized on Taylorist principles, the organization has no particular commitment to continuing the status quo. In such cases the dominance of Taylorism is due more to inertia and the longer-established position of industrial engineering relative to more behaviorally oriented approaches. There are other instances, however, in which Job Enrichment must reckon with new and vigorous applications of Taylorism.

One of these is the approach to production control known as short interval scheduling (SIS). A system of short interval scheduling begins with an existing work arrangement, and it does not usually make significant changes in work flow beyond adjusting obvious inefficiencies.

Using sophisticated timing devices and technology, the industrial engineer conceptually separates the work process into a series of control-oriented action steps. Then he carefully times the various steps to determine, on the average, how many of them can be performed in a given period—usually one hour.

Up to this point we are dealing with work measurement as widely understood. The next step moves into the realm of job design. Several employees are assigned to scheduling work. As the work comes in, they batch it on the basis of the average times developed in the time study. The heart of SIS is to break work down into batches of such a size that a worker can perform his or her assigned operation on the batch within a specified interval—again, usually one hour.

The number of employees assigned solely to batching, scheduling, and logging output can differ, depending on the work processes involved. In a typical group of 80 to 100 employees, there may be from four to six schedulers.

Use of a SIS system is based on the assumption that the resulting increase in productivity will more than offset the cost of removing several employees from direct production work to do nothing but batch and schedule. The deeper assumption—the familiar underlying assumption of Taylorism—is that workers will be vastly more productive if their work flows in highly standardized pathways and spares them the need to make time-consuming decisions.

It should be clear from a reading of this book that short interval scheduling tends to remove from jobs many elements closely linked with Job Enrichment. Are the two approaches, then, incompatible?

There probably is no single answer. However, the following points can be made: Frst, since SIS basically accepts any existing flow of work, it might be possible to redesign a work situation to provide for more enrichment in some of the implementing concepts and still retain SIS. In such a situation the improvement of motivating potential in the job might be considerable, but it would still be less than could be achieved by giving employees greater say in the batching and scheduling of their own work.

Second, in many cases Job Enrichment can produce as great a productivity improvement as SIS. In deciding whether Job Enrichment is feasible, the existence of SIS is only one factor. But if the investment in the SIS system is substantial, and the advantages of Job Enrichment are not convincing, it may be wise not to attempt Job Enrichment in a work group using SIS—at least not as its first introduction into the organization.

Third, the Job Enrichment practitioner should make clear to management from the start that it may not be able to have both enriched jobs and short interval scheduling. The practitioner then has an obligation to make clear what the advantages or drawbacks of each may be.

Finally, if existing jobs are highly repetitive and otherwise bad in terms of motivation, but it is impossible or highly impractical to change them, then it may be virtually imperative to have SIS. Its advantage in such cases would be to impose the structure of short time horizons on tasks that might otherwise seem endless and undifferentiated. This possible advantage, however, may be of little value. The key point is that if poor jobs are left unchanged, people are likely to develop intensely adverse feelings about the work and seek every opportunity to avoid it. In such a situation control systems such as SIS may well be imperative. However, the costs are heavy in terms of minimal production and staff turnover.

THE ROLE OF FEASIBILITY STUDIES

The case of short interval scheduling and Job Enrichment ultimately comes down to a number of questions to be answered objectively. It is the role of a sound feasibility study to provide these answers. As we noted in Chapter 6, the diagnostic tools of Job Enrichment are rapidly increasing in precision. A feasibility study properly using the available tools should be able to:

- Determine whether job content and structure are major factors in nonproductive work behavior.
- Identify precisely which aspects of the job are at fault.
- Suggest steps to be taken by way of remedy.
- Identify factors in the immediate job situation or the larger organization which might limit chances of success.

The increasing scope of Job Enrichment diagnosis increases both the practitioner's chances of making a good case for Job Enrichment and his obligation to be objective in doing so. Although the feasibility study can provide volumes of facts and knowledge crucial to diagnosis, the practitioner must eventually recommend courses of action. In making recommendations, the practitioner will often have in mind that the task is at least partially to remedy excesses of job fragmentation and restriction. The challenge to the practitioner, however, is not to trade it for excesses of his or her own, but to help the client find the most favorable tradeoff of technological and human needs.

DESIGNING TRUE SOCIOTECHNICAL SYSTEMS

Professor Louis Davis of UCLA, Professor Eric Trist of Wharton, and other organization theorists have put considerable emphasis on the idea of the workplace as the meeting ground of two subsystems, the social and the technical. It is a truism of systems theory that individual subsystems tend to maximize their own performance rather than that of the entire system. It is part of the long heritage of Taylorism that in the typical work organization the technical subsystem has more often been allowed to optimize its performance.

The results in performance of the total system have not all been bad by any means. Davis has noted, however, that the total sociotechnical system is not completely closed. It is permeable to "leaking" of values in both directions, inward and outward.

Advocates of Job Enrichment do not—should not—want the long favoring of the technical system replaced with an equally unsuitable alternative; the design of work in the name of job satisfaction with no regard for technological imperatives. But they do believe that the two kinds of needs can be harmonized. And they must be harmonized, because the sociotechnical system is increasingly permeated by values from outside the workplace—values which say that workers want satisfying, motivating jobs. The company that provides such jobs is taking a vital action to ensure its high productivity.

In most cases jobs must be enriched within existing technological systems. In a few companies, however, there is a growing effort to build in Job Enrichment at the first stages of systems design. The new assembly plants of Volvo AB, mentioned in the case histories, are an outstanding example. There are other cases as well, but the total number, relative to the size of world industry, is still small.

To give human and social values equal weight with technological values in systems design requires changed attitudes in most organizations. What is easily overlooked is that this can also require structural changes in work organization. The first step is likely to be closer *ad hoc* teamwork between industrial engineering and some source of behavioral science input—such as an internal or external consultant, an Organization Development department, or a specially trained staff within personnel.

A further step—one which we have observed in a few client organizations—is the enhancement of existing systems-design/industrial-engineering capability with special training in Job Enrichment and other behavioral science applications.

This is a welcome and significant trend. The objective should not be Job Enrichment per se, or industrial engineering per se. The objective is *enlightened design of the total sociotechnical system*. The rigor of industrial engineering methods and the insights and growing precision of Job Enrichment can be combined in a model of systems design appropriate to increasing productivity in a time of changing demands on the organization.

REFERENCES

1. "Industrial Engineers and Behavioral Scientists—A Team Approach to Improved Productivity," *Personnel Magazine* (July/August 1967).

2. "The Industrial Engineer Moves Up to the Driver's Seat, *Management Review*, (March 1972).

3. "Human Resource Planning: Foundation for a Model," Vincent S. Flowers and Bernard A. Cook, *Personnel*, (Jan.-Feb. 1974).

Epilogue

There is great unrest in our working society. Manifestations of this are numerous and will increase in frequency and magnitude.

The alert organization is the one that recognizes the symptoms, understands the sociotechnical reasons behind them and is courageous enough to go to work on the problem.

This is slow, arduous, painful work. It has taken years to firmly entrench both our work methods and work systems, and our assumptions about people at work. Our society is paying a staggering price for human underutilization.

To paraphrase the British statesman and orator, Edmund Burke, "All that is necessary for the forces of evil to take over in the world are for enough good men (and women) to do nothing."

It's clearly up to us. We must move ahead.

About the Authors

Formed in 1967, Roy Walters & Associates, Inc., is a management consulting firm located in Glen Rock, N.J. The staff now includes the following:

ROY W. WALTERS, *President*

After graduation from the University of Pittsburgh, Roy Walters was employed in numerous line and staff positions by the Bell Telephone Co. of Pennsylvania. In 1960 he was transferred to AT&T as Director of Employment and Development.

At AT&T he won recognition as a leading exponent and developer of new philosophies, methods, and programs for the utilization of human resources. He was responsible for the first empirical research into applications of job enrichment.

In 1967 he established Roy W. Walters & Associates. The firm's success in redesigning jobs for maximum motivation and performance has established Roy as "Mr. Job Enrichment." He is a popular speaker before business and professional groups and has published many articles on motivation management. He is a member of the American Society for Training and Development, the Sales Executive Club and the American Society for Personnel Administration.

JOHN V. HICKEY, JR.
Manager of Research and Publications

John Hickey began his involvement with the behavioral sciences at Harvard College, where he studied
both psychology and anthropology and worked as an
undergraduate assistant in the university's Psychological Laboratories.

After graduation he spent three years in the
United States Army, in a variety of intelligence assignments in the United States and Europe.

Before becoming associated with the Walters firm,
he pursued a career in publications for management.
He was a technical textbook editor for Prentice-Hall,
Inc., reports editor for The Conference Board, and
senior editor for the Conover-Mast Div., Cahners
Publishing. He has written extensively on virtually
all aspects of management, economic, technological,
and human. Both as an editor and as a member of
Walters & Associates, he has taken part in numerous
organizational studies in such varied fields as air-
lines, banking, food processing, personnel, health care,
insurance, government, textiles and metal-working.

ROBERT JANSON, *Vice President*

Bob Janson participated with Roy Walters in the Bell
System's original job enrichment research and trials.
Before joining Walters & Associates, he was a District Manager for the New York Telephone Co., with
responsibility for several hundred employees and supervisors. He has had consulting experience in job
redesign projects in a wide variety of manufacturing
and service organizations—steel, textiles, chemicals,
banking, and insurance, to name a few industries.

Besides numerous articles in personnel and train-
ing journals, he has contributed chapters to Robert
N. Ford's *Motivation through the Work Itself* and to
Van Nostrand's *New Perspectives in Job Enrichment.*
He is a frequent speaker on motivation through job
design.

FRANK J. KAVENEY, *Senior Associate*

Frank Kaveney received a BS degree in engineering from the University of Massachusetts and was soon hired by the New Jersey Bell Telephone Co. He held a number of line and staff positions in both the engineering and plant departments before being appointed a District Plant Manager. After serving in this position for three years, he was appointed Director of New Jersey Bell's Initial Management Development Program, geared especially to high-potential college hires. In this capacity he did extensive college recruiting for the Bell System.

Frank became associated with Dr. Robert N. Ford of AT&T. He eventually assumed responsibility for coordinating New Jersey Bell's Job Enrichment efforts and directed some 25 projects.

Since joining Walters & Associates, he has served as consultant to many corporations' human resource management programs. His clients have included companies in banking, autos, chemicals, research and development, and heavy manufacturing, among others.

W. PHILIP KRAFT, JR., *Vice President*

Before joining Walters & Associates Phil Kraft was an executive of New York Telephone Co., both as head of its largest commercial district and as a key internal consultant on manpower utilization. An expert in implementation methods and training, he has consulted extensively in such widely varied companies as banks, brokerage firms, manufacturers, insurance companies, drug manufacturers, advertising agencies, sales organizations, and independent telephone systems.

He has conducted numerous training workshops and seminars in job enrichment theory and implementation. Author of many articles on human utilization, he has also contributed to *New Perspectives in Job Enrichment, Handbook of Modern Office Management,* and the landmark HEW study, *Work in America.*

PETER LANDRIGAN, *Senior Associate*

Upon graduation from St. Lawrence University, Peter
Landrigan joined Chemical Bank in New York. After
completing an executive training program, he took on
assignments in branch administration, labor relations, and bank operations. For three years he was
administrator of Chemical Bank's extensive job enrichment program.

In his most recent work Peter has worked closely
with industrial engineers. Their joint goal was a philosophy of systems design integrating work measurement and job design principles for better use and
motivation of employees.

KENNETH L. PURDY, *Senior Associate*

Specializing in work organization as well as job enrichment, Ken Purdy has represented Walters & Associates with many clients in the United States and
Canada. He has trained internal consultants, managers, and supervisors and directed management
team-building efforts. Like other members of the
Walters firm, Ken has practical experience as a line
manager—in Commercial Operations with the Bell
System. As an internal consultant with Bell, he was
a pioneer in practical applications of job enrichment.

He has contributed numerous articles and papers
to the literature on job design and the quality of
work—including chapters on job enrichment with
Roy Walters in the *Handbook of Modern Office Management* and *The Encyclopedia of Management*.

Index

DATE DUE

5. 06. '82	
6. 10. '82	
5. 14. '86	
11. 25. 87	
NOV 07 '90	
OCT 3 0 '91	
NOV 3 0 1995	
DEC 2 0 2004	